KU-200-798

THE BEDFORD SERIES IN HISTORY AND CULTURE

The Nazi State and German Society

A Brief History with Documents

Robert G. Moeller

University of California, Irvine

BEDFORD/ST. MARTIN'S   Boston ♦ New York

For Bedford/St. Martin's

Publisher for History: Mary V. Dougherty
Director of Development for History: Jane Knetzger
Senior Editor: Heidi L. Hood
Developmental Editor: Laura Arcari
Editorial Assistant: Jennifer Jovin
Production Supervisor: Sarah Ulicny
Executive Marketing Manager: Jenna Bookin Barry
Project Management: Books By Design, Inc.
Index: Books By Design, Inc.
Text Design: Claire Seng-Niemoeller
Cover Design: Richard DiTomassi
Cover Photo: Crowds cheer and salute Nazi leader Adolf Hitler as he appears on the balcony of the Deutscher Hof Hotel, Nuremberg, during a visit to the city, September 5, 1938. Getty Images.
Composition: TexTech International
Printing and Binding: RR Donnelley & Sons Company

President: Joan E. Feinberg
Editorial Director: Denise B. Wydra
Editor in Chief: Karen S. Henry
Director of Marketing: Karen R. Soeltz
Director of Editing, Design, and Production: Marcia Cohen
Assistant Director of Editing, Design, and Production: Elise S. Kaiser
Manager, Publishing Services: Emily Berleth

HAMMERSMITH AND WEST
LONDON COLLEGE
LEARNING CENTRE

- 6 DEC 2012

331791   £19-99
943.086 MOE
TRAVEL - HIST
3WKS

Library of Congress Control Number: 2009921708

Copyright © 2010 by Bedford/St. Martin's

All rights reserved. No part of this book may be reproduced, stored in a retrieval system, or transmitted in any form or by any means, electronic, mechanical, photocopying, recording, or otherwise, except as may be expressly permitted by the applicable copyright statutes or in writing by the Publisher.

Manufactured in the United States of America.

4   3   2   1   0
f   e   d   c   b

For information, write: Bedford/St. Martin's, 75 Arlington Street, Boston, MA 02116   (617-399-4000)

ISBN-10: 0-312-45468-6
ISBN-13: 978-0-312-45468-5

Acknowledgments

Acknowledgments and copyrights appear at the back of the book on pages 194–96, which constitute an extension of the copyright page.

Distributed outside North America by PALGRAVE MACMILLAN.

WITHDRAWN

THE BEDFORD SERIES IN HISTORY AND CULTURE

The Nazi State and German Society

A Brief History with Documents

THE LEARNING CENTRE
HAMMERSMITH AND WEST
LONDON COLLEGE
GLIDDON ROAD
LONDON W14 9BL

HAMMERSMITH WEST LONDON COLLEGE

331791

Related Titles in
THE BEDFORD SERIES IN HISTORY AND CULTURE
Advisory Editors: Lynn Hunt, *University of California, Los Angeles*
David W. Blight, *Yale University*
Bonnie G. Smith, *Rutgers University*
Natalie Zemon Davis, *Princeton University*
Ernest R. May, *Harvard University*

Foreword

The Bedford Series in History and Culture is designed so that readers can study the past as historians do.

The historian's first task is finding the evidence. Documents, letters, memoirs, interviews, pictures, movies, novels, or poems can provide facts and clues. Then the historian questions and compares the sources. There is more to do than in a courtroom, for hearsay evidence is welcome, and the historian is usually looking for answers beyond act and motive. Different views of an event may be as important as a single verdict. How a story is told may yield as much information as what it says.

Along the way the historian seeks help from other historians and perhaps from specialists in other disciplines. Finally, it is time to write, to decide on an interpretation and how to arrange the evidence for readers.

Each book in this series contains an important historical document or group of documents, each document a witness from the past and open to interpretation in different ways. The documents are combined with some element of historical narrative—an introduction or a biographical essay, for example—that provides students with an analysis of the primary source material and important background information about the world in which it was produced.

Each book in the series focuses on a specific topic within a specific historical period. Each provides a basis for lively thought and discussion about several aspects of the topic and the historian's role. Each is short enough (and inexpensive enough) to be a reasonable one-week assignment in a college course. Whether as classroom or personal reading, each book in the series provides firsthand experience of the challenge—and fun—of discovering, recreating, and interpreting the past.

Lynn Hunt
David W. Blight
Bonnie G. Smith
Natalie Zemon Davis
Ernest R. May

Preface

The Nazi State and German Society addresses a topic about which virtually all students know something, but it challenges preconceptions that often come from television, movies, and the limited coverage of German fascism in high school textbooks. It seeks to make the familiar unfamiliar by inviting students to view Adolf Hitler and the Nazi state through a range of perspectives.

The study of National Socialism remains stunningly relevant to an understanding of the contemporary world. It yields insights into questions that continue to plague us today. Why would citizens in a democratic republic willingly give up fundamental civil liberties? What allows an authoritarian regime to take power, and why do some authoritarian regimes receive overwhelming popular support? Why are authoritarian regimes so concerned with the structure of the family and individual choices about sexual preference? What makes it possible for them to identify certain groups as "enemies of the state" and to move toward the social isolation and even physical extermination of those groups without encountering massive resistance? Because the study of National Socialism can help us to formulate answers to these questions, it can illuminate the present as well as the past.

The primary sources in this collection illustrate how the Nazis used force and repression to maintain order, but they also suggest why millions of Germans enthusiastically embraced a regime that dramatically restricted their civil liberties and denied them fundamental freedoms. Although there is no shortage of collected works featuring primary source documents related to National Socialism, no other college-level text offers students as broad a range of perspectives in such a manageable and accessible format. This collection includes documents that illustrate the nature of Nazi propaganda and policies, as well as those that allow students to explore how the Nazi state invaded the daily lives of Germans, dictating who should and who should not have children, what music they should listen to, and what art they should see. The sources demonstrate the ways in which anti-Semitic messages, conveyed by laws and propaganda, shaped the views of young people who grew up in Germany in the 1930s. They also capture multiple voices, from Nazi leaders such as Hitler, Heinrich Himmler, and Joseph Goebbels to everyday people: a rabbi's wife who endured anti-Semitism in the 1930s, a soldier deployed to the eastern front, survivors of concentration camps, a woman who lived through the bombing of Hamburg, college students who died because they opposed the Nazis, and a woman who witnessed the arrival of the Soviet Red Army in Danzig in the spring of 1945. In addition, the documents reveal what Americans knew, or should have known, about the Nazi state, drawing on the acute observations of journalist William L. Shirer and articles from the *New York Times*. A selection of images encourages students to consider visuals as primary sources.

This volume contextualizes the sources through a brief introduction that explains the rise of National Socialism, describes life in the Nazi state, discusses Hitler's expansive war of aggression in Europe, and recounts how the systematic persecution of Jews culminated in the creation of massive killing facilities in eastern Europe, where the Nazis sought to carry out the Final Solution. A headnote introduces each document, providing students with the context they need to make sense of the source, and gloss notes explain unfamiliar terms and references. Following the documents are additional student aids, including a chronology of major events from 1914 to 1945, a list of questions for consideration that invite students to engage critically with the sources they have read, and a selected bibliography for those who want to go beyond this basic introduction.

All the selections in the book have been taken from English-language translations. We have maintained the spelling conventions that appear in the original editions.

ACKNOWLEDGMENTS

I am grateful to series advisory editor Lynn Hunt for her inspirational model as a teacher, her friendship, and her encouragement to undertake this project. Without her belief that I could pull it off, I would never have tried. At Bedford/St. Martin's, I thank Mary Dougherty, who encouraged me to "dare to omit," and Jane Knetzger, Katherine Meisenheimer, Heidi Hood, and Jennifer Jovin, who left no e-mail unanswered and patiently dealt with my chronic insecurity. Emily Berleth and Nancy Benjamin expertly guided the copyediting and production of the book. Laura Arcari was a wonderful developmental editor. She brought enormous intelligence, insight, and good judgment to the project, and I cannot begin to express my gratitude for all she accomplished. Working with her was a pleasure from beginning to end.

Several other people have influenced this work. My approach to teaching the Nazis was profoundly shaped by my experience presenting the complex history of National Socialism to some twelve hundred first-year students a year during a three-year cycle of the University of California, Irvine's Humanities Core Course, a team-taught introduction to the humanities. Teaching this course with my friends Julia Lupton and Vivian Folkenflik constantly made me aware that sometimes less *can* be more. My work over the past decade or so with middle and high school teachers in Orange County, California, has helped me to think critically about how to make history accessible without dumbing things down. I have also benefited from the responses of a number of "focus groups"—students who have sat through my lecture classes on Hitler and the Germans. Along the way, I have received useful critical responses from Frank Biess, Jane Caplan, David Crew, Geoff Eley, Heide Fehrenbach, Harold Marcuse, and Uta Poiger. The following manuscript reviewers offered helpful advice: Brady Brower, Weber State University; Rebecca Friedman, Florida International University; Peter Fritzsche, University of Illinois at Urbana–Champaign; Derek Hastings, Ferris State University; Jeffrey Plaks, University of Central Oklahoma; and J. B. Shank, University of Minnesota. Patricia Steimer helped me to clean up my prose and say more clearly what was on my mind. Gedina Bergstrom provided invaluable research assistance and offered astute comments on what did and did not work.

I dedicate the book to Lynn Mally, a superb scholar and teacher whose advice I (almost) always take, and Nora Mally, an unabashedly enthusiastic fan of American musical theater, who inspired me to bring Mel Brooks and "Springtime for Hitler" into the classroom and this book.

Robert G. Moeller

Contents

PART ONE

Introduction: Understanding Nazi Germany

In the early part of the twenty-first century—more than half a century after the Third Reich was defeated by a massive military coalition headed by the United States, the Soviet Union, and Great Britain— Hitler and the Nazis remain powerful symbols of the worst possible villains imaginable. The regime that promoted a terrifying principle of racial purity, incarcerated many of its own citizens in concentration camps because of their political or religious views or their sexual orientation, started a world war, and attempted to murder all European Jews was the twentieth century's icon of absolute evil.

At the start of the twenty-first century, German history provided a point of reference for U.S. president George W. Bush when he compared the Iraqi dictator Saddam Hussein to Hitler. It was also the stuff of box office hits. In 2004, millions went to see *The Downfall*, an Oscar-nominated German film about Hitler's last days in Berlin. A year later, as political leaders in Washington, Moscow, Berlin, London, Paris, and Tokyo grappled with how best to commemorate the sixtieth anniversary of the end of World War II, Hitler was again front-page news. He even appeared on Broadway as a character in the Tony Award–winning musical *The Producers*, about a Broadway producer who tries to con investors by selling 100 percent of the shares in his show many times over, then staging a musical designed to flop. The

1

show, called *Springtime for Hitler*, becomes a hit, and the producer ends up in jail for defrauding his investors. At the Tony Awards ceremony, writer and composer Mel Brooks, an American Jew who was stationed in Germany with the U.S. Army during the Second World War, ironically included the Führer (the German word for "leader" used by Hitler and adopted by others to describe his central role in Nazi Germany) among those he thanked for his success—"for being such a funny guy on stage."[1]

Nazi Germany continues to fascinate, a source of historical analogy, melodrama, and satire and a ubiquitous presence on television and the Internet. Perhaps this should come as no surprise. The initial triumph of National Socialism, Nazi aggression, the horrors of the Final Solution, the staggering death tolls of the war the Nazis unleashed, and the geopolitical division of the post-1945 world between the United States and the Soviet Union, the superpowers most responsible for defeating Nazism, define the history of the twentieth century.

Hitler and the Nazis have taken on almost mythical status—historical phenomena long since drowned in printer's ink, smothered in celluloid, and awash in the hypertext of cyberspace. But in some ways, myth has come to be a substitute for history. For many people, Hitler exists outside any understanding of the historical context that made him possible.

What many people know about the Nazis comes from sources such as movies, television, even the historical analogies offered up by the White House, but rarely from history books. To be sure, there's no shortage of historical scholarship on National Socialism,[2] but often scholars spend too much time writing for other scholars and not enough time presenting their findings in a way that is accessible to general readers. Scholars also do the work of analysis and interpretation for readers, rather than inviting them to offer their own interpretations of complex historical phenomena. This book is based on the belief that readers can most readily gain an understanding of Hitler and the Nazi regime if they are given the opportunity to analyze critically key documents about the politics, culture, and society of Germany from the end of the First World War to the defeat of the Third Reich.

The documents include political speeches and important laws, but they also touch on subjects that intersect more directly with daily life—how the Nazi regime regulated young people, what conceptions of masculinity and femininity it promoted, which kinds of music and art it tolerated and which it prohibited, how it regulated sexuality, and how ordinary people responded to the regime's policies. Examining these themes can provide insights into the dynamics of the Nazi state, making clear that the Third Reich sought not only to dominate the continent of Europe but also to regulate people's personal lives, breaking down the barriers between public and private.

Although people today sometimes see Nazi Germany as a throwback to an age of barbarism, it was instead an extremely modern state. This book demonstrates that and also focuses on what led millions of Germans to sacrifice individual rights and personal freedoms in the interest of collective goals and national security. The documents allow readers to consider not only what forms of repression the Nazis used to stay in power but also what carrots accompanied those sticks and how millions of Germans, without coercion, could support the regime so enthusiastically.[3]

In twenty-first-century America, we tend to take democratic institutions for granted, but the experience of Germany in the years between the First and Second World Wars indicates how fragile democracy can be and how vital it is to understand the forces that threaten it. This book invites readers to take seriously the complex set of factors that allowed Hitler to become German chancellor in January 1933 and remain in power for the next twelve years.

THE WEIMAR REPUBLIC AND THE RISE OF THE NAZI PARTY

The story presented in this book begins with the First World War, when an enthusiastic Austrian named Adolf Hitler enlisted in the Bavarian army (Document 1). Like many other German-speaking central Europeans, Hitler believed that the war would create a truly unified German empire—that is, that success in battle would solidify and expand Germany's power and prestige in Europe and the world. Instead, four years later, in 1918, Germany surrendered to the Allies.

During the war, a state-regulated wartime economy, privation, and shortages of all basic necessities spawned considerable domestic discontent among German workers. At the end of the war, this discontent bubbled up in political demands for the overthrow of the authoritarian imperial government, led by the kaiser, in which elected parliamentary representatives had very little power. On November 9, 1918, the leaders of the Social Democratic party, inspired by Marxist ideology and hopeful that a democratic Germany would emerge from the collapse of the old regime, called for the creation of a German republic.

Two days later, Germany accepted the armistice that ended the war. Although Social Democratic leaders confronted challenges from the radical left, which drew its inspiration from the Bolshevik Revolution that had rocked Russia in late 1917, they successfully pushed for national elections to create a broad-based political coalition that would draft a constitution for a democratic Germany. Despite this success, many on the radical right saw the German defeat in the war as a source of profound humiliation. Hitler and many others believed that the war effort had been compromised by dissidents, including Marxists and Jews, who had infected the home front and undermined military morale. Socialists, they claimed, had played on divisions defined by economic status and been responsible for eroding national unity.

Along with Hitler, most Germans shared the view that the Treaty of Versailles, the document hammered out by the victors in 1919 at a former palace of the French kings outside Paris, was profoundly unjust. The victorious Allies laid exclusive blame for starting the war at the feet of the Germans, took away Germany's colonies and some German territory in Europe, drastically reduced the size of its army, and demanded monetary reparations to compensate them for their losses during the war. Throughout the 1920s and early 1930s, the political demands of Hitler and many other right-wing nationalists focused on revising the postwar settlement of Versailles and the democratic changes introduced by those they called "November criminals," the socialists who had created the democratic republic at the war's end, accepted the armistice agreement, and played a major role in drafting the German constitution in the town of Weimar in early 1919.

During this time, however, Hitler and those who shared his views were on the political margins. By 1922, the promise of a democratic socialist revolution in Russia had been betrayed, and the Bolsheviks exercised one-party rule and repressed any opposition. In contrast, the democratic government in Germany lasted for more than a decade, surviving the ravages of the postwar inflation of the German currency, economic instability, and challenges from both monarchist sympathizers and fringe groups such as Hitler's on the right and the Communists, inspired by Moscow, on the left. The German constitution defined the authority of a freely elected parliament and president, and, at least until the late 1920s, millions of Germans—some more enthusiastically than others—were willing to support this new form of government.

The democratic republic that had its capital in Berlin continued to bear the name of the town in which its constitution was drafted. The

Weimar Republic affirmed basic civil liberties such as freedom of religion and speech. It guaranteed the right of working people to organize to represent their interests. It granted the vote to women, one year before the United States and twenty-five years before France. And it created the political framework within which it was possible to discuss reform and experimentation in many other areas. Accompanying women's political emancipation were visions of their cultural and economic emancipation. Although few women ultimately attained it, the ideal of the "new woman"—economically independent, educated, in charge of her own fate, and no longer relegated to hearth and home—was promoted in magazine advertisements, films, novels, and popular songs and by feminist political organizations (Document 3). Sexual reformers pushed to increase women's access to sex education and information on birth control, to end the prohibition of abortion, and to abolish the parts of the criminal code that outlawed male homosexual activity (Document 2). The Weimar Republic was also known as a place where artistic creativity and experimentation were encouraged and celebrated. Germany in the 1920s was incredibly modern, and from all over Europe and North America, those who sought to see what shape the future might take—politically, economically, culturally, sexually, and artistically—flocked to Germany.

What appealed to some, however, frightened others. Weimar's openness to modernity and experimentation caused concern among those who remained unconvinced that democratic political institutions could succeed and feared that too much innovation too quickly would destroy traditional institutions and values. Many civil servants—employees of state and local government offices, including schoolteachers and university professors—had come of age before the First World War and remained deeply skeptical of democracy. Rural dwellers worried that Social Democratic leaders would favor urban workers, to the disadvantage of the agrarian sector. And even though the German army had been dramatically trimmed by the Treaty of Versailles, those officers who remained were no friends of democracy or social and cultural experimentation.

Antidemocratic leanings did not, however, translate automatically into support for Hitler or endorsement of his vision of a revived right-wing nationalism that excluded Jews and rejected the principles of parliamentary democracy. Hitler headed the National Socialist German Workers' Party (Nationalsozialistische Deutsche Arbeiterpartei, or NSDAP), also known as the Nazi party. Those who sought to disparage the party coined this name, which echoed the derogatory term

"Sozi," used to refer to the Social Democratic party. The Nazis railed against Communists and Jews—who, according to them, had international connections and stood outside the "national community" (Document 4)—and denounced liberal ideals of the equality of women and men (Document 6). But until the late 1920s, the National Socialists did not do well in local, state, or federal elections. Despite its claims to be a workers' party, the NSDAP polled poorly with wage earners, most of whom remained loyal to the Social Democratic party, and the Nazis were outdistanced by other nationalist political groups.

In November 1923, Hitler attempted to follow Benito Mussolini's October 1922 "march on Rome," the move that had led to the establishment of an authoritarian regime in Italy, with what became known as the Beer Hall Putsch. He took control of a right-wing political meeting at a beer hall in Munich and proposed marching from Munich to Berlin to overthrow the Weimar Republic. His effort was a debacle. Hitler and his followers never made it beyond the Munich city limits, and he landed in jail, convicted of trying to overthrow the state. He served only a fraction of his five-year sentence, however, and was paroled by the end of 1924. While imprisoned, he wrote *Mein Kampf* (*My Struggle*), which was published in 1925. The book was anything but an overnight success, and it would be almost another decade before this rambling, repetitive, incoherent rant became an essential part of the home libraries of millions of Germans (Document 5).

In fact, it was not until the national elections of September 1930 that the Nazi party emerged as a credible political force. In 1928, Hitler's party won only 2.6 percent of the popular vote. Two years later, the NSDAP captured 18.3 percent of the vote, allowing it to send into the German parliament a cadre of brown-uniformed representatives, who now commanded a national platform for their attacks on Weimar democracy and those they held responsible for German disunity. This list included not only the Social Democrats and the Communists but also the victorious Allies, who had imposed the terms of the Treaty of Versailles; feminists; and Jews, who, they claimed, should be permanently excluded from the national community (*Volksgemeinschaft*). Just over half a million in number, not even 1 percent of the German population in 1933, Jews were public enemy number one for the Nazis. No group loomed larger in Hitler's worldview. But until Hitler became chancellor in January 1933, Nazi anti-Semitism often took a backseat to anticommunism and attacks on the Weimar Republic (Document 7).

The Nazis effectively used a highly organized propaganda machine to convey their message, creating the image of a party of change, dynamism, and movement; tailoring appeals to specific interests; and creating organizations for occupational groups including farmers, civil servants, and women, whose occupation was presumed to be housewifery and motherhood. Such electoral tactics are powerful evidence of how mistaken it would be to see the Nazis as antimodern. Hitler's well-oiled political apparatus was highly sophisticated, targeting different voting blocs in a way that calls to mind the use of focus groups and public opinion surveys today. There is also no question that for at least some Nazis, hearing the charismatic Führer speak resulted in something akin to a religious conversion (see the cover of this book, the image below, and Document 8).

Rhetoric, propaganda, and the aura surrounding Hitler were effective tools of the Nazis, but it was the world economic crisis of 1929 that ultimately allowed them to make significant political gains. Between the Nazis' dismal electoral showing in 1928 and their much better results in 1930, an economic slowdown that had begun in 1928 took on truly catastrophic proportions. It was worsened by the stock market crash in the United States in October 1929.) The economic prosperity of the mid-1920s had been financed in part with American loans. Now banks in the United States, struggling to survive, cut off

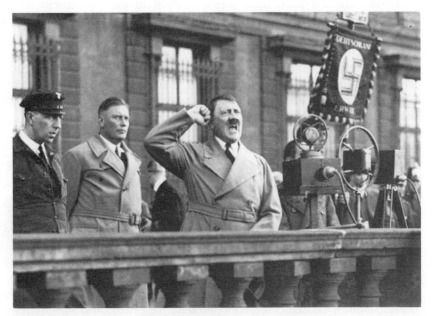

Hitler speaking in Berlin, April 4, 1932.
Research Library, The Getty Research Institute, Los Angeles, California (920024).

the supply of capital and called in outstanding loans. Unemployment soared, hitting about one in three German workers. According to some reports, by early 1932 the total number of jobless and their dependents reached thirteen million, around 20 percent of the population. In heavy industrial areas, where production took a nosedive, unemployment was even higher. ⁄

As political outsiders who had never exercised power at the national level, the Nazis were ideally positioned to attack the inability of democratically elected governments to solve Germany's problems. Although industrial workers—those most directly affected by the Depression—continued to vote mainly for Communists and Social Democrats, these two groups were deeply divided. In some cases, Communist diatribes against Weimar politics could be as savage as those of the Nazis. The split between Communists and Social Democrats meant that the Nazis faced no unified opposition on the left.

The deepening economic crisis affected all Germans, and in Nazi political appeals, it became emblematic of everything that was wrong with the Weimar Republic. Germany's multiparty system and an electoral law that allowed for parliamentary representation in proportion to the popular vote ensured that no party ever commanded a majority, even the smallest party had representation in the parliament, and political decisions could be reached only after a multiparty coalition had been cobbled together. The fragility of these political constructions and the inability of parliament to provide meaningful responses to the economic crisis led to the repeated dissolution of both state and federal parliaments and calls for new elections. Because elections were incapable of producing a stable government, the Nazis claimed that they made no difference. In Weimar's fourteen years in existence, on average, each ruling cabinet lasted a little less than eight months, one indication of why Weimar was never able to give birth to a robust form of democratic governance. The Nazis could convincingly argue that the Weimar Republic was broken, even if not all Germans would have agreed that it was beyond repair or that the Nazis were the ones best qualified to fix it.

The Nazis continued to win electoral gains by effectively presenting themselves as the best possible alternative to the status quo in a political landscape where options were extremely limited. They emerged as the one party capable of unifying millions of Germans who were ready for a dramatic political change, even if the party offered little specific information about what that change might entail. The Nazis also sought new allies by significantly revising their political program and abandoning any claim to being primarily a workers' party. Hitler now emphasized that his highest priority was to combat the threat of the German Communist party and the political power of the Social Democratic party and the trade union movement.

Although the Nazis never achieved a political majority and there is evidence that by late 1932 electoral support for the party was waning, in early 1933 the popularly elected president, Paul von Hindenburg, who had the authority to appoint the chancellor, gave in to pressure from conservative politicians to name Hitler to this position. They argued that if Hitler led a coalition government in which the Nazis controlled only a limited number of ministerial posts, Nazi radicalism would be contained, and Nazi votes in parliament would create the basis for an end to the political instability of the previous years. Although some historians have described January 1933 as the Nazi seizure of power, Hitler didn't have to break down the door to the chancellery; he was invited to walk through it by President von Hindenburg. His followers celebrated his rise to power with a massive demonstration in Berlin that captured the imagination of millions of Germans who were hoping for a better future (Document 9). Like many Germans, Hindenburg believed that Hitler would tone down his rhetoric once he was in office and that a cabinet made up of conservatives who were not Nazis would rein him in (Document 10).

Such optimism was short-lived. In February, at Hitler's behest, Hindenburg exercised his powers to dissolve parliament and called for new elections. Later that month, a former Dutch Communist who advocated violent direct action as a mode of political protest set fire to the Reichstag building, home of the German parliament. The Nazis seized on this event as an excuse to intensify attacks on the left. They conjured up a Bolshevik conspiracy bent on overthrowing the state. Moving quickly to consolidate Nazi authority, the government suspended a range of civil liberties, including freedom of expression, the press, and assembly, justifying these actions by pointing to the threat allegedly presented by the left. Hitler unleashed the police and storm troopers (Sturmabteilung, or SA), the paramilitary organization financed by the Nazi party, on Communists, Social Democrats, and trade unionists, driving some into political exile, others into concentration camps, and still others into silence. The most effective sources of opposition to the Nazis were quickly eliminated (Document 11). Completely erasing any distinction between Social Democrats and Communists, Hitler emphasized that "our fight against Marxism will be relentless, and . . . every movement which allies itself to Marxism will come to grief with it."[4]

In early March, new parliamentary elections still did not yield a Nazi majority. Despite the virtual silencing of opposition parties, the Nazis won only 43.9 percent of the popular vote. A parliamentary coalition headed by the Nazis was, however, ready to use democratic means to end democratic governance. The Enabling Act, passed in March, was opposed only by the Social Democrats; the Communist party had been banned in early March. Hitler's cabinet could now assume complete responsibility for introducing new laws. One of its first laws, passed in July, eliminated all political parties except the NSDAP. Hitler's continued commitment to proceeding by legal means assuaged the fears of many middle-class Germans that the Nazis would operate outside the law, making it possible for them to look past the regime's consistent reliance on extra-legal violence to maintain its authority, crush opponents, and quiet dissent.

LIFE IN NAZI GERMANY

Nazi policies were backed by force — the police and the Gestapo (Geheime Staatspolizei, or state secret police). But the state did not have to coerce most Germans to accept the end of parliamentary democracy and the institution of one-party authoritarian rule. Millions of Germans welcomed the suppression of the political left, the destruction of the trade union movement, the end of parliamentary wrangling, and Hitler's promise that he would lead Germany into a brighter future. They also welcomed signs of the return of economic prosperity and programs that promised to even out social inequality and create new opportunities for workers (Document 12). Those who still required encouragement and instruction to embrace Nazi rule needed to look no further than the Ministry for Popular Enlightenment and Propaganda, headed by Joseph Goebbels, whose responsibilities included oversight of many forms of cultural production and the media. For the Nazis, propaganda did not manipulate; rather, it educated and illuminated (Document 13). The propagandistic message of power, infallibility, confidence, and authority was also clearly conveyed at the carefully orchestrated annual Nazi party congresses in the city of Nuremberg (Document 14).

Hitler went to great lengths to reassure important organizations, especially the Catholic Church and the military, that he would not challenge their authority (Document 15). Plans to bring Protestant Christianity into a unified structure headed by an enthusiastic supporter of Hitler, however, ran into opposition from many Protestant clerics. Although they insisted on religious autonomy from the Nazi state (Document 16), they stopped far short of openly challenging the regime's political authority. The main targets of Nazi political violence in the spring and summer of 1933 were trade unionists, Social Democrats, and Communists, all lumped together by Hitler and his followers as "Marxists" and "November criminals," the groups the Nazis held responsible for Germany's woes. The Nazis also attacked other highly visible symbols of Weimar modernity, such as movements for sexual reform. In early May, a student organization torched the library of Magnus Hirschfeld's Institute for Sexual Science in Berlin. Hirschfeld, well known as a leading champion of sexual reform and homosexual rights, was also a Jew (see Document 2). The Nazis could hate him for more than one reason. Hirschfeld was outside Germany at the time, but the crowd burned as many as ten thousand of the books in his library. This was only one of countless events nationwide in which books considered "un-German" were publicly put to the torch.

Through a process called "coordination," the Nazis brought cultural institutions, sports clubs, professional organizations, and the press into line with Nazi principles, purging those who did not meet the racial, political, sexual, and religious criteria of the Nazi state. Thousands of political activists, artists, scientists, composers, musicians, writers, and other opponents of the Nazis, as well as many German Jews, left the country, resulting in a major loss of intellectual talent. Among those who fled were scientist Albert Einstein, novelist Thomas Mann, philosopher Hannah Arendt, and Austrian-born film director Fritz Lang.

The regime's attempts to promote a National Socialist aesthetic, free of Jewish influence and the experimental tendencies of Weimar, were exemplified by its attitude toward artistic production. For the Nazis, what Weimar had fostered was "degenerate art," a very broad label that included the work of artists on the political left, such as Otto Dix and George Grosz, whose depictions of disabled veterans of World War I carried a strong pacifist and antiwar message, but also Franz Marc, whose landscapes featured whimsical cows, excoriated because they were unrealistic fantasies that no German farmer could possibly recognize. The work of many non-German artists, including Paul Klee, Marc Chagall, and Wassily Kandinsky—all very much at home on the Weimar cultural scene—also was banned. In place of an abstract art that allegedly misrepresented reality and created only confusion, the Nazis substituted a realist "German art" that featured muscular male nudes, a militarized masculinity often conveyed by swords and other military regalia, big-breasted blond women ready to suckle a newborn (a vision of femininity that was firmly tied to women's maternal responsibilities), noble peasants, solemn cows, and Hitler in every imaginable pose (Document 17). For the Nazis, music could also be degenerate. Perhaps not surprisingly, they outlawed American jazz, which they claimed was the pernicious product of one racially inferior group, African Americans, promoted by another, Jews (Document 18). But they also forbade the performance of the music of much-loved classical composers such as Felix Mendelssohn. For the Nazis, Mendelssohn's baptism as a Christian did not alter his racial classification as a Jew. Many artists, composers, and musicians left Germany, and the cultural impoverishment of the Third Reich translated into the incalculable cultural enrichment of Britain, the United States, and many other countries in the world.

Those who remained in Germany and resisted the regime risked being sent to concentration camps, although Hitler reassuringly told the public that these facilities were committed only to reeducation and rehabilitation (Document 19). But, in fact, prisoners found themselves under the arbitrary control of the Nazi police state (Document 20). Before 1938, the camps interred relatively few Jews. Instead, those incarcerated included mainly political and religious opponents, such as Jehovah's Witnesses, who rejected all state authority; so-called asocials—prostitutes, vagrants, drunks, or those whom the Nazis deemed not fit for the "national community"; and male homosexuals, whose sexuality made them both criminals and outsiders in a society that celebrated heterosexual families with many children. Although the camps provided a potent warning of what might await any opponent of the regime, many Germans agreed that the earliest inmates deserved their fate and were best kept out of the way.

Hitler also made it clear that he would brook no opposition from within the ranks of the Nazi faithful. After 1933, some enthusiastic Nazis had been disappointed to see that Hitler had not made a clean break with the past. They still hoped for the "second revolution," in which the Nazis would not compromise with conservative elites. In particular, Ernst Röhm, an early backer of Hitler who headed the SA, felt that the state and the military had not ensured that all political and military leaders were loyal Nazis. Röhm not only wanted to see committed Nazis and storm troopers take over military and state offices, however. He also was critical of the conservative moral order that condemned his homosexual inclinations. On the night of June 30, 1934, following Hitler's orders, units of the Schutzstaffel (SS, Protection Squad) put an end to Röhm's aspirations, killing him and several other opponents of the regime. The Night of Long Knives, as it became known, made clear to Germans that Hitler would not hesitate to move against his followers, and his actions met with broad popular support from those who were critical of Röhm on both political and moral grounds (Document 21).

At the annual party rally the following fall, Hitler assured the party faithful that he would not forget those who had brought him to power, and in a highly orchestrated spectacle, he affirmed the unity of the Nazi movement. But the Röhm assassination made clear that the power of the SA would be carefully circumscribed even as the authority of the SS steadily expanded. Although the SS had its origins as a special group charged with protecting Hitler, by the mid-1930s, under Heinrich Himmler, who became head of the SS and controlled the Gestapo, it attained independent status and assumed more and more police powers, including responsibility for running the concentration camps and implementing Nazi racial policy.

Although Hitler relied heavily on force and terror to eliminate opposition, the Third Reich was also founded on "positive" conceptions of the unity and equality of all those who could claim "Aryan" status, defining what historians Michael Burleigh and Wolfgang Wippermann have called the "racial state."[5] "Aryan" had originally been used in the nineteenth century to describe speakers of Germanic languages. For the Nazis, it became synonymous with a German whose family history revealed no traces of racial mixing and who was thus assumed to be racially superior. Women played a vital role in the Aryan race because they knew best "what is necessary so that a race does not die out" (Document 22). Promoting healthy Aryan families was a central part of Nazi domestic policy (Document 23). In 1933, the Nazi state adopted a law that granted loans to young married couples, if the wife agreed to leave wage work and devote herself exclusively to motherhood. Intensifying prosecution of violations of Paragraph 218 of the criminal code, which outlawed abortion, was another part of this radically pronatalist regime. The Nazis were also intent on organizing boys and girls at a young age in order to indoctrinate them in the Nazi worldview. Accompanied by a constant drumbeat of Nazi ideology, the Hitler Youth (Hitler Jugend) and the League of German Girls (Bund deutscher Mädel) provided young people with all sorts of activities (Document 24). The overwhelming majority of German young people were happy to wear the swastika and raise their arms in the Hitler salute.

Although the science behind the Nazi racial theory was highly suspect and constantly subject to revision, Nazi conceptions of race divided outsiders and insiders. Heading the roll call of outsiders were Jews, but they were not the only ones who were driven from the "national community." The Nazis also viewed all people of African descent as inferior. Reality sometimes powerfully challenged ideology and racial doctrine. In 1936, the Olympic Games in Berlin gave the Nazis an opportunity to welcome the world to the new Germany, putting on display the evidence of Aryan racial superiority. Much to their dismay, Jesse Owens, an African American, walked away with four gold medals (Document 25). Still, if Owens could go home with the gold, for all Afro-Germans who were primarily the children of German women and black French colonial troops who had been recruited during World War I and ended up occupying parts of Germany after the war, no such exit route existed. In 1937, the Nazis ordered that all children of these postwar unions should be sterilized.

Joining Jews and Afro-Germans on the list of outsiders were Gypsies (Sinti and Roma; Document 29). Also highly suspect were individuals judged to have serious mental illnesses or to be bearers of hereditary diseases; more than 360,000 of them were sterilized (Document 26). And those whose mental or physical disabilities or terminal illnesses made their lives "worthless," according to the Nazis, were subject to murder. In a famous dramatic film from 1941, *Ich klage an* (*I Accuse*), director Wolfgang Liebeneiner made the case for "euthanasia" and also provided a stunning example of the Nazis' use of the immensely popular film medium to convey their views (Document 27). The euthanasia campaign claimed some 267,000 lives in Germany and Nazi-occupied Europe. Homosexual men also were persecuted. Although Paragraph 175 of the criminal code, which outlawed same-sex activity between men, had been on the books since 1871, provisions of the law were dramatically expanded in 1935 (Document 28). Between 1933 and 1945, the Nazis prosecuted about 50,000 homosexual men, two-thirds of whom received jail sentences. Lesbians were excluded from criminal prosecution because, according to Nazi legal experts, lesbians were not as aggressive and predatory as male homosexuals and because, at least potentially, lesbians could become mothers and contribute to the goal of an ever-expanding racially fit population. In a society that placed such a high priority on motherhood, however, lesbians could hardly be open about their sexual orientation.

Of all the Third Reich's perceived enemies, none were more threatening and dangerous to Hitler than Jews. From the party's early history, Hitler made clear that anti-Semitism was at the core of his worldview. Although the Nazi party downplayed attacks on Jews in its electoral propaganda before 1933, once in power Hitler pursued both legal means and extra-legal violence to push German Jews to the margins of society—the "social death" that preceded the Nazi plan to exterminate all Jews.[6] The Nazis launched a constant anti-Semitic barrage in popular magazines, radio broadcasts, newspapers, posters, and primers used to teach young Germans reading, writing, and arithmetic. One popular, highly melodramatic film from 1940, *Jud Süss* (*The Jew Süss*), directed by Veit Harlan, depicted eighteenth-century Jews as attempting to integrate themselves into German society in order to corrupt and undermine it. The underlying message was that Jews had always been a threat to Germans.

Anti-Semitism also became part of Germany's official legal policy. The Law for the Protection of German Blood and German Honor and the Reich Citizenship Law, collectively called the Nuremberg Laws because they were proclaimed at the annual Nazi party conference held in that city in September 1935, defined the status of German Jews, robbed them of their citizenship, criminalized their sexual relations with persons of "German or racially related blood," and restricted their activities in ways that anticipated the accelerating erosion of their rights in the years that followed (Document 30). Memoirs written by German Jewish survivors yield rich insights into the daily tyranny that they encountered during the 1930s (Documents 31 and 32).

German Jews responded by creating cultural, social welfare, and educational institutions to replace those to which they no longer had access. Many also chose emigration, but leaving Germany was not easy. Tight immigration policies in countries such as Britain and the United States limited the places to which German Jews could flee. Liquidating property in an economic climate where Aryans offered Jews less and less for their belongings made it difficult to amass the necessary capital to emigrate. Many German Jews also were tied to Germany by strong bonds of language and culture. And because Hitler was never explicit about his intentions, it was possible for some German Jews to believe that things would get no worse.

On the night of November 9, 1938, the SA obliterated any hopes that the regime's anti-Semitic trajectory would be halted or reversed (Document 33). Responding to the news that a seventeen-year-old Polish Jew had assassinated Ernst vom Rath, a foreign service officer at the German embassy in Paris, the SA used massive force against Jews across Germany, and their acts were sanctioned by the Nazi leadership. Because the windows of so many Jewish businesses and synagogues were shattered, leaving the streets of German and Austrian cities littered with shards of glass, the event became known as Kristallnacht, or the "Night of Broken Glass." For the first time, German Jews were arrested in large numbers, and the barrage of anti-Semitic legislation that followed was a clear indication that there was no longer any place for Jews in Germany. In January 1939, all German Jewish men were required to add "Israel" to their legal names. The counterpart for women was "Sara." Jews were now publicly placed even further outside the Nazis' national community. Kristallnacht triggered a wave of German Jewish emigration, but the state's move to seize Jewish assets, combined with the continued resistance of many nations to accept Jewish immigrants, meant that for some there was no option but to remain in Germany and face a terrifying future. Historians estimate that between 270,000 and 300,000 Jews, about three-fifths of the 1933 population, were ultimately able to leave Germany, but the Nazis would later apprehend about 30,000 of them during World War II in other parts of Europe.

After the Nazi takeover, German society was increasingly treacherous for those excluded from the national community. But by the late 1930s the future looked bright for insiders who could document a racially acceptable genealogy and who supported the state that governed them. Most Germans were pleased with what the Führer had accomplished, and Joseph Goebbels could point to a thriving economy approaching full employment in his propagandistic attempts to surround Hitler with a myth of infallibility.[7]

GERMANY GOES TO WAR

Most Germans enthusiastically applauded the signs of the reassertion of Germany's position as a major political power in Europe and Hitler's determined efforts to reverse the post–World War I settlement and the restrictions of the Versailles treaty. In 1935, Hitler publicly announced that he was rejecting limits on German military rearmament, and a military buildup that had begun in secret now took place in the open. In 1936, he ordered the military occupation of parts of western Germany declared off-limits to German troops at Versailles, and his action triggered no international response. There were many signs that the

German economy was gearing up to support even more aggressive actions, and Hitler purged the military, the Foreign Ministry, and the Economics Ministry of anyone who questioned his plans to accelerate Germany's preparation for war.

In March 1938, German troops marched into Austria, ostensibly in response to the Austrian people's desire to join the Greater German Reich, also called the Third Reich. (The Nazi state was called the Third Reich because it claimed to be the successor to two earlier regimes, the Holy Roman Empire, dissolved in 1806, and the German Empire, or Deutsches Reich, of 1871 to 1918.) Austrian Jews were now subject to the anti-Semitic measures that had already been put in place in Germany. Germans in the western part of Czechoslovakia, the Sudetenland, which bordered Germany, were the next group that, according to Hitler, sought to be incorporated into the Third Reich. When the Czechoslovakian government threatened to resist Nazi intentions, it received no support from French, British, or Soviet political leaders, who, along with other European powers, feared another war. In October 1938, German troops marched into the Sudetenland. Still facing no apparent opposition, Hitler sent troops into what remained of the Czech state in March 1939. The successful outcome of these high-stakes geopolitical gambles only enhanced Hitler's status and popularity in Germany, contributing to the widespread belief that the Führer could do no wrong.

Hitler's next target was Poland. In August 1939, he struck a bargain with Soviet leader Joseph Stalin. Hitler agreed not to stand in the way of the Soviet Union's expansion of its "sphere of influence" to include eastern Poland and other parts of eastern Europe, in return for Stalin's promise not to oppose German aggression in the rest of Poland. When the agreement became public, world leaders had difficulty believing that the Nazis had signed a nonaggression pact with the nation that was the birthplace of communism. For Stalin's part, he feared that if Germany's invasion of Poland prompted no international reaction, the Soviet Union would be next in line. Hitler justified the Nazi invasion of Poland in September by conjuring up the threat posed to ethnic Germans by their Polish neighbors (Document 34). He hoped that the French and British would join the Soviet Union on the sidelines, doing nothing to stop German aggression, but on September 3, 1939, they declared war on Germany. The Second World War had commenced.

For the rest of 1939 and 1940, no one could halt the Nazi advance. The German army rolled over Poland in weeks, wiping out the Polish army and killing untold numbers of civilians. Many German civilians followed the army into Poland, encouraged by the state to see themselves as enlightened colonizers, ready to establish order, create a new home for Germans, and seize territory that had been "mismanaged" by the Poles. The Nazis forcibly removed the Polish population to make room for ethnic Germans imported from other parts of Poland and southern and eastern Europe (Documents 35 and 36). Hitler next looked to the north and west, and by the end of June 1940, the German army had conquered Denmark, Norway, Belgium, Luxembourg, Holland, and France. In these early victories, Germans found powerful evidence that Hitler would make good on his promise to restore German greatness. Army recruits, most of whom were seeing combat for the first time, marched into France, elated to reverse the outcome of the First World War (Document 37). But German expansion ended at the English Channel. Hitler's attempt to bomb the British into submission was met with determined resistance and the commitment of Prime Minister Winston Churchill to oppose the Nazis with "blood, sweat, toil and tears."

Stymied in the west, Hitler turned back to the east, preparing for an attack on the Soviet Union by first subjugating Greece and Yugoslavia. Dubbed Operation Barbarossa, the invasion of the Soviet Union on June 22, 1941, significantly expanded the scope of the war. In the Soviet Union, the Nazis sought not only to defeat Bolshevism and eliminate the imagined "Judeo-Bolshevik" threat, but also to expand into territories that could be settled by racially pure Germans. The Versailles treaty had denied Germany any rights to an empire outside Europe. In the Soviet Union, the Third Reich sought to create such an empire *within* Europe, a space into which a "people without space," the Aryans crammed into Germany, could expand. From the start, the Nazis viewed the war in the east as a race war, aimed at eliminating racially inferior Slavs and Jews in order to open up a new homeland for the racially superior Aryans (Document 38).

The Red Army and the Russian winter blocked the German advance (Document 39). In December 1941, Germany added to its list of foes by declaring war on the United States. Hitler was convinced that the way to keep the United States out of the war in Europe was to involve it in a war in the Pacific with Japan, which was also led by a militaristic authoritarian regime bent on its own agenda of imperialist expansion in Asia. When the Japanese attacked the United States at Pearl Harbor on December 7, Hitler supported their aggression and four days later declared war on the United States. Hitler believed that by the time America mobilized an army big enough to enter the

European war, a German victory over the Soviet Union would have left the Nazis virtually unbeatable. Hitler's declaration of war against the United States also allowed him to link the war to anti-Semitism, and he denounced Roosevelt as allied with "the Jew, in his full satanic vileness." As historian Saul Friedländer has written, "By formally declaring war on the United States . . . Hitler had closed the circle of his enemies in a world war of yet-unknown fury."[8]

Hitler's expectation of a quick victory over the Soviet Union was not fulfilled. During the spring and summer of 1942, the Germans regrouped and continued to move into Russia, but winter returned, halting their progress and creating the conditions that allowed the Red Army to capture one of the most important German military contingents at Stalingrad, where the Germans suffered a major defeat in February 1943. Attempts by Propaganda Minister Goebbels to translate unequivocal defeat into a call for "total war," a struggle that involved civilians on the home front just as much as soldiers on the battlefront, may have worked on party loyalists (Document 40), but for many Germans, Stalingrad marked a turning point in the war, the moment when things began to go from bad to worse.

Defeat at Stalingrad was not the only major setback. By late 1942, British and American troops went on the offensive against the German troops that had invaded northern Africa in 1941 to support Hitler's Italian allies. By May 1943, the Allies had won a major victory, defeating the Germans and Italians. The final battle at the city of Tunis was dubbed "Tunisgrad." Two months later, British and American forces invaded Sicily, and the fascist dictator Mussolini was deposed. A new government signed an armistice with the Allies, but the Germans continued to occupy Italy and fought fiercely. The Allies pushed on into the country, finally taking Rome in June 1944.

Although the British remained wary of initiating a ground war against the Germans on the western front and the Americans needed time to move men and war materiel into place for the invasion of France, British prime minister Winston Churchill and U.S. president Franklin D. Roosevelt agreed that they would intensify the air war over Germany. German fighter pilots and antiaircraft battalions on the ground downed many Allied bombers, but British and American strategists remained committed to the air war. U.S. pilots dropped their bombs by day, and their British counterparts filled the skies over Germany at night. Bad weather and poor visibility, antiaircraft fire, and the limits of bombing technology meant that the Allies had limited success taking out industrial plants, but by using more and more incendiary bombs, they could level the dense urban housing in which industrial workers lived, driving workers from their homes and undermining domestic morale. The use of this tactic resulted in devastating firestorms that killed hundreds of thousands and left German cities in ruins. In this way, Allied bombers brought the war home to Germany (Document 41). Surviving the bombs defined life in German cities. Although some people in Britain and the United States questioned the moral legitimacy of military tactics targeting noncombatants, the Allies' official position was that the Germans had been the first ones to bomb civilians indiscriminately in Rotterdam, London, and Coventry, and they had no one but themselves to blame for the destruction that fell from the skies.

THE PERSECUTION OF THE JEWS AND THE FINAL SOLUTION

While German soldiers fought against the Soviet, British, and American troops, and Germans on the home front dodged Allied bombs, the Nazis continued to prosecute the other war that had dramatically intensified in 1939. The enemies in this war were European Jews. Hitler explicitly linked the two dimensions of the Nazis' war before the invasion of Poland, proclaiming in January 1939 that if a world war began, "the result will not be the Bolshevization of the earth and with it the victory of Jewry, but the annihilation of the Jewish race in Europe."[9]

After September 1939, prophecy translated into policy. Poland and the Soviet Union were home to millions more Jews than resided in Germany, and the SS enthusiastically took on the task of regulating the fate of Jews there. In Poland and the occupied parts of the Soviet Union, the Nazis established ghettos—sealed-off parts of big cities, where they concentrated the Jewish population from the surrounding territory, isolating them and killing countless thousands through starvation and overwork (Document 47). They also used "mobile killing squads" and special police units, groups that worked in cooperation with the regular army, to carry out mass executions, rounding up the entire Jewish populations of occupied towns, in some cases forcing them to dig their own graves and then shooting them. The mobile killing squads attempted to recruit collaborators in places such as Latvia and Ukraine where the local population shared their anti-Semitic views and willingly participated in the attempt to make these regions *judenrein*, "free of Jews" (Documents 45 and 46). Some German soldiers proved to be willing accomplices, assisting in the work of these squads. In addition to Jews, the squads killed non-Jewish partisans, Communists, and any civilians suspected of attempting to resist the Nazis. Historians estimate that as many as 2 million people, 1.3 million of whom were Jewish, were murdered by these squads and their collaborators.

The SS continued to explore ways to carry out mass murder more efficiently. Impressed by the successful use of poison gas in the euthanasia program, the SS began to see this as an answer to the "Jewish question." Killing Jews by gassing began at Chelmno, renamed Kulmhof by the Germans, in December 1941. After the Wannsee Conference, named for the villa in Berlin where leading Nazis met in January 1942 to outline the "final solution," the SS tremendously increased its capacity to conduct mass murder, designating additional camps that were specifically committed to this goal at Belzec, Sobibor, Treblinka, Majdanek, and Auschwitz-Birkenau (Document 49). Historians estimate that the Nazis murdered three million Jews in these facilities. Although gas killed many at these six sites and at other concentration camps, death rates also soared because of unhygienic conditions, disease, medical experiments, the violence of SS guards, and starvation (Document 50).

In the year following the Wannsee Conference, the rate of mass murder accelerated rapidly. Historian Doris Bergen calculates that in early 1942, "75 percent of the Jews who would be murdered in the Holocaust were still alive." A year later, "75 percent of the approximately 6 million who would be killed were already dead."[10] From all parts of Nazi-controlled Europe, Jews were shipped by railroad car to killing facilities in Poland. Jews who were able to escape or elude the Nazis remained active in the underground resistance movement throughout Europe (Document 48).

For German Jews, cut off from all sources of information and all but completely isolated from their neighbors, the future remained terrifyingly uncertain (Document 42). As of September 1941, all Jews older than age five were legally obliged to wear the six-pointed "Jewish star." Clearly identified as a group apart, Jews could only imagine what awaited them next. Faced with an ever-expanding catalog of legal restrictions and charged with organizing their own deportation (Document 43), they received virtually no support from other Germans, who feared for their own safety, chose not to imagine what happened to Jews deported to the east, and perhaps stood to gain by taking control of the apartments, houses, and household goods that Jews left behind. Some also enthusiastically applauded policies aimed at "cleansing" Germany of all vestiges of "Jewish influence." After the German defeat in May 1945, many Germans would claim to have had no knowledge of what was happening to their Jewish neighbors. But millions looked on as Jews were deported (Document 44), and thousands more participated directly in the mass murder of Jews. Silence and willful forgetting should not be confused with ignorance.

THE LIMITS TO RESISTANCE

As the war progressed, the authority of the Gestapo and the SS grew, and the opportunities for Germans to question, let alone resist, the Nazi state were virtually nonexistent. Even dancing to American swing music was suspect (Document 51), and anyone who told a joke directed at Nazi leaders might end up facing the Gestapo (Document 52). Rare calls for open opposition, such as those made in 1942 and 1943 by the White Rose, a secret student organization led by Sophie and Hans Scholl at the University of Munich, were punished with death (Document 53). In July 1944, a secret coalition of military officers that included Colonel Claus von Stauffenberg tried to end the war by attempting to assassinate Hitler in a plot code-named Operation Valkyrie. The military conspirators planned to seize control of the army and major German cities once Hitler was dead (Document 54). But the plot failed. The bomb Stauffenberg planted in Hitler's headquarters in East Prussia went off, but it did not kill the Führer. Stauffenberg was quickly apprehended and executed.

There is no question that the ubiquitous presence of the Nazi terror apparatus limited the possibility of resistance, but it is also important to emphasize that domestic morale in Germany remained at a high level right up to the end of the war. The overwhelming majority of the military command also remained loyal to Hitler. By the end of the war, the greatest source of resistance to the Third Reich within Germany came not from Germans, but from enslaved foreign workers, hauled to Germany to replace men sent to the front (Document 55).

THE LAST DAYS OF THE NAZI REGIME

In June 1944, the Allies finally invaded France. As they pushed eastward, the Red Army pushed westward. In Germany, the air war intensified, as German defenses proved increasingly unable to fend off U.S.

and British planes. On the home front, men ages sixteen to sixty were mobilized in local militias called the *Volkssturm*, and by the end of the war, boys as young as sixteen were conscripted into the regular army (Document 56). To the havoc wreaked by the air war was added the influx of millions of Germans from eastern Europe and the parts of eastern Germany conquered by the Red Army. These expellees— mostly women, children, and elderly men—fled in advance of Soviet soldiers, who showed little mercy to those who did not abandon their homes. Many Red Army soldiers marked their victory by raping German women. According to some estimates, as many as 1.5 million German women were raped (Document 57). Some expellees reported that as they fled before the Red Army, they crossed paths with concentration camp inmates driven west by their SS guards on death marches, in an attempt to prevent Soviet forces from capturing evidence of the worst crimes of the Nazi regime.

By early 1945, with enemy armies pushing forward on both fronts and British and American bombers dominating the skies over Germany, the Nazi defeat was inevitable. Still, the German army continued to fight ferociously on the eastern front, and from Berlin Hitler declared that he would never capitulate. The Nazis also continued to carry out the mass murder of Jews in the areas they controlled. As the Allies advanced from east and west, however, they liberated the big killing facilities and concentration camps, revealing to the world the horrific crimes the Nazis had committed (Document 58). By late April, even Hitler realized that German defeat was imminent. In a melodramatic gesture characteristic of the Führer's larger-than-life persona, Hitler married his longtime companion, Eva Braun, and they celebrated their honeymoon by committing suicide (Document 59). Within days, the Third Reich had surrendered unconditionally, and the war in Europe was over.

British, American, and Soviet soldiers, joined by troops and partisan forces from many other nations, had defeated German fascism, and Germany was now occupied by the victors. From mid-July to early August, the "Big Three" met in Potsdam, a town close to Berlin. Franklin D. Roosevelt, who had led the United States throughout the war, had died on April 12 and been replaced by Harry Truman. In the midst of the negotiations at Potsdam, Winston Churchill was voted out of office in Britain and replaced by Clement Attlee. Joseph Stalin still represented the Soviet Union. The Big Three divided Germany into four zones. Each of them would occupy one zone, leaving the fourth for the French. The geopolitical division of the globe between communism and democracy was already taking shape, and the Potsdam

Conference would be the last time the major powers that had defeated the Nazis would meet on friendly terms. For more than four decades, the division of Germany outlined at Potsdam would be an abiding legacy of the war the Germans had started in September 1939.

The victorious Allies also agreed to put major Nazi war criminals on trial. Twenty-four leading Nazis were indicted by the international tribunal, which met in Nuremberg, the city that had hosted the annual Nazi party congresses. The trial began in November 1945 and lasted almost eleven months. Twelve defendants were sentenced to death by hanging, and seven others received long prison sentences. One was deemed too ill to stand trial, and another committed suicide before the trial began. Three were acquitted. The extraordinary documentary record compiled by the prosecutors continues to be a vital source of information about the Third Reich. The trial also established a legal precedent for the international prosecution of war criminals.[11]

We continue to be overwhelmed by the Nazis' systematic murder of some six million European Jews, a number that would have been much higher had the Nazi state not been defeated. As many as 27 million Soviet soldiers and civilians also had died by the time the shooting stopped. Among them were 3.3 million Soviet POWs—well over half of all those captured by the Germans—who had died under German supervision.

In the spring of 1945, most Germans did not focus on the damage inflicted on others by the Nazi regime, however. Rather, they mourned their own losses, and those losses were considerable. By the time the German army unconditionally surrendered on May 8, 1945, Allied bombs had killed more than 400,000 Germans. In many big cities as much as 70 percent of housing stock was destroyed, leaving some 7.5 million Germans homeless. Another 12 million or so expellees fled their homes in late 1944 and 1945, seeking to escape the Red Army as it advanced into eastern Europe and then into eastern Germany. The best data available indicate that about 500,000 of them had been killed in the process. The war left many German families without fathers, husbands, sons, and brothers. More than 5 million Germans in uniform lost their lives before the shooting stopped, well over half of them on the eastern front. The first postwar census recorded that there were 2,242 available women for every 1,000 adult men who might seek a spouse.

For some 11 million more Germans in uniform, the war ended in Allied prisoner of war camps. Although most German POWs found their way back to Germany by the end of 1948, POWs continued to straggle home from the Soviet Union until January 1956. About 1 million men died before being released from Soviet camps. Other losses were registered not in death rates and destruction, but in the borders that were redrawn at Potsdam, which would define a Germany divided between a communist East and a democratic West until the country was reunified in 1990.

Sorting through this troubling history continues to preoccupy historians and remains central to the political identity of contemporary Germany. In the last sixty or so years, many Germans—including the sons and daughters, and the grandsons and granddaughters, of those who lived through the Nazi era—have accepted collective responsibility for National Socialism, the Final Solution, and the Second World War. Not surprisingly, the past in all its complexity remains quite present in Germany today. But that past can also tell those outside Germany much about the tension between a society's desire for security and citizens' demands for the robust defense of civil liberties. It offers a gripping case study of the sources of modern racism and reveals how the celebration and elevation of some groups can lead to the exclusion and extermination of others. It reminds us that authoritarian regimes depend not just on repression and coercion but also on their ability to insinuate their ideology into the daily lives of their citizens. And it has much to tell us about how ordinary people can come to support an authoritarian regime and enable it to undertake unbelievably horrendous acts. Nazi Germany fundamentally defined world history in the twentieth century, and it sadly remains a vital point of reference for our understanding and analysis of authoritarian regimes, state-organized terror, and mass murder today.[12]

NOTES

[1] Andrew Buncombe, "Mel Brooks 'Thanks' Hitler for Twelve Tony's," *The Independent*, June 5, 2001.

[2] I could not have written this introduction or completed the headnotes for the documents without drawing on this scholarship heavily. See the bibliography at the end of the book.

[3] Peter Fritzsche, *Germans into Nazis* (Cambridge, Mass.: Harvard University Press, 1998).

[4] Richard J. Evans, *The Coming of the Third Reich* (New York: Penguin Press, 2004), 321. See also Richard J. Evans, *The Third Reich in Power, 1933–1939* (New York: Penguin Press, 2005); and Evans, *The Third Reich at War, 1939–1945* (London: Allen Lane, 2008). I have drawn heavily on Evans's excellent account in this introduction.

[5]Michael Burleigh and Wolfgang Wippermann, *The Racial State: Germany, 1933–1945* (New York: Cambridge University Press, 1991).

[6]Marion A. Kaplan, *Between Dignity and Despair: Jewish Life in Nazi Germany* (New York: Oxford University Press, 1998).

[7]Ian Kershaw, *The "Hitler Myth": Image and Reality in the Third Reich* (Oxford: Oxford University Press, 1989).

[8]Saul Friedländer, *The Years of Extermination: Nazi Germany and the Jews, 1939–1945* (New York: HarperCollins, 2007), 279. See also the first volume of this extraordinarily important work, Saul Friedländer, *Nazi Germany and the Jews*, vol. 1, *The Years of Persecution, 1933–1939* (New York: HarperCollins, 1997).

[9]Quoted in Friedländer, *Nazi Germany and the Jews*, 310.

[10]Doris L. Bergen, *War and Genocide: A Concise History of the Holocaust* (Lanham, Md.: Rowman & Littlefield, 2003), 175. Bergen provides an excellent concise summary.

[11]Michael R. Marrus, *The Nuremberg War Crimes Trial, 1945–46: A Documentary History* (Boston: Bedford/St. Martin's, 1997).

[12]For an excellent general introduction to current historiography on Nazi Germany, see Jane Caplan, ed., *Nazi Germany, 1933–1945* (Oxford: Oxford University Press, 2008).

PART TWO

The Documents

1

The Weimar Republic and the Rise of the Nazi Party

1

ADOLF HITLER

On His Hopes for Germany in 1914, from Mein Kampf

1925

In August 1914 at the start of World War I, Adolf Hitler, an Austrian by birth, joined the Bavarian army and the German cause. Hitler reflected on his war experiences in his book Mein Kampf *(*My Struggle*), written while he was in jail after his failed attempt to overthrow the Weimar Republic in November 1923. In this passage, Hitler clearly expresses the hopes for national unity and a decisive victory shared by millions of Germans in 1914. His comments help us understand his sense of humiliation and resentment over the defeat Germany was dealt in 1918.*

The struggle of the year 1914 was not forced on the masses—no, by the living God—it was desired by the whole people.

People wanted at length to put an end to the general uncertainty. Only thus can it be understood that more than two million German men and boys thronged to the colors for this hardest of all struggles, prepared to defend the flag with the last drop of their blood.

From Adolf Hitler, *Mein Kampf*, trans. Ralph Manheim (Boston: Houghton Mifflin, 1971), 161–64.

To me those hours seemed like a release from the painful feelings of my youth. Even today I am not ashamed to say that, overpowered by stormy enthusiasm, I fell down on my knees and thanked Heaven from an overflowing heart for granting me the good fortune of being permitted to live at this time. . . .

For the last time in many years the people had a prophetic vision of its own future. Thus, right at the beginning of the gigantic struggle the necessary grave undertone entered into the ecstasy of an over-flowing enthusiasm; for this knowledge alone made the national upris-ing more than a mere blaze of straw. The earnestness was only too necessary; for in those days people in general had not the faintest con-ception of the possible length and duration of the struggle that was now beginning. They dreamed of being home again that winter to con-tinue and renew their peaceful labors. . . .

As a boy and young man I had so often felt the desire to prove at least once by deeds that for me national enthusiasm was no empty whim. It often seemed to me almost a sin to shout hurrah perhaps without having the inner right to do so; for who had the right to use this word without having proved it in the place where all playing is at an end and the inexorable hand of the Goddess of Destiny begins to weigh peoples and men according to the truth and steadfastness of their convictions? Thus my heart, like that of a million others, over-flowed with proud joy that at last I would be able to redeem myself from this paralyzing feeling. I had so often sung *"Deutschland über Alles"* and shouted *"Heil"* at the top of my lungs, that it seemed to me almost a belated act of grace to be allowed to stand as a witness in the divine court of the eternal judge and proclaim the sincerity of this con-viction. For from the first hour I was convinced that in case of a war— which seemed to me inevitable—in one way or another I would at once leave my books. Likewise I knew that my place would then be where my inner voice directed me. . . .

On the third of August, I submitted a personal petition to His Majesty, King Ludwig III,[1] with a request for permission to enter a Bavarian regiment. The cabinet office certainly had plenty to do in those days; so much the greater was my joy to receive an answer to my request the very next day. With trembling hands I opened the doc-ument; my request had been approved and I was summoned to report to a Bavarian regiment. My joy and gratitude knew no bounds. A few

---

[1]Ludwig III was the last king of the German state of Bavaria. His reign ended when Germany was declared a republic in November 1918.

days later I was wearing the tunic which I was not to doff until nearly six years later.

For me, as for every German, there now began the greatest and most unforgettable time of my earthly existence. Compared to the events of this gigantic struggle, everything past receded to shallow nothingness. Precisely in these days, with the tenth anniversary of the mighty event approaching, I think back with proud sadness on those first weeks of our people's heroic struggle, in which Fate graciously allowed me to take part.

2

MAGNUS HIRSCHFELD

Sexual Catastrophes

1926

The Weimar years witnessed debates over sexual identity and sexual reform. Magnus Hirschfeld (1868–1935), one of Germany's best-known sex researchers, headed the Institute for Sexual Science in Berlin and wrote widely on sexuality. In this excerpt from his book Sexual Catastrophes: Pictures from Modern Sexual and Married Life, *Hirschfeld argues that because homosexuality is a "natural, in-born disposition," it makes no sense to criminalize it. He lobbied against Paragraph 175 of the criminal code, which prohibited sexual relations between men. A political leftist, Hirschfeld was also Jewish. Out of the country when Hitler came to power, he learned in May 1933 that the Nazis had destroyed his library and looted his institute. He died in France in 1935.*

There is a reluctance to speak about the fact of homosexuality. To understand it requires serious consideration, which means intellectual exertion. So some plead that the topic is not respectable enough for them. Understanding homosexuality presupposes a psychological

From Magnus Hirschfeld, *Sexual Catastrophes: Pictures from Modern Sexual and Married Life* in *The Weimar Republic Sourcebook*, ed. Anton Kaes, Martin Jay, and Edward Dimendberg (Berkeley: University of California Press, 1994), 700–701.

reorientation, a self-liberation from the tutelage of the legislator who ignorantly subsumes homosexuality and depravity under the same concept.

What is homosexuality? The sexual inclination of men to male, women to female persons. There have been decades of fruitless controversy as to whether homosexuality is endogenous—that is, inborn—or acquired through training, habit, seduction, etc.

Modern research, based on the biological law that the opposite sex is latent in every individual, has elaborated the following formula:

> In every living being born of the union of two sexes, the characteristics of one sex are to be identified to varying degrees alongside those of the other.

The key to this formula derives from a fact discovered by embryological science in the previous century: unisexuality is a later development subsequent to an original bisexuality. This is to be observed in plants but also in animals, such as snails.

It is therefore a fact that homosexuality is an inborn condition, that is, a matter of constitution. Typical initial symptoms are demonstrable in homosexuals as early as the seventh and eighth, indeed, even in the third and fourth year of life.

If one carries this thought process through to the conclusion that homosexuality is a natural, in-born disposition, then the moral condemnation of homosexuality can only be regarded as an injustice and Paragraph 175 of the criminal code as a remnant of medieval conceptions.

The criminal prosecution of homosexuality is based on the fundamental juridical principle that legitimate interests are to be defended against violation. But what interests are violated by a homosexual act? Salacious (to use the technical term) sexual involvement with children is already punishable by a prison sentence on the basis of other articles in the criminal code. The age at which children are no longer protected could also be appropriately raised. The homosexual rape of adults, on the other hand, is inconceivable; mutual consent is a necessary condition of homosexual activity, which takes place in private without violating the interests of third parties. . . .

Once . . . the essence of homosexuality has been recognized, it is the obligation of every fair-minded person to speak out for the elimination of an injustice that already produces more victims and claims by the hour.

3

ELSA HERRMANN

This Is the New Woman

1929

In the 1920s, the Weimar Republic became known throughout Europe for its encouragement of all sorts of experimentation—musical, artistic, even sexual. Though a global phenomenon, the "new woman"—characterized by her short hair, androgynous dress, and independence—seemed to be particularly at home in Germany. Elsa Herrmann described this new woman in a 1929 book. Although this vision was well beyond the reach of many urban working-class women and posed a threat to more traditional women of all classes, in this excerpt Herrmann suggests some of the ways in which conceptions of appropriate femininity were subject to redefinition in the Weimar years.

To all appearances, the distinction between women in our day and those of previous times is to be sought only in formal terms because the modern woman refuses to lead the life of a lady and a housewife, preferring to depart from the ordained path and go her own way. In fact, however, the attitude of the new woman toward traditional customs is the expression of a worldview that decisively influences the direction of her entire life. The difference between the way women conceived of their lives today as distinguished from yesterday is most clearly visible in the objectives of this life.

The woman of yesterday lived exclusively for and geared her actions toward the future. Already as a half-grown child, she toiled and stocked her hope chest for her future dowry. In the first years of marriage she did as much of the household work as possible herself to save on expenses, thereby laying the foundation for future prosperity, or at least a worry-free old age. In pursuit of these goals she helped her husband in his business or professional activities. She frequently accomplished incredible things by combining her work in the

From Elsa Herrmann, *This Is the New Woman*, in *The Weimar Republic Sourcebook*, ed. Anton Kaes, Martin Jay, and Edward Dimendberg (Berkeley: University of California Press, 1994), 206–7.

household with this professional work of her own, the success of which she could constantly observe and measure by the progress of their mutual prosperity. She believed she had fulfilled her life's purpose when income deriving from well-placed investments or from one or more houses allowed her and her husband to retire from business. Beyond this, the assets saved and accumulated were valued as the expression of her concern for the future of her children.

... The woman defined exclusively by her status as a lady determined the occasions when she would allow herself to be seen in public by considering the possible advantages to herself and her family, a standpoint that would often determine the selection of the places she would frequent and where she would vacation. . . .

Her primary task. . . she naturally saw to be caring for the well-being of her children, the ultimate carriers of her thoughts on the future. Thus the purpose of her existence was in principle fulfilled once the existence of these children had been secured, that is, when she has settled the son in his work and gotten the daughter married. Then she collapsed completely, like a good racehorse collapses when it has maintained its exertions up to the very last minute. . . .

In stark contrast, the woman of today is oriented exclusively toward the present. That which is is decisive for her, not that which should be or should have been according to tradition.

She refuses to be regarded as a physically weak being in need of assistance — the role the woman of yesterday continued to adopt artificially — and therefore no longer lives by means supplied to her from elsewhere, whether income from her parents or her husband. For the sake of her economic independence, the necessary precondition for the development of a self-reliant personality, she seeks to support herself through gainful employment. It is only too obvious that, in contrast to earlier times, this conception of life necessarily involves a fundamental change in the orientation of women toward men which acquires its basic tone from concerns of equality and comradeship.

The new woman has set herself the goal of proving in her work and deeds that the representatives of the female sex are not second-class persons existing only in dependence and obedience but are fully capable of satisfying the demands of their positions in life. . . .

The people of yesterday are strongly inclined to characterize the modern woman as unfeminine because she is no longer wrapped up in kitchen work and the chores that have to be done around the house. Such a conception is less informative about the object of the judgment than the ones making it, who have adopted a view about the essence of the sexes based upon various accidental, external features. The concepts *female* and *male* have their ultimate origin in the erotic sphere and do not refer to the ways in which people might engage in activity. A woman is not female because she wields a cooking spoon and turns everything upside down while cleaning, but because she manifests characteristics that the man finds desirable, because she is kind, soft, understanding, appealing in her appearance, and so on.

4

ADOLF HITLER

Anti-Semitic Speech

April 12, 1922

In January 1919, the German Workers' party joined a host of right-wing parties on the fringes of German politics. In February 1920, the party changed its name to the National Socialist German Workers' Party (Nationalsozialistische Deutsche Arbeiterpartei, or NSDAP), commonly known as the Nazis. By 1922, Hitler had established himself as the party's most effective and charismatic leader. In this speech reprinted in the party newspaper, Völkischer Beobachter *(People's Observer), Hitler makes explicit that his anti-Semitism is tied to his hatred of all parties on the left. He refers to the immigration of eastern European Jews, in many cases refugees from Polish anti-Semitism, immediately after World War I, and he suggests that the Russian Revolution of 1917 led to a state controlled by Jews. In the Weimar Republic, the two main leftist parties—the Social Democratic party, which supported democracy, and the Communist party, which favored a Bolshevik-style workers' revolution—were in fact often bitter political enemies. But Hitler did not differentiate between the various positions on the left, and he tied them all to Jews.*

I ask you: Did the Jews have an interest in the collapse of 1918? It is possible for us to discuss that objectively today. You are undoubtedly aware that on a comparative basis very few Jews have suffered at all. Let no one tell me: Oh, the poor Eastern Jew! Of course, they did

From Louis L. Snyder, ed., *Hitler's Third Reich: A Documentary History* (1981; repr., Chicago: Nelson-Hall, 1988), 27–30.

not possess anything to begin with, for the simple reason that they lived in a country which they had robbed and stripped to the bone for centuries. They never have been nor will they ever be productively active.

They were poor when they came here. But look at any Oriental after he has been here for five or six years. Look at those millions of workers in Berlin in 1914 and look at them today. Now they are thinner; their clothes ragged and torn; they are poverty-stricken.

And now take a look at the 100,000 Jews from the East who came here during the first years of the war. Most of them have gotten rich and even own automobiles. That is so not because the Jews are more clever, because I challenge you to say that millions of decent and hardworking citizens are only stupid people.

The only reason is that these 100,000 Jews were never really ready to work in an honorable manner in a national organism for the common good of all. From the beginning they regarded the whole national organism as nothing more than a hothouse in which they could thrive.

The Jew has not become poorer. Slowly he is puffing himself up. If you do not believe me, take a look at our health resorts. There you find two kinds of people: the German who tries to catch a breath of fresh air for the first time in a long while and who wants to recuperate; and the Jew, who goes to the resorts as a means of getting rid of his excess fat. . . .

That same Jew, who was a Majority Socialist or an Independent[1] in those days of November 1918, led you then and he leads you now. He can be either an Independent or a Communist, but he remains the same.

And just as he did not look after your interests at that time but after the interests of his own capital and his own race, so today he will certainly not lead you in the struggle against his race and against his capital. . . .

Today in Soviet Russia millions are starving and dying. Some 30 million so-called "proletarians" lie prostrate, digging roots and grass from the soil in order to prolong their lives even for a few days, or for a few weeks. . . . The four hundred Soviet commissars of Jewish nationality are not suffering, nor are the thousands of deputy commissars. Quite the opposite. All the wealth which the "proletarians" in their madness took from the so-called "bourgeois" in order to fight against so-called capitalism, is now concentrated in the hands of the Soviet commissars. . . .

---

[1]During World War I, the Social Democratic party split into Independents and Majority Socialists. The two groups reunified after the war.

... Millions of men lost their last ruble, which they had saved honestly, honorably, and with great care. These millions of rubles now became the property of those who as leaders had not done anything at all and who are not doing anything now except to starve and bleed the people.

And now, my dear fellow countrymen, do you really believe that those people who are doing the same thing here[2] will end the revolution of 1918? They do not want to end the Revolution because there is no need for them to do so.

The Aryan looks upon work as the foundation of the national community. The Jew looks upon work as a means of exploiting others. The Jew never works as a productive creator but rather always with the idea of becoming a master. He works unproductively, utilizing and profiting from the work of others.

... The Jew is the ferment of the decomposition of people. This means that it is in the nature of the Jew to destroy, and he must destroy, because he lacks altogether any idea of working for the common good. It is of no matter whether or not the individual Jew is decent or not. He possesses certain characteristics given to him by nature and he never can rid himself of those characteristics. The Jew is harmful to us. ...

I say this: My feeling as a Christian leads me to be a fighter for my Lord and Saviour. It leads me to the man who, at one time lonely and with only a few followers, recognized the Jews for what they were, and called on men to fight against them, and who, believe me, was greatest not as a sufferer but as a fighter. ...

As a Christian and as a man with boundless love, I read that passage which told how the Lord finally gathered His strength and used the whip in order to drive the money-changers, the vipers, and the cheats from the temple.

Today, some two thousand years later, I understand with deep emotion Christ's tremendous struggle on behalf of the world against the Jewish poison. I understand it all the more by the fact that He has given His blood on the cross in this struggle. It is not just my duty as a Christian to allow myself to be cheated, but it is my duty to be a champion of truth and of right. ...

I ask this question of those who today call us agitators: "What do you have to offer the common people in the way of a belief they might

[2]Revolutionary workers who unsuccessfully promoted a Bolshevik-type seizure of power following World War I and Social Democrats who declared the democratic Weimar Republic.

hold to?" Nothing at all. For you yourself do not believe in your own prescriptions.

Such is the mightiest mission of our movement—to give the searching and bewildered masses a new, strong belief, a belief which will not leave them in these days of chaos, to which they will swear and abide by. . . .

Two thousand years ago a man was similarly denounced by this particular race which today denounces and blasphemes all over the place, by a race which agitates everywhere and which regards any opposition to it as an accursed crime. That man was dragged before a court and they said: He is arousing the people! So He, too, was an agitator! And against whom? Against "God," they cried. Indeed, He is agitating against the "god" of the Jews, because that "god" is nothing more than money.

5

ADOLF HITLER

On the Use of Mass Meetings, from Mein Kampf

1925

In 1925, when Mein Kampf *was published, the Nazis were still an extremely insignificant political party.* Mein Kampf *would become a best-seller only after Hitler became chancellor in January 1933. His insights in this excerpt on political tactics would profoundly influence Nazi strategy in the second half of the 1920s.*

All great, world-shaking events have been brought about, not by written matter, but by the spoken word. . . .

While the speaker gets a continuous correction of his speech from the crowd he is addressing, since he can always see in the faces of his listeners to what extent they can follow his arguments with understanding and whether the impression and the effect of his words lead to the desired goal—the writer does not know his readers at all. Therefore,

From Adolf Hitler, *Mein Kampf*, trans. Ralph Manheim (Boston: Houghton Mifflin, 1971), 469–71, 478–79.

to begin with, he will not aim at a definite mass before his eyes, but will keep his arguments entirely general. By this to a certain degree he loses psychological subtlety and in consequence suppleness. And so, by and large, a brilliant speaker will be able to write better than a brilliant writer can speak, unless he continuously practices this art. . . .

. . . He will, if he is a brilliant popular orator, not be likely to repeat the same reproach and the same substance twice in the same form. He will always let himself be borne by the great masses in such a way that instinctively the very words come to his lips that he needs to speak to the hearts of his audience. And if he errs, even in the slightest, he has the living correction before him. As I have said, he can read from the facial expression of his audience whether, firstly, they *understand* what he is saying, whether, secondly, they can *follow the speech as a whole*, and to what extent, thirdly, he has *convinced* them of the *soundness* of what he has said. If—firstly—he sees that they do not understand him, he will become so primitive and clear in his explanations that even the last member of his audience has to understand him; if he feels—secondly—that they cannot follow him, he will construct his ideas so cautiously and slowly that even the weakest member of the audience is not left behind, and he will—thirdly—if he suspects that they do not seem convinced of the soundness of his argument, repeat it over and over in constantly new examples. He himself will utter their objections, which he senses though unspoken, and go on confuting them and exploding them, until at length even the last group of an opposition, by its very bearing and facial expression, enables him to recognize its capitulation to his arguments.

Here again it is not seldom a question of overcoming prejudices which are not based on reason, but, for the most part unconsciously, are supported only by sentiment. To overcome this barrier of instinctive aversion, of emotional hatred, of prejudiced rejection, is a thousand times harder than to correct a faulty or erroneous scientific opinion. False concepts and poor knowledge can be eliminated by instruction, the resistance of the emotions never. Here only an appeal to these mysterious powers themselves can be effective; and the writer can hardly ever accomplish this, but almost exclusively the orator. . . .

The mass meeting is also necessary for the reason that in it the individual, who at first, while becoming a supporter of a young movement, feels lonely and easily succumbs to the fear of being alone, for the first time gets the picture of a larger community, which in most people has a strengthening, encouraging effect. The same man, within a company or a battalion, surrounded by all his comrades, would set out on an attack with a lighter heart than if left entirely on his own. In the crowd he always feels somewhat sheltered, even if a thousand reasons actually argue against it.

But the community of the great demonstration not only strengthens the individual, it also unites and helps to create an *esprit de corps*. The man who is exposed to grave tribulations, as the first advocate of a new doctrine in his factory or workshop, absolutely needs that strengthening which lies in the conviction, of being a member and fighter in a great comprehensive body. And he obtains an impression of this body for the first time in the mass demonstration. When from his little workshop or big factory, in which he feels very small, he steps for the first time into a mass meeting and has thousands and thousands of people of the same opinions around him, when, as a seeker, he is swept away by three or four thousand others into the mighty effect of suggestive intoxication and enthusiasm, when the visible success and agreement of thousands confirm to him the rightness of the new doctrine and for the first time arouse doubt in the truth of his previous conviction — then he himself has succumbed to the magic influence of what we designate as "mass suggestion." The will, the longing, and also the power of thousands are accumulated in every individual. The man who enters such a meeting doubting and wavering leaves it inwardly reinforced: he has become a link in the community.

6

ELSBETH ZANDER

Tasks Facing the German Woman

January 23, 1926

The Nazis railed against the "new woman" of Weimar (see Document 3), but this did not mean that women had no place in the Nazi party. Elsbeth Zander, a Nazi activist who headed an organization called the German Women's Order, which was tied to the Nazi party, describes in this article from the Völkischer Beobachter *her belief in a Nazi world in which women should remain separate from men but equal in terms of their contribution to the movement. Femininity for Zander definitely did not*

From Elsbeth Zander, "Tasks Facing the German Woman," in *Hitler's Voice: The Völkischer Beobachter, 1920–1933*, by Detlef Mühlberger (Oxford: Peter Lang, 2004), 2:326–27.

mean passivity. Zander's organization was dissolved in 1931 when the National Socialist Women's Organization (NS-Frauenschaft) became the representative of women in the party.

Napoleon I was once asked what was missing in France and he replied: "We lack mothers!" Our era also loudly demands German mothers, for those who will try—through true motherly love, through good understanding and sisterly comradeship—to heal the wounds which a gruesome fate has inflicted on us. The woman should, and the mother must, be the guardian of her family, of her home. But she has also in this terrible time of distress the sacred duty to look beyond her boundaries and, if it is necessary, go beyond these in order to fulfil her duty in the struggle for the well-being of our Fatherland. . . . German youth demands the careful hand of the mother, needs her kind, understanding eye when the great desire shines forth from the eyes of youth: "German mothers, lead us to the pure heights of truth!" . . .

. . . We represent the viewpoint: "The German can only be helped by Germans!" That is why the German welfare system must be controlled again by Germans. For he who through necessity has learned to love his people above all others, has learned also to hate all of the enemies of his people. And that is why it is important to demonstrate clean living to our youth, to teach it that strength lies only in purity. It is also important in the struggle for the most sacred goals to stand next to the German male as a comrade. The German woman must also be the guardian of German honour, for she suffers as much from humiliation and shame as the German male, if not more deeply. The German male will one day fight with the sword for the freedom of the Fatherland, but the German female shall fight for it with unshakeable belief, with endless love and loyal hope, in unceasing painstaking and detailed work, by bridging the social divide. She will bandage the wounds resulting from the struggle and the distress endured by our people. She must give the tired new energy. We do not wish to have anything to do with those who, with the help of our internal enemies, fight to secure our freedom. Clear and without compromise we support those who fight and strain for the purity of the *völkisch*[1] idea, who really want to construct a social state.

. . . We women must, through our quiet, honest work, inspire the German male to do noble things once more! The German woman shall and must again be worth sacrificing for. . . .

---

[1] German term most simply translated as "national"; used by the Nazis to invoke a sense of a racial identity grounded in heredity.

. . . German mothers, lead us to the heights of pure truth. The prerequisite for victory is to educate our youth, the future generation, to be pure and true.

7

ADOLF HITLER

Adolf Hitler's Manifesto
September 10, 1930

The Nazis first claimed national attention in September 1930 when they won more than 18 percent of the vote in the parliamentary elections. In the article excerpted here, published four days before the elections, Hitler lays out the party's political platform. Note that he is far clearer about what he rejects than he is about what he hopes to accomplish.

The Judgement of 14 September

On 14 September the German people are once again to hold court and give sentence. The practical answer of the questions which the people should consider leads continuously only to one result:

All that has been previously promised and assured by the political parties has not been attained.

The parties of the manual worker promised an improvement in the situation of the German worker!

His situation has deteriorated!

The parties of industry and big business promised the salvation of the German economy, of German industry:

The German economy and the whole of German industry is going under!

The parties have promised our peasantry to save agriculture from ruination!

If the salvation experienced up to now continues for another 10 years there will be nothing left of the independent German farmer!

From Adolf Hitler, "Adolf Hitler's Manifesto," in *Hitler's Voice: The Völkischer Beobachter, 1920–1933*, by Detlef Mühlberger (Oxford: Peter Lang, 2004), 1:395–96, 400–401, 403–4.

The parties of the middle classes have assured the *Mittelstand*[1] that they will prevent its destruction:

The German Mittelstand *is heading towards its complete decline at a most rapid rate!* . . .

How They Have Lied

Not only in purely party terms have the successes of our political movements failed to materialise, but also by and large in the political, national and economic sphere have their activities been fateful for our people!

The Revolution was launched with lies.

The armistice was based on lies.

The necessity of surrendering our fleet rested on lies.

Our people have been deceived. . . .

With lies one determined that Germany should sign the so-called peace Treaty of Versailles. . . .

And when today the attempt is made even to talk about a reconstruction of the German economy or of our society, then that is a deception. . . .

Which Are the Traitor-Parties?

For 11 years these parties have lied.

Marxism lied about the advantages of the cheap administration of the Republic, of the reduction of indirect taxes and the overcoming of capitalism, of the end to militarism, of eternal peace etc.

People, what has happened?!

The bourgeois national parties lied about the reconstruction of a powerful Reich, the reinstatement of the monarchy, the removal of class division, the strengthening of the military, the re-establishment of the boundaries of 1914, the recovery of the colonies etc.

And people, what has happened?!

The religious parties lied about overcoming anti-Christ, lied about the salvation of the family, lied about the moral elevation of the people, of the rescue of the family, of the strengthening of religion, of the battle against immorality, of the cleansing of public life etc.

And German people, judge for yourselves, what has happened?!

And the economic parties lied about rescuing the economy, lied about rescuing agriculture, rescuing the *Mittelstand*, rescuing small

[1] Small-scale entrepreneurs who owned their own businesses.

businesses, rescuing tourism, rescuing house ownership, rescuing the victims of inflation etc. etc.

And now judge for yourselves, German people, what has happened?!

The pacifist-democratic parties lied about the re-entry of Germany on the global stage, of a change in attitude of our enemies, of the usefulness of the League of Nations, of the conscience of the world, of cultural solidarity etc. etc.

And again people judge, what has happened?!

A terrible reality!

One occupation after another, one social estate after another, all are being destroyed.

Today we stand before the revelation of the greatest political system of lies of all time. For decades the parties have blinded our people with these lies, for decades they have been led towards ruination, and now that it is no longer possible to help them through great lies, they reach as a last resort to personal slander, to the small lie in the political electoral struggle.

German people, cast your glance back into the past and you will in future no longer be able to believe one word of these terrible swindlers and terrible liars!

Whatever they try to advance to support their old parties today can be nothing else but lies. . . .

What We Want

Through its victory the National Socialist Movement will overcome the old class and estate mentality. It will allow the reconstitution of a people out of the estate madness and class nonsense.

It will educate the people to iron decisiveness.

It will overcome democracy and enhance the authority of the personality.

It will give back to the German people their damaged rights through the brutal advocacy of the fundamental principle that one does not have the right to hang the little man as long as the greatest criminals are left unpunished and in peace. . . .

Smash the Interest Parties to Pieces

. . . If the right conclusions are drawn, then the 14 September 1930 can see the beginning of a tremendous German transformation, out of which a new German power will grow.

Millions today suspect the fate that awaits us. Let them have the strength to avert it!

The slogan of 14 September can only be: "Smash the political bank-rupts of all our old parties!"

Destroy those who subvert our national unity!

8

ALBERT SPEER

On Joining the Nazi Movement in 1931

1969

Albert Speer (1905–1981) was Hitler's chief architect, and in 1942 he became minister of armaments and war production. A little more than a decade earlier, he went to hear Hitler speak in Berlin. Like many other university-educated Germans, an elite group recruited almost exclusively from the conservative upper middle class, he was skeptical of Hitler, convinced that he was a "fanatic in uniform." In this excerpt from his memoirs, originally published in German in 1969 after he served a twenty-year sentence for war crimes, Speer records how he became a convert to the Nazi cause.

Hitler was delivering an address to the students of Berlin University, and the Institute of Technology. My students urged me to attend. Not yet convinced, but already uncertain of my ground, I went along. The site of the meeting was a beer hall called the Hasenheide. Dirty walls, narrow stairs, and an ill-kept interior created a poverty-stricken atmosphere. This was a place where workmen ordinarily held beer parties. The room was overcrowded. It seemed as if nearly all the students in Berlin wanted to see and hear this man whom his adherents so much admired and his opponents so much detested. A large number of professors sat in favored places in the middle of a bare platform. Their presence gave the meeting an importance and a social acceptability

From Albert Speer, *Inside the Third Reich: Memoirs by Albert Speer*, trans. Richard and Clara Winston (New York: Simon & Schuster, 1997), 15–18.

that it would not otherwise have had. Our group had also secured good seats on the platform, not far from the lectern.

Hitler entered and was tempestuously hailed by his numerous followers among the students. This enthusiasm in itself made a great impression upon me. But his appearance also surprised me. On posters and in caricatures I had seen him in military tunic, with shoulder straps, swastika armband, and hair flapping over his forehead. But here he was wearing a well-fitted blue suit and looking markedly respectable. Everything about him bore out the note of reasonable modesty. Later I learned that he had a great gift for adjusting—consciously or intuitively—to his surroundings.

As the ovation went on for minutes, he tried, as if slightly pained, to check it. Then, in a low voice, hesitantly and somewhat shyly, he began a kind of historical lecture rather than a speech. To me there was something engaging about it—all the more so since it ran counter to everything the propaganda of his opponents had led me to expect: a hysterical demagogue, a shrieking and gesticulating fanatic in uniform. He did not allow the bursts of applause to tempt him away from his sober tone.

It seemed as if he were candidly presenting his anxieties about the future. His irony was softened by a somewhat self-conscious humor; his South German charm reminded me agreeably of my native region. A cool Prussian could never have captivated me that way. Hitler's initial shyness soon disappeared; at times now his pitch rose. He spoke urgently and with hypnotic persuasiveness. The mood he cast was much deeper than the speech itself, most of which I did not remember for long.

Moreover, I was carried on the wave of the enthusiasm which, one could almost feel this physically, bore the speaker along from sentence to sentence. It swept away any skepticism, any reservations. Opponents were given no chance to speak. This furthered the illusion, at least momentarily, of unanimity. Finally, Hitler no longer seemed to be speaking to convince; rather, he seemed to feel that he was expressing what the audience, by now transformed into a single mass, expected of him. It was as if it were the most natural thing in the world to lead students and part of the faculty of the two greatest academies in Germany submissively by a leash. Yet that evening he was not yet the absolute ruler, immune from all criticism, but was still exposed to attacks from all directions. . . .

. . . The peril of communism, which seemed inexorably on its way, could be checked, Hitler persuaded us, and instead of hopeless unemployment, Germany could move toward economic recovery. He had mentioned the Jewish problem only peripherally. But such remarks did not worry me, although I was not an anti-Semite; rather, I had Jewish friends from my school days and university days, like virtually everyone else. . . .

. . . I applied for membership in the National Socialist Party and in January 1931 became Member Number 474,481.

It was an utterly undramatic decision. Then and ever afterward I scarcely felt myself to be a member of a political party. I was not choosing the NSDAP, but becoming a follower of Hitler, whose magnetic force had reached out to me the first time I saw him and had not, thereafter, released me. His persuasiveness, the peculiar magic of his by no means pleasant voice, the oddity of his rather banal manner, the seductive simplicity with which he attacked the complexity of our problems—all that bewildered and fascinated me. I knew virtually nothing about his program. He had taken hold of me before I had grasped what was happening.

9

MELITA MASCHMANN

A German Teenager's Response to the Nazi Takeover in January 1933

1963

Melita Maschmann, daughter of a middle-class family, was a teenager in January 1933 when Hitler came to power. Her memoir, first published in German in 1963, is composed as a letter to a childhood friend, a Jew. In it Maschmann attempts to explain why she was attracted to the Third Reich. In this excerpt, she describes Hitler's extraordinary appeal to young people as he assumed the office of chancellor in January 1933.

There must be many answers to the question—what caused young people to become National Socialists at that time. For people at a certain stage of adolescence the antagonism between the generations, taken in conjunction with Hitler's seizure of power, probably often

From Melita Maschmann, *Account Rendered: A Dossier on My Former Self*, trans. Geoffrey Strachan (London: Abelard-Schuman, 1964), 10–12, 16.

played a part in it. For me it turned the scale. I wanted to follow a different road from the conservative one prescribed for me by family tradition. In my parents' mouths the words "social" or "socialist" had a scornful ring. They used them when they waxed indignant over the hunchback dressmaker's desire to play an active part in politics. On January 30, 1933, she [the dressmaker] announced that a time was now at hand when servants would no longer have to eat off the kitchen table. My mother always treated her servants correctly but it would have seemed absurd to her to share their company at table.

No catchword has ever fascinated me quite as much as that of the "National Community" (*Volksgemeinschaft*). I heard it first from the lips of this crippled and care-worn dressmaker and, spoken on the evening of January 30, it acquired a magical glow. The manner of my first encounter with it fixed its meaning for me: I felt it could only be brought into being by declaring war on the class prejudices of the social stratum from which I came and that it must, above all, give protection and justice to the weak. What held my allegiance to this idealistic fantasy was the hope that a state of affairs could be created in which people of all classes would live together like brothers and sisters.

On the evening of January 30 my parents took us children, my twin brother and myself, into the centre of the city. There we witnessed the torchlight procession with which the National Socialists celebrated their victory. Some of the uncanny feel of that night remains with me even today. The crashing tread of the feet, the sombre pomp of the red and black flags, the flickering light from the torches on the faces and the songs with melodies that were at once aggressive and sentimental.

For hours the columns marched by. Again and again amongst them we saw groups of boys and girls scarcely older than ourselves. What was I, who was only allowed to stand on the pavement and watch, feeling at my back the icy blast which emanated from my parents' reserve? Hardly more than a chance spectator, a child who was still given schoolgirl stories for Christmas. And yet I longed to hurl myself into this current, to be submerged and borne along by it. . . .

. . . The boys and girls in the marching columns did count. Like the adults, they carried banners on which the names of their dead were written.

At one point somebody suddenly leaped from the ranks of the marchers and struck a man who had been standing only a few paces away from us. Perhaps he had made a hostile remark. I saw him fall to the ground with blood streaming down his face and I heard him cry out. Our parents hurriedly drew us away from the scuffle, but they had not been able to stop us seeing the man bleeding. The image of him haunted me for days.

The horror it inspired in me was almost imperceptibly spiced with an intoxicating joy. "For the flag we are ready to die," the torch-bearers had sung. It was not a matter of clothing or food or school essays, but of life and death. For whom? For me as well? I do not know if I asked myself this question at that moment, but I know I was overcome with a burning desire to belong to these people for whom it was a matter of life and death.

Whenever I probe the reasons which drew me to join the Hitler Youth, I always come up against this one: I wanted to escape from my childish, narrow life and I wanted to attach myself to something that was great and fundamental. This longing I shared with countless others of my contemporaries. . . .

I believed the National Socialists when they promised to do away with unemployment and with it the poverty of six million people. I believed them when they said they would reunite the German nation, which had split into more than forty political parties, and overcome the consequences of the dictated peace of Versailles. And if my faith could only be based on hope in January 1933, it seemed soon enough to have deeds to point to.

10

NEW YORK TIMES

Germany Ventures

January 31, 1933

After their 1930 electoral breakthrough, the Nazis continued to score political successes. In the July 1932 national parliamentary elections, the Nazis captured a little more than 37 percent of the vote. By January, President Hindenburg's advisers convinced him that the only way to achieve political stability would be to make Hitler, head of the largest

From "Germany Ventures," editorial, *New York Times*, January 31, 1933.

*party in parliament, chancellor. In his first cabinet, Hitler was joined by
only two other members of the Nazi party, leaving many Germans—and
the author of this editorial in the* New York Times—*to believe that
Hitler's radicalism would be contained. The writer could not have been
more mistaken.*

It would be useless to try to disguise the qualms which the news from
Berlin must cause to all friends of Germany. At the head of the Government of the German Republic has been placed a man who has
openly scorned it and vowed that he would destroy it as soon as he
could set up the personal dictatorship which was his boasted aim.
That he has not attained. A majority of the Cabinet which he, as Chancellor, has been forced to accept would be strongly opposed to him if
he sought to translate the wild and whirling words of his campaign
speeches into political action. On the outside stand the powerful
organizations of German labor, ready to resist, by a general strike if
need be, any open movement to set up a Fascist Dictator in Germany.
It is announced that the national finances will be kept in strong and
conservative hands. Germany's foreign policy will remain unchanged.
Best assurance of all is the fact that President Hindenburg will retain
supreme command prepared to unmake Hitler as quickly as he has
made him, in case the safety and honor of the Reich require it.

There is thus no warrant for immediate alarm. It may be that we
shall see the "tamed Hitler" of whom some Germans are hopefully
speaking. Always we may look for some such transformation when a
radical or demagogue fights his way into responsible office. . . . Yet it
cannot be concealed that Germany has entered upon a perilous political adventure. In addition to a disturbing effect at home, it may cause
grave apprehensions abroad. Public men in Great Britain and France
will follow every phase of the Hitler experiment with the deepest concern. All will depend upon the ability or disposition of Chancellor
Hitler to rise to his new opportunity.

Much of his old electoral thunder has either been stolen from him
or has died down into a negligible rumble. The more violent parts of
his alleged program he has himself in recent months been softening
down or abandoning. He now has a chance to show the world whether
he is anything more than a flighty agitator who has almost unaccount-
ably captivated the middle classes and the flaming youth of Germany.
Judgment should be suspended until it is more clearly known what
course he will elect to pursue. But anxiety will not be relaxed nor vigi-

lance abated so long as it is uncertain whether the new Chancellor of
Germany is going to urge and seek to compel the German people to
take a leap into the dark. The step already taken is undeniably critical,
and every subsequent one will be closely watched in the hope that the
dominant German instinct for order, and the determination which Germans have repeatedly shown to stand by and defend and preserve
their republic, may again triumph over every danger suddenly rising
in their path.

11

JOHN HEARTFIELD

Adolf, the Superman: Swallows Gold and Spouts Tin

1932

*Helmut Herzfelde was so outraged by German nationalism in the First
World War that in protest he changed his name to John Heartfield
(1891–1968). After the war, Heartfield joined the Communist party. He
believed that art should serve an explicitly political purpose. He used a
new method called photomontage to produce images that were critical of
the Nazis. His images often adorned the covers of mass-circulation illus-
trated newspapers aimed at working-class audiences. When Hitler became chancellor in 1933, Heartfield left Germany, but he continued to
use his art to resist National Socialism while in exile. Heartfield created
his image, used as a poster in the 1932 national elections, based on a
widely circulated photograph of Hitler giving a speech (see page 7).
Using the photomontage technique, he superimposed an X-ray and
images of a swastika, the Iron Cross, and many coins. The caption reads,
"Adolf, the Superman: Swallows Gold and Spouts Tin."*

Research Library, The Getty Research Institute, Los Angeles, California (87-S194). © 2008
Artists Rights Society (ARS), New York/VG Bild-Kunst, Bonn.

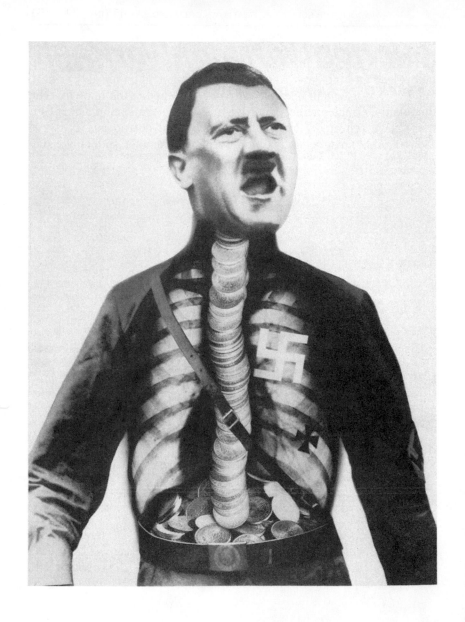

2

Life in Nazi Germany

12

Reports on the Sources of Working-Class Support for the Nazis and the Limits to Opposition

1935–1939

These secret reports from Social Democrats in Germany to the Social Democratic Party leaders in exile offer insights into the boundaries between discontent and opposition and the widespread political apathy that Social Democrats believed characterized many Germans in the 1930s. They also reveal what led some working-class Germans to support the National Socialist regime. The Nazis could take credit for the improvement of the economy. They also introduced inexpensive popular entertainment and state-subsidized holidays to demonstrate that they were serious about leveling social divisions among Germans. Established in November 1933, the organization that sponsored these activities was called Strength through Joy (Kraft durch Freude, or KdF). The KdF also led workers to believe that they might one day own the "people's car," the Volkswagen, which was also known as the KdF-Wagen. Of course, the Nazis accompanied these carrots with sticks, completely destroying any opposition parties.

From Detlev J. K. Peukert, *Inside Nazi Germany: Conformity, Opposition, and Racism in Everyday Life*, trans. Richard Deveson (New Haven, Conn.: Yale University Press, 1987), 240, 195; Jeremy Noakes and Geoffrey Pridham, eds., *Nazism, 1919–1945: A Documentary Reader*, vol. 2, *State, Economy, and Society, 1933–1939* (Exeter, U.K.: University of Exeter Press, 2000), 159, 397.

[1935]

The purpose of all the National Socialist organisations is the same.
Whether we are talking of the Labour Front or Strength through Joy,
the Hitler Youth or Labour Service, in each case the organisation's
purpose is the same: to "include" or "look after" the "national comrades," to make sure that they are not left to their own devices and, as
far as possible, to see that they do not come to their senses at all. Just
as empty restless activity prevents a person from doing any serious
work, so the National Socialists are forever providing excesses of
excitement with the express aim of preventing any real communal
interests or any form of voluntary association from arising. Ley[1]
recently said as much quite openly: "national comrades" were not to
have a private life, and they should certainly give up their private
skittles club. The aim of this organisational monopoly is to rob the
ordinary man of all independence, to suffocate whatever initiatives
he might take to create even the most primitive forms of voluntary
association, to keep him at a distance from anyone who is like-minded
or merely sympathetic, to isolate him and at the same time to bind
him to the state organisation. The effects are inevitable. Occasionally
one can hear working men or women express their appreciation of
Strength through Joy, and comment: "Nobody ever bothered about us
before." Sure enough, the state did not previously regard it as its job
to send rotas of working men and women off to the theatre in their
"free time." Previously, it was a point of pride for the workers to
"bother" about such things for themselves. But many people will
prefer the state-run forms of pleasure and "relaxation" because they
are less trouble. If that is the way things are, then clearly it cannot
be just a side-issue for us to show the workers that one or another particular achievement has come about because they stood firm, "shoulder to shoulder": this task becomes a central feature of illegal active
work.

The essence of fascist control of the masses is compulsory organisation on the one hand and atomisation on the other.

---

[1]Robert Ley (1890–1945) was the leader of the German Labor Front, the Nazi organization that sought to organize all German workers.

[1936]

KdF events have become very popular. Even ordinary workers can afford these walking trips, since they are generally cheaper than private hikes.

Almost all national comrades rate KdF as one of National Socialism's really creditable achievements. KdF sports courses are enjoying greater and greater popularity, even among older people. Everyone can take part. . . .

KdF is now running weekly theatre trips into Munich from the countryside. Special theatre trains are coming to Munich on weekdays from as far away as 120 km. It has therefore been made easy for people from the countryside to go to the theatre in the city. The trips are very popular. . . .

I attended a KdF swimming course in which over 50 took part, and I have to admit there was very little Party atmosphere. The participants were all ordinary people. There were scarcely any "Heil Hitlers." Coming from the old workers' sports clubs as we did, we felt at home, so to speak. I was doubtful about taking part in a KdF function at first, but there is really no alternative. I was all the more pleasantly surprised to find that there was absolutely nothing National Socialist about the way the course was organised and run.

It is pretty generally the case now that you can't avoid Kraft durch Freude if you want to travel or take part in sport. So a lot of our comrades who used to be in the Outdoor Club, for example, are availing themselves of the opportunity of going on trips with KdF. There is simply no other choice.

The average worker is primarily interested in work and not in democracy. People who previously enthusiastically supported democracy show no interest at all in politics. One must be clear about the fact that in the first instance men are fathers of families and have jobs, and that for them politics take second place and even then only when they expect to get something out of it.

Many people reject participation in illegal activity on account of this basic attitude. They consider it pointless and that one only ends up in jail because of it. But that does not by any means imply that they are going over to the Nazis.

An important point—it even seems to me the crucial point for our policy—is the fact that our people are averse to any unpatriotic attitudes. While it is true that they are in favour of an international understanding they feel that in the first instance they are Germans. One cannot drive it out of them.

[1938]

Strength through Joy is very popular. The events appeal to the yearning of the little man who wants an opportunity to get out and about himself and to take part in the pleasures of the "top people." It is a clever appeal to the petty bourgeois inclinations of the unpolitical workers. For such a man it really means something to have been on a trip to Scandinavia, or even if he only went to the Black Forest or the Harz Mountains, he imagines that he has thereby climbed up a rung on the social ladder. . . .

[1939]

. . . For a large number of Germans the announcement of the people's car came as a pleasant surprise. There developed a real KdF-Car psychosis. For a long time the KdF Car was a big talking point among all classes of population. . . . With the KdF Car the leadership of the Third Reich has killed several birds with one stone. In the first place, it removes for a period of several years money from the German consumer which he would otherwise spend on goods which cannot be supplied. Secondly, and that is the most important thing, they have achieved a clever diversionary tactic in the sphere of domestic politics. This car psychosis, which has been cleverly induced by the Propaganda Ministry, keeps the masses from becoming preoccupied with a depressing situation. Hitler has acquired domestic political credit with the car savers until the delivery of the car. For, it is well-known that, while they are saving up for a particular commodity, people are prepared to make quite a lot of sacrifices. Another aspect must not be overlooked. Despite all the export subsidies paid by other countries for their cars, the KdF car will be at least half the price of an equivalent car from the other exporting countries. In all the markets of northern and southern Europe, Asia, South and Central America, everywhere where the market is open, the KdF Car will beat all the other mass produced cars. . . .

13

JOSEPH GOEBBELS

The Tasks of the Ministry for Propaganda

March 15, 1933

Joseph Goebbels (1897–1945) joined the Nazi party in 1922 and quickly won a reputation for his oratorical skills and his political savvy. In March 1933, Goebbels became the Minister for Popular Enlightenment and Propaganda, a position created by Hitler, which ultimately encompassed responsibility for art, culture, education, and the media. In the following excerpts from an address to journalists, he outlines how he intends to combine the two tasks suggested in the title of his office. The Nazi state did not hesitate to use repression to enforce its beliefs, but Goebbels's speech also suggests what the Nazis believed could be accomplished with education and persuasion. Before Germany surrendered in May 1945, Goebbels instructed an SS doctor to poison Goebbels's six children. He then ordered another SS man to shoot him and his wife, Magda.

There can no longer be any doubt that since 30 January[1] a national revolution has been carried through in Germany, a revolution that in a single bound has moulded historical events in the course of six to eight weeks in a way that in normal times would require ten or twenty or even thirty years. No one can be in any doubt either that none of these events can be reversed or that, on the contrary, everyone, both in Germany and the world at large, must come to terms with the National Revolution and the events that it has brought about. Whether one supports or opposes this revolution and these consequences is in this context a matter of absolutely no importance. I see the establishment of this new Ministry for Popular Enlightenment and Propaganda

[1]The date in 1933 on which Hitler became chancellor.

From Joseph Goebbels, "The Tasks of the Ministry for Propaganda," in *The Third Reich: Politics and Propaganda*, by David Welch, 2nd ed. (London: Routledge, 2002), 173–75.

as a revolutionary act of government because the new Government has no intention of abandoning the people to their own devices and locking them up in an airless room. This Government is, in the truest sense of the word, a People's Government. It derives from the people and it will always execute the people's will. I protest most passionately against the notion that this Government is the expression of some reactionary will and that we are reactionaries. . . . We want to give the people what belongs to them, albeit in a different form from what has been the case under parliamentary democracy. . . .

The name of the new ministry tells us quite clearly what we mean by this. We have founded a Ministry for Popular Enlightenment and Propaganda. These two titles do not convey the same thing. Popular enlightenment is essentially something passive; propaganda, on the other hand, is something active. We cannot, therefore, be satisfied with just telling the people what we want and enlightening them as to how we are doing it. We must, rather, replace this enlightenment with an active Government propaganda, a propaganda that aims at winning people over. It is not enough to reconcile people more or less to our regime, to move them towards a position of neutrality towards us, we want rather to work on people until they are addicted to us, until they realise, in the ideological sense as well, that what is happening now in Germany not only must be allowed, but can be allowed. In this respect the National Socialist Movement has already done an enormous amount of preparatory work. . . .

Propaganda—a much-maligned and often misunderstood word. The layman uses it to mean something inferior or even despicable. The word "propaganda" always has a bitter after-taste. But, if you examine propaganda's most secret causes, you will come to different conclusions; then there will be no more doubting that the propagandist must be the man with the greatest knowledge of souls. I cannot convince a single person of the necessity of something unless I have got to know the soul of that person, unless I understand how to pluck the string in the harp of his soul that must be made to sound. It is not true that propaganda presents merely a rough blueprint; it is not true that the propagandist does no more than administer complex thought processes in rough form, in a raw state, to the masses. Rather, the propagandist must not just know the soul of the people in general but must also understand the secret swings of the popular soul from one side to another. The propagandist must understand how to speak not only to the people in their totality but also to individual sections of the population: to the worker, the peasant, the middle class; he must understand how to speak to both the south German and the north German; he must be able to speak to different professions and to different faiths. The propagandist must always be in a position to speak to people in the language that they understand. These capacities are the essential preconditions for success.

14

WILLIAM L. SHIRER

Description of the Nazi Party Rally in Nuremberg

September 4–5, 1934

In September 1934, Hitler traveled to Nuremberg to address a huge crowd of enthusiastic followers at the annual meeting of the Nazi party, famously captured in Leni Riefenstahl's documentary Triumph of the Will *(1935). This event exemplified the Nazis' keen sense of how to stage a political spectacle. William Shirer (1904–1993), an American journalist who lived in Europe in the 1920s and 1930s, was in Nuremberg for the weeklong affair and recorded his impressions in his diary. In this excerpt, he vividly describes the delirious enthusiasm Hitler was able to awaken in his followers.*

Nuremberg, September 4
Like a Roman emperor Hitler rode into this mediæval town at sundown today past solid phalanxes of wildly cheering Nazis who packed the narrow streets that once saw Hans Sachs and the *Meistersinger.*[1] Tens of thousands of Swastika flags blot out the Gothic beauties of the place, the façades of the old houses, the gabled roofs. The streets, hardly wider than alleys, are a sea of brown and black uniforms. I got

---

[1] Hans Sachs is the central figure in Richard Wagner's opera *Die Meistersinger von Nürnberg* (*The Master Singers of Nuremberg*).

From William L. Shirer, *Berlin Diary: The Journal of a Foreign Correspondent, 1934–1941* (Boston: Little, Brown, 1941), 16–19.

my first glimpse of Hitler as he drove by our hotel, the Württemberger Hof, to his headquarters down the street at the Deutscher Hof, a favourite old hotel of his, which has been remodeled for him. He fumbled his cap with his left hand as he stood in his car acknowledging the delirious welcome with somewhat feeble Nazi salutes from his right arm. He was clad in a rather worn gaberdine trench-coat, his face had no particular expression at all—I expected it to be stronger—and for the life of me I could not quite comprehend what hidden springs he undoubtedly unloosed in the hysterical mob which was greeting him so wildly. . . .

About ten o'clock tonight I got caught in a mob of ten thousand hysterics who jammed the moat in front of Hitler's hotel, shouting: "We want our Führer." I was a little shocked at the faces, especially those of the women, when Hitler finally appeared on the balcony for a moment. They reminded me of the crazed expressions I saw once in the back country of Louisiana on the faces of some Holy Rollers who were about to hit the trail. They looked up at him as if he were a Messiah, their faces transformed into something positively inhuman. If he had remained in sight for more than a few moments, I think many of the women would have swooned from excitement. . . .

NUREMBERG, SEPTEMBER 5

I'm beginning to comprehend, I think, some of the reasons for Hitler's astounding success. Borrowing a chapter from the Roman church, he is restoring pageantry and colour and mysticism to the drab lives of twentieth-century Germans. This morning's opening meeting in the Luitpold Hall on the outskirts of Nuremberg was more than a gorgeous show; it also had something of the mysticism and religious fervour of an Easter or Christmas Mass in a great Gothic cathedral. The hall was a sea of brightly coloured flags. Even Hitler's arrival was made dramatic. The band stopped playing. There was hush over the thirty thousand people packed in the hall. Then the band struck up the *Badenweiler March*, a very catchy tune, and used only, I'm told, when Hitler makes his big entries. Hitler appeared in the back of the auditorium, and followed by his aides, Göring,[2] Goebbels, Hess,[3] Himmler, and the others, he strode slowly down the long centre aisle

[2]Hermann Goering (or Göring) (1893–1946) was designated by Hitler as second-in-command in the Third Reich. He held several offices, including commander-in-chief of the Luftwaffe.
[3]Rudolf Hess (1894–1987), Hitler's private secretary for many years, was made deputy leader of the Nazi party in 1933.

while thirty thousand hands were raised in salute. It is a ritual, the old-timers say, which is always followed. Then an immense symphony orchestra played Beethoven's *Egmont* Overture. Great Klieg lights played on the stage, where Hitler sat surrounded by a hundred party officials and officers of the army and navy. Behind them the "blood flag," the one carried down the streets of Munich in the ill-fated putsch.[4] Behind this, four or five hundred S.A. standards. When the music was over, Rudolf Hess, Hitler's closest confidant, rose and slowly read the names of the Nazi "martyrs"—brown-shirts who had been killed in the struggle for power—a roll-call of the dead, and the thirty thousand seemed very moved.

In such an atmosphere no wonder, then, that every word dropped by Hitler seemed like an inspired Word from on high. Man's—or at least the German's—critical faculty is swept away at such moments, and every lie pronounced is accepted as high truth itself.

[4] Hitler's Beer Hall Putsch in November 1923.

15

Concordat between the Holy See and the German Reich
July 20, 1933

In 1933, approximately 32 percent of the German population was Catholic, and about 63 percent was registered as Evangelical (Protestant). The Catholic Church feared that the Nazis might threaten its control over religious practice and the religious education of Catholic youths. Hitler moved swiftly to ensure church leaders that they had nothing to fear. In return, the church agreed to refrain from partisan political activity and to accept the dissolution of the Catholic Center party. By negotiating an agreement called a concordat with the Vatican, led by Pope Pius XI, the Nazi state also gained legitimacy on the world stage.

From "Concordat between the Holy See and the German Reich," in *The Nazi Germany Sourcebook: An Anthology of Texts*, ed. Roderick Stackelberg and Sally A. Winkle (London: Routledge, 2002), 156–60.

His Holiness Pope Pius XI and the President of the German Reich,[1] moved by a common desire to consolidate and enhance the friendly relations existing between the Holy See and the German Reich, wish to regulate the relations between the Catholic Church and the State for the whole territory of the German Reich in a permanent manner and on a basis acceptable to both parties. They have decided to conclude a solemn agreement, which will supplement the Concordats already concluded with certain individual German states, and will ensure for the remaining states fundamentally uniform treatment of their respective problems. . . .

Article 1. The German Reich guarantees freedom of profession and public practice of the Catholic religion.

It acknowledges the right of the Catholic Church, within the limit of those laws which are applicable to all, to manage and regulate her own affairs independently, and, within the framework of her own competence, to publish laws and ordinances binding on her members. . . .

Article 16. Before bishops take possession of their dioceses they are to take a loyalty oath either to the governor (*Reichsstatthalter*) of the state concerned, or to the President of the Reich, according to the following formula:

> Before God and on the Holy Gospels I swear and promise, as becomes a bishop, loyalty to the German Reich and to the state of ____. I swear and promise to honor the legally constituted government and to cause the clergy of my diocese to honor it. In the performance of my spiritual office and in my solicitude for the welfare and the interests of the German Reich, I will endeavor to avoid all detrimental acts which might endanger it.

. . .

Article 22. With regard to the appointment of Catholic religious instructors, agreement will be arrived at as a result of mutual consultation on the part of the bishop and the government of the state concerned. Teachers who have been declared by the bishop unfit for the further exercise of their teaching functions, either on pedagogical grounds or by reason of their moral conduct, may not be employed for religious instruction so long as the problem remains.

Article 23. The retention of Catholic denominational schools, and the establishment of new ones, is guaranteed. In all parishes in which parents or guardians request it, Catholic elementary schools will be

[1]The President of the German Reich was Paul von Hindenburg, who had appointed Hitler to the position of Chancellor.

established, provided that the number of pupils available appears to be sufficient for a school managed and administered in accordance with the standards prescribed by the state, due regard being given to the local conditions of school organizations.

Article 24. In all Catholic elementary schools only such teachers are to be employed as are members of the Catholic Church, and who guarantee to fulfill the special requirements of a Catholic school.

Within the framework of the general professional training of teachers, arrangements will be made which will secure the formation and training of Catholic teachers in accordance with the special requirements of Catholic denominational schools. . . .

In witness hereof, the plenipotentiaries have signed this Concordat. Signed in two original exemplars.
In the Vatican City, 20 July 1933

[signed] Eugenio, Cardinal Pacelli
[signed] Franz von Papen[2]

[2]Cardinal Pacelli, the Vatican's representative, would become Pope Pius XII in 1939. Von Papen was the vice chancellor under Hitler in 1933.

16

PROTESTANT CHURCH LEADERS

Declaration of Independence from the Nazi State

October 21, 1934

Hitler proposed that the German Christians, a Protestant organization that had supported Hitler before he became chancellor, should take control of a unified national German Evangelical Church that would include all German Protestants. Many Protestant church leaders resisted this plan, and, in October 1934, they rejected the institutional authority of the new church. They insisted on clerical control of all religious matters and

From Jeremy Noakes and Geoffrey Pridham, eds., *Nazism, 1919–1945: A Documentary Reader*, vol. 2, *State, Economy, and Society, 1933–1939* (Exeter, U.K.: University of Exeter Press, 2000), 390.

claimed that religion and Nazi ideology should not mix. The Confessing Church, as this movement was called, was ruled by its own synod, a council that represented all member churches. It existed in an uneasy relationship with the Nazi state, and in the late 1930s some of its leaders were arrested, but it never moved into open opposition to the Nazis. Most of its members supported Nazi policy as long as it did not directly affect religious practice. The histroy of the Confessing Church indicates the limits imposed on the Nazis' attempts to transform all aspects of German society. This 1934 pronouncement by church leaders makes explicit the division between the German Christians and the newly created Confessing Church.

1. We declare that the Constitution of the German Evangelical Church has been destroyed. Its legally constituted organs no longer exist. The men who have seized the Church leadership in the Reich and the states have divorced themselves from the Christian Church.

2. In virtue of the right of Churches, religious communities and holders of ecclesiastical office, bound by scripture and confession, to act in an emergency, the Confessional Synod of the German Evangelical Church establishes new organs of leadership. It appoints as leader and representative of the German Evangelical Church, as an association of confessionally determined Churches, the Fraternal Council of the German Evangelical Church and from among it the Council of the German Evangelical Church to the management leadership. Both organs are composed and organized in accordance with the confessions.

3. We summon the Christian communities, their pastors and elders, to accept no directives from the present Church Government and its authorities and to decline cooperation with those who wish to remain obedient to this ecclesiastical governance. We summon them to observe the directives of the Confessional Synod of the German Evangelical Church and its recognized organs.

17

ADOLF HITLER

Opening Address at the House
of German Art in Munich

July 19, 1937

The Nazis believed that all forms of culture—from popular music and movies to opera and art—played a crucial role in conveying Nazi ideology. This was at no time clearer than in July 1937 at the opening of the House of German Art, a museum in Munich built to display and celebrate the type of Aryan art of which Hitler approved. In the same year, an exhibition of some 650 works titled Entartete Kunst *(Degenerate Art) toured Germany and Austria. Some of the artists, such as Otto Dix and George Grosz, were Germans associated with communism who used their art to critique capitalism and militarism. Others, such as the Swiss Paul Klee and the Russian Wassily Kandinsky, were "degenerate" because their work was considered too modern and abstract. And still others, such as Marc Chagall, were so labeled because they took up themes of Jewish culture. If the degenerate art exhibition included the wrong sort of art, the House of German Art was dedicated to the right sort. It featured bombastic sculptures of muscle-bound male nudes, often carrying weapons, and highly realistic paintings of chaste female nudes, intended to embody a desexualized femininity, as well as landscapes and portraits of Hitler. In these excerpts from his address opening the museum, Hitler, himself a failed painter, waxes eloquent on his view of art and the artist.*

As in politics, so in German art-life, we are determined to make a clean sweep of empty phrases. Ability is the necessary qualification if an artist wishes his work to be exhibited here. People have attempted to recommend modern art by saying that it is the expression of a new age; but art does not create a new age, it is the general life of peoples which fashions itself anew and often looks for a new expression.... A

From Adolf Hitler, opening address, House of German Art, July 19, 1937, in Jeremy Noakes and Geoffrey Pridham, eds., *Nazism, 1919–1945: A Documentary Reader*, vol. 2, *State, Economy, and Society, 1933–1939* (Exeter, U.K.: University of Exeter Press, 2000), 205–6.

new epoch is not created by *littérateurs* but by the fighters, those who really fashion and lead people, and thus make history. . . . It is either impudent effrontery or an almost inconceivable stupidity to exhibit to people of today works which perhaps ten or twenty thousand years ago might have been made by a man of the Stone Age. They talk of primitive art, but they forget that it is not the function of art to retreat backwards from the development of a people: its sole function must be to symbolize that living development.

The new age of today is at work on a new human type. Men and women are to be healthier and stronger. There is a new feeling of life, a new joy in life. Never was humanity in its external appearance and in its frame of mind nearer to the ancient world than it is today. . . . This, my good prehistoric art stutterers, is the type of the new age, but what do you manufacture? Misformed cripples and cretins, women who inspire only disgust, men who are more like wild beasts, children who, were they alive, must be regarded as under God's curse. And let no one tell me that that is how these artists see things. From the pictures sent in for exhibition it is clear that the eye of some men portrays things otherwise than as they are, that there really are men who on principle feel meadows to be blue, the heaven green, clouds sulphur-yellow, or, as perhaps they prefer to say, "experience" them thus. I need not ask whether they really do see or feel things in this way, but in the name of the German people I have only to prevent these miserable unfortunates, who clearly suffer from defects of vision, attempting with violence to persuade contemporaries by their chatter that these faults of observation are indeed realities or from presenting them as "art." There are only two possibilities here. Either these "artists" do really see things in this way and believe in what they represent. Then one has only to ask how the defect in vision arose, and if it is hereditary the Minister for the Interior will have to see to it that so ghastly a defect of vision shall not be allowed to perpetuate itself. Or if they do *not* believe in the reality of such impressions but seek on other grounds to burden the nation with this humbug, then it is a matter for a criminal court. There is no place for such works in this building. . . .

The artist does not create for the artist. He creates for the people, and we will see to it that the people in future will be called in to judge his art. No one must say that the people has no understanding for a really valuable enrichment of its cultural life. . . . The people in passing through these galleries will recognize in me its own spokesman and counsellor. It will draw a sigh of relief and gladly express its agreement with this purification of art. And that is decisive: an art which cannot count on the readiest and most intimate agreement of the great mass of the people, an art which must rely upon the support of small cliques, is intolerable. Such an art only tries to confuse, instead of gladly reinforcing, the sure and healthy instinct of a people. The artist cannot stand aloof from his people. This exhibition is only a beginning, but the end of Germany's artistic stultification has begun.

18

"Degenerate Music" Brochure

1939

Paralleling the traveling exhibition of degenerate art (Document 17) was an exhibition of degenerate music (Entartete Musik). The Nazis were particularly critical of American jazz. As this poster makes clear, they associated it with African Americans, whom they deemed racially inferior, and Jews, whom they charged with disseminating and promoting this "primitive" form of cultural expression throughout the world. The image was used as the cover of a brochure for the traveling exhibition, which opened in 1938. The guide was written by Dr. H. S. Ziegler, a state official who was the director of the National Theater in Weimar and a Nazi party leader.

Deutsches Historisches Museum Picture Archive, Berlin.

19

NEW YORK TIMES

Report on a Visit to a Reich Prison Camp
July 26, 1933

By the summer of 1933, the Nazis had established concentration camps, announced officially as facilities that could imprison and rehabilitate "enemies of the state," "reeducating" them in ways that would allow them to return to the "national community" (Volksgemeinschaft)*. Communists and Socialists made up most of the earliest inmates. By the late 1930s, they were joined by homosexual men, Jehovah's Witnesses, those deemed "asocial" by the Third Reich, Sinti and Roma (called* Zigeuner *or gypsies), and, in ever-growing numbers after November 9, 1938, Jews (see Document 33). Public knowledge of the camps was widespread, and as this article from the* New York Times *makes clear, Americans were not ignorant of them.*

DACHAU, BAVARIA, July 25.—The name of this idyllic little town, situated about a half-hour's automobile ride from Munich, has become a word of dread throughout Bavaria.

All the Bavarians, noted for their racy unreservedness of speech, pray these days with a mock drollery designed to beguile genuine apprehension:

> Please. Lord, make me dumb,
> So I won't to Dachau come.

For on the edge of Dachau is the big Bavarian concentration camp for political prisoners. Many a man has landed there, because of an incautious word or too much confidence in supposed comrades or friends. The Nazi Secret State Police, like the Cheka[1] of Russia, has agents everywhere, and any criticism of the new régime and even lack

---

[1] The secret police unit, predecessor to the KGB, that was created at the time of the Bolshevik Revolution.

From "Times Writer Visits Reich Prison Camp," *New York Times*, July 26, 1933.

of proper enthusiasm for it are punished as "sabotage" of the Nazi up-building program.

Such "saboteurs and killjoys" are sentenced to an indefinite period of training and education in the new and only true dogma of national salvation and for this purpose are sent to what are euphemistically called "educational camps," where in rigid discipline and hard labor they are converted from egotistical Marxists or liberals to good Nazis who place service to the State above service to themselves. . . .

The prisoners accept their confinement as a blow of revolutionary fate against which it is futile to rave. The older prisoners and "trusties" soon break in the new ones and the latter quickly learn that in view of the indefiniteness of their stay, good behavior and the quickest possible conversion to Nazism are their only chance of release. The intellectually honest are out of luck. . . .

Surrounding the camp is a seven-foot wall topped off with barbed wire and a short distance beyond have been placed barbed wire entanglements. Between the wall and the entanglements there are patrols of guards clad in grey green service denim. They are armed with rifles while machine guns are strategically placed and manned by alert crews with fingers at the triggers ready to mow down the rebellious or check any flight. . . .

Dachau is ruled by both prison regulations and rules of military discipline. That is apparent on the prisoners. Under a smiling sky, there was not a smile in the 2,000. They looked sour, grim, sullen, sad or merely apathetic. Thoughts of other things than the beauty of nature and the peacefulness of the scene obviously engaged their minds. And dark were the looks which greeted the Deputy Commander accompanying the correspondent.

20

GABRIELE HERZ

Description of an Early
Concentration Camp for Women
1937

Gabriele Herz (1886–1957), Jewish and Austrian by birth, married Emil Herz in 1910 and moved with him to Berlin, where they raised four children and lived a comfortable middle-class life. Once the Nazis took control, Emil lost his job, and he and Gabriele began to consider leaving Germany. In 1936, she visited Italy and on her return was arrested as a "returning émigré," subject to incarceration for breaking a Nazi law of which she was completely unaware. While authorities determined whether she had engaged in activities abroad that might be a threat to the government, Herz spent six months in Moringen, the first German concentration camp established exclusively for women. Her memoir, written after her release in 1937, provides insights into the early camps, ostensibly created for the "instruction" of inmates (see Document 19). Camps like this one dotted all of Germany, and their inmates were for the most part political enemies of the Nazis, not Jews. Herz was struck in particular by the deep convictions of Communists, whose allegiance to Moscow placed them outside the Nazis' national community, and Jehovah's Witnesses, whose religious beliefs dictated that they not subject themselves to a secular state.

MORINGEN, LATE OCTOBER 1936

. . . Yes, the Communists here are made of stern stuff. Confronted with the steadfastness of their convictions, external pressures prove completely futile. Even if Hitler piles triumph upon triumph, the women in Moringen are firmly convinced of the ultimate victory of the communist ideal, which they see being fulfilled in the construction of the Soviet state. For all their aspirations to independence and despite their frequent criticisms of the Russian system, they are spiritually

---

From Gabriele Herz, *The Women's Camp in Moringen: A Memoir of Imprisonment in Germany, 1936–1937*, trans. Hildegard Herz and Howard Hartig, ed. Jane Caplan (New York: Berghahn Books, 2006), 85, 94–95, 110–11, 150–51, 158–59.

71

dependent on Moscow. Moscow is the sun around which they orbit and from which they receive their light. It is in the light of this vision that they grapple with the great ideological dilemmas: individuality or community, freedom or coercion, democracy or dictatorship. The Russian model remains the standard, not only on questions of working conditions, on wages and the forty-hour week, but also on personal and even intimate matters, on love, marriage, extra-marital affairs, birth control, and child rearing. With consummate vigilance, in fact, the women monitor the successive phases in the development of the relationship between state and family [in the Soviet Union]. They are critical of the [state's] initial indifference to marriage, its facilitation of divorce, the attempts to weaken the status of parents and to strengthen the independence of children often raised in state institutions. They offer their opinions, sometimes approving, sometimes disapproving, on how these attitudes have been changing, gradually returning to the affinities of the past, right up to the recent official declaration that "the family, as the primary social cell, is of supreme value to all structures of the state."

Politically I cannot agree with the Communists, especially their spiritual leaders, the five [former] members of the federal and state parliaments. Their dialectic does not appeal to me, and I disapprove of this egalitarianism, equalization without individual evaluation, the overestimation of reason at the expense of emotion, the whole thoroughly materialistic ideology. But from the human point of view, I have the greatest respect for these strong and principled personalities, for their steadfastness and their moral integrity. I am happy to put up with their various minor faults. Even the simplest of these women, or perhaps especially they, are generally likable people. I seize every opportunity to expand my personal relationships and hence my knowledge of human nature. . . .

MORINGEN, EARLY NOVEMBER 1936

A genuine dilemma, almost an ordeal, is presented by the handling of nature's physical needs. For the one hundred women here there is only a single lavatory with two seats, side by side. There is a frightening crush early in the morning after we get up and in the evening before we go to bed. The room cannot be locked, and thus the lucky occupants of the two seats at any given time are besieged by the other waiting and impatient women and are goaded to hurry with antagonistic or sarcastic remarks.

"Are you working in slow motion in there, or what? Gretl, my God, do you ever have good digestion!"

"That bean soup seems to have agreed with you pretty well. You've turned the loudspeaker on again. Hey, we can hear you already! Beans, beans, the musical fruit, the more you eat the more you toot."

Personally, I have trained myself to wake up at 5:30 A.M. sharp. With the first sound of the signal bell, I rush down the stairs to be the first to reach the lavatory, where I spend a few minutes of solitude. Then, with a quick "Good morning" to the sleepy matron, I hurry back upstairs to the sleeping quarters, where my companions are slowly rising, and punch my straw mattress into the prescribed shape.

Space in the lavatory, already tight enough to begin with, is restricted even more by the buckets brought here from the sleeping quarters in the early morning hours, further by two huge garbage pails and a cabinet containing cleaning materials and shoe polish. Every object that is so worn out and useless that no one would dare offer it directly to anybody else is brought here. Given the intense and pervasive poverty, however, and behind the veil of anonymity, as it were, these items find their admirers and are put to new uses. Sardine tins are transformed into soap dishes, twine—a much sought-after item—into shoelaces, cloth remnants into neckties, a chemise into warm mittens.

At the same time, the lavatory also serves as a "beauty parlor." Every Monday former federal representative Anna Löser sets up her stool here and attends gratis to anyone who turns up. The scissors are the property of the "hairdresser"; the "customers" must provide their own razor blades, towel, and cream.

The lavatory offers yet another, distinctive attraction. Throughout the entire course of the day, there is not a single minute during which you can be alone with yourself. In the day room, during the exercise period, in the sleeping quarters, you are always together with your comrades in misfortune. But the desire for occasional solitude is overwhelming. From time to time, even if only for a little while, you would like to be able to lose yourself in thought, undisturbed by the others, by their sight, by their talking, by their movements. Forever crowded into this compulsory community, how can you summon the inner peace and composure necessary to think about a difficult letter, to draft a petition? Where can you share an important piece of news with a friend without all ears in the vicinity pricking up? There is only one room for all that—the lavatory. It is visited relatively infrequently in the afternoon hours. To be sure, in addition to the odor the cold is also a nuisance, since the windows are kept open for ventilation even when there is frost on the ground. But you can easily put up with that. And because every woman understands how absolutely necessary a little solitude is, everyone is respectful whenever others, driven by the same desire, visit this place. You simply don't see them. You withdraw discreetly, unless, of course, you are spoken to. . . .

MORINGEN, LATE NOVEMBER 1936
. . . The Bible Students[1] have refused to accept any role in the Winter Relief Campaign.[2] For them the state is fundamentally a creation of Satan; consequently, any order from the state derives from Satan, too. Their refusal was extremely awkward for the director. He had to take a stand on the matter but was apparently reluctant to administer severe reprisals. He's surprisingly well versed in the Holy Scriptures himself, and it has often given him considerable pleasure to put the biblical knowledge of the Jehovah's Witnesses to the test with little-known quotations. So now he tried to win the devout women over with biblical references. "Your conduct places you in flagrant contradiction to divine law. Charity, relief of the poor is the duty of each and every one of the faithful. Isaiah preaches 'Is it not [your duty] when you see the naked, to clothe him, and not to turn away from your own flesh and blood?' [Isaiah 58:7]."

"But it is also written in the Gospel according to Matthew: 'Watch out for false prophets. They come to you in sheep's clothing, but inwardly they are ferocious wolves' [Matthew 7:15]," Magdalene Mewes, serving as spokeswoman for the Bible Students, responded bluntly.

It was hard for the director to restrain himself. "Winter Relief is required by the state. Paul commands explicitly in his Epistle to the Romans: 'Everyone must submit himself to the governing authorities' [Romans 13:1]."

"And Paul continues in the same sentence: 'There is no authority except that which God has established' [Romans 13:1]," objected Magdalene Mewes. "But God cannot have promoted this new state, for Paul says in a different passage, in his Epistle to the Corinthians: 'For God is not a God of disorder but of peace' [I Corinthians 14:33]. In today's Germany, where exactly does peace prevail?"

[1]Jehovah's Witnesses.
[2]Nazi program whereby local party leaders and the SA collected clothing and goods for the needy.

The director abandoned the theological realm and gave worldly inducements a try. "Everyone who contributes to the Winter Relief can request one article of clothing from the inventory for herself and one for her children."

"'What good will it be for a man if he gains the whole world, yet forfeits his soul?' [Matthew 16:26]," Magdalene Mewes, citing Matthew, declined indignantly.

The director finally lost his patience. He fumed at the women: "I could easily break this foolish resistance with the right kind of measures, such as reducing the daily food rations, or corporal punishment or confinement. But I'm reluctant to turn fools into martyrs. Nevertheless, I'm not prepared to allow this resistance to proceed without reprisal. I am therefore ordering your complete physical isolation. You will be removed from the Great Hall, from all contact with any other prisoners, and you will be housed in a separate cell."

"Luke says: 'Blessed are you when men hate you, when they exclude you and insult you and reject your name as evil' [Luke 6:22]," Magdalene Mewes encouraged her companions.

"Since this punishment apparently makes so little impression on you," the director continued, "I hereby strengthen it with a renewal of the mail embargo. This time it applies to you and you alone and will be in effect for six weeks in the first instance."

That was a heavy blow. The women knew only too well, from previous sad experience, what this mail embargo means. For a moment, even Magdalene Mewes was speechless. Then she pulled herself together, and her voice, at first a little shaky, became resonant, joyfully triumphant, buoyed by inner strength: "Who cares about letters? Thus speaks Paul to all of the righteous: 'You yourselves are our letter, written on our hearts, known and read by everybody. You show that you are a letter from Christ . . . written not with ink but with the Spirit of the living God, not on tablets of stone but on tablets of human hearts' [II Corinthians 3:2–3]."

The director held no power over these zealots. Far from hurting them with his punishment, he had actually fulfilled their most secret wishes. Their isolation, which even excluded them from communal exercise with us, was seen by them, quite seriously, as preferential treatment, as a reward for lives lived in service to God. Now completely together among themselves, with no diversion from any other activities, with no need to worry about those with different views, they dedicated themselves from dawn to dusk to the study of the Holy Scriptures and indulged in the most esoteric of interpretations, comparisons, and allegories. Undisturbed, they could now imagine the horror of the imminent end of the world, the details of Armageddon, the impending final battle between the righteous and the unrighteous. They could fantasize about the miracle of the Last Judgment and the splendor of the kingdom of righteousness, newly established by Jesus himself. The mail embargo was not too high a price to pay for this freedom to organize their lives completely around their religious desires and needs. In any case, the few letters that they had exchanged with their relatives up to then were less the expression of their personal experiences than an accumulation of impersonal biblical quotations.

The Jehovah's Witnesses had lost little and gained much. Whenever we happened to meet up with them, they would whisper to us, with joy and conviction: "God does not forsake his own." . . .

MORINGEN, LATE FEBRUARY 1937

Our situation here is becoming ever more hopeless and unbearable. Almost every day brings new burdens and new deprivations. . . .

With not the faintest ray of hope, with no motivation from within, with no faith in a brighter future, you trudge along, exhausted and resigned. Everything makes you sick. The overcrowding and the wretchedness of your surroundings, the monotony of the food, the loathsome "clinkclank," as the tin dishware is known here, the pitchers and mugs of damaged enamel. You find the stupid, hostile matrons disgusting. Often, you find even your friends disgusting: you know them too well, their mannerisms, their whole attitude. Mostly, you find yourself disgusting: you don't want to look at yourself any longer, always in the same dress that you have to wear constantly, day in, day out. You don't want to think the same thoughts any longer, they keep slamming, dazed and confused, into the same brick walls. The whole pointlessness and meaninglessness of the camp is disgusting. When will this misery finally end? Will we be buried alive here forever?

Our existence in Moringen is like artificial life in a vacuum under a bell jar. We have been removed from the circulation of real life. The principles of meaningful existence do not apply to us. By order of the state, we have been denied any responsibility, any real participation. We can no longer care for our families, for husband and child, can no longer earn money to meet our own needs, no matter how modest, cannot give any advice, cannot be of any use. We are no longer the subject of events, merely their object. At this time of momentous upheaval we sit helplessly in the background, at the mercy of the enemy; we have to put our hands in our laps and do what we're told. . . .

BERLIN, LATE MARCH 1937
... On March 17, 1937, I left the women's camp in Moringen.

The little local train traveled slowly. But for me it was still traveling too fast. Inwardly, I couldn't keep up. The conflict of emotions, the constant fluctuation between joy and melancholy befuddled me. . . .

I ride, I ride. Cities, villages fly past. Names resound in my ears, names that once meant a great deal to me but now ring hollow. I hear Magdeburg, Brandenburg, Potsdam. But I don't know where I am.

Then suddenly: "Berlin, Zoological Garden. Berlin, Zoological Garden."

From the other end of the platform, otherwise deserted now at midnight, my children's voices call out: "Mother! Mother!" My daughter, my son are hanging round my neck. My husband is standing in front of me. He cannot speak. Neither can I.

I have written these final pages in Berlin, in our home. It's all a dream. And I am not yet awake.

Only with difficulty am I able to come to terms with my new situation. Surely it's wrong, but I am unable to enjoy my freedom. The large house with its many comfortable and attractive rooms depresses me. I still live in Moringen. I don't want to sit at our table with its bountiful, nutritious fare—in Moringen people are hungry. I don't want to take part in my visitors' often trivial conversations—in Moringen the conversations are all about the most profound of questions, about freedom, life, and death. The lovely avenues, their trees resplendent with the first green of spring, the stately villas, the wide streets, the people, all dressed up, out for a stroll—I don't want to see them. Facing me is always the suffering, the sorrow, the despair of my companions in Moringen.

Gradually, by force of necessity, I find my way back to reality. I am also gradually able to help Ehm, my husband. He is expending his entire energy to press ahead with our emigration. "Let us not linger one day longer than we must," he says constantly. "Better to abandon everything here, house and belongings. Let us just get away from this land of Nazi criminality, of unfathomable barbarity."

At last. At last. Our passports, our papers have all been put in order.

Tomorrow we cross the German frontier.

21

Reports on Working-Class Attitudes toward the Murder of SA Leader Ernst Röhm

1934–1935

On June 30, 1934, Hitler deployed the SS to carry out a "blood purge" against Ernst Röhm and his followers. A close comrade of Hitler's since the Führer's earliest days in the Nazi party, Röhm was the leader of the storm troopers (Sturmabteilung, or SA), the Nazis' brown-uniformed paramilitary organization. Although Röhm's criticism of the military leadership was the most important reason for the purge, referred to as the Night of Long Knives, Hitler also justified it by pointing to Röhm's homosexuality. How Germans viewed this act is suggested by the reports of German Social Democratic Party leaders in exile.

The immediate result of the murders was great confusion, both as regards the way they were viewed and as regards their future political consequences. On the whole, Hitler's courage in taking decisive action was stressed the most. He was regarded practically as a hero. Hitler's slandering of the victims, their homosexuality and their 30,000 Mark meals, was at first also adjudged heroic. As to what the repercussions of the events of 30th June and their aftermath will be, an agreed and definitive answer cannot yet be given. Our comrades report that Hitler has won strong approval and sympathy from that part of the population which still places its hopes in him. To these people his action is proof that he wants order and decency. Other sections of the population have been given cause for thought.

East Saxony: A small businessman told me that he and his colleagues had known for a long time that Hitler was going to strike at Röhm and his associates. He still sees Hitler, even now, as an utterly honourable man who wants the best for the German people. It is only Hitler's hangers-on who have been preventing him from working for the people, and now he has got rid of them. When I tried to explain to him

From SOPADE, "Reports on Germany," Detlev J. K. Peukert, *Inside Nazi Germany: Conformity, Opposition, and Racism in Everyday Life*, trans. Richard Deveson (New Haven, Conn.: Yale University Press, 1987), 71–72.

that Hitler alone bore the responsibility for all the murders, these and earlier ones, he said: "Still, the main thing is, he's got rid of the Marxists." He also said that Hitler undoubtedly still had as much support among the majority of the people as he did before, especially as he was now cleaning out the dreadful SA, who had done Germany great damage. Wages would definitely be cut now, and industry would be able to get back to work and start earning money. He still swears by Hitler as a superhuman being, even if he is a murderer many times over.

Bavaria: 1st report. By slaughtering his "best friends" Hitler has forfeited none of his mass support as yet; rather, he has gained. Reports from different parts of Bavaria are unanimous that people are expressing satisfaction that Hitler has acted so decisively. He has produced fresh proof that he will not settle for second-best and that he wants decency in public life.

22

ADOLF HITLER

Speech to the National Socialist Women's Organization

September 8, 1934

During the Weimar Republic, many organizations emerged to champion women's rights and advocate women's equality with men. Once the Nazis came to power, Social Democratic, Jewish, and Communist organizations were crushed, and other organizations were merged into the National Socialist Women's Organization. In the following excerpts from his address to this body in 1934, Hitler makes clear that for him, a woman's primary responsibility is as a mother, and he associates the language of women's emancipation with the Jews. Note, however, that even as he praises women for their "strength of feeling" and "ever patient devotion," he also applauds them as "the most loyal, fanatical comrades-in-arms," who are "fighters" in the "struggle" for the "common preservation of life." Bearing a child is, he

From Adolf Hitler's speech to the National Socialist Women's Organization, in *The Nazi Germany Sourcebook: An Anthology of Texts*, ed. Roderick Stackelberg and Sally A. Winkle (London: Routledge, 2002), 182–84.

notes, a "battle" that a mother "wages for the existence of her people." For Hitler, motherhood was not a private affair; rather, mothers served not only their families but also the higher goals of the Nazi state.

The phrase "women's liberation" is a phrase invented only by Jewish intellectualism, and its content is shaped by the same spirit. The German woman never needed to be emancipated in the really good times of German life. She possessed exactly the gifts that nature had perforce given her to manage and preserve, exactly as man in his good times never needed to fear that he would be forced out of his role in relation to woman.

His place was least of all threatened by woman. It was only when he himself was not certain about what his responsibility was that woman's eternal instinct for self-preservation and preservation of the people began to rebel. A change of roles not in accord with nature began with this rebellion, and it lasted until both sexes returned once again to the roles that an eternally wise providence assigned to them.

If one says that man's world is the state, man's world is his struggle, his readiness to act on behalf of the community, then one could perhaps say that the world of woman is a smaller one. For her world is her husband, her family, her children, and her home. But where would the larger world be if no one wanted to look after the smaller world? How could the larger world exist, if there were no one who would make the cares of the smaller world the content of their lives? No, the large world is founded on this small world! This large world cannot exist, if the small world is not stable. Providence assigned to woman the cares of a world that is particularly her own, and it is only on this that man's world can be shaped and constructed.

That is why these two worlds are never in conflict. They complement each other, they belong together, as man and woman belong together.

We feel it is not appropriate when woman forces her way into man's world, into his territory; instead we perceive it as natural when these two worlds remain separate. One world is characterized by strength of feeling, strength of the soul! The other world is characterized by strength of vision, toughness, determination, and willingness to act. In the former case this strength requires the willingness of woman to commit her life to preserve and increase the family unit; in the latter case this power requires from man the readiness to provide security.

Whatever sacrifices man makes in the struggles of his people, woman makes in the struggle for the preservation of her people in family units. What man offers in heroic courage on the battlefield, woman offers in ever patient devotion, in ever-patient suffering and endurance. Each child that she brings into the world is a battle that she wages for the existence of her people. Both man and woman must therefore value and respect each other, when they see that each accomplishes the task that nature and providence have ordained. Out of this separation of functions there will necessarily come mutual respect.

It is not true, as Jewish intellectualism maintains, that respect depends on overlapping spheres of activity of the sexes; instead respect requires that neither sex try to do what rightly is the task of the other. In the final analysis respect comes from each side knowing that the other is doing everything necessary to maintain the whole! . . .

Woman, because she springs from the root of life, is also the most stable element in the preservation of a people.

In the last analysis she has the most infallible sense for what is necessary so that a race does not die out, because it is above all her children who will be the first to be affected by that misfortune.

Man is often psychologically too erratic to find his way immediately to these fundamental truths. Only in good time and with a good education will man come to know exactly what his responsibility is. For many years we National Socialists have therefore opposed bringing woman into political life, a life that in our eyes is unworthy of her. A woman once said to me: "You must see to it that women get into the parliament, because only they can ennoble it." "I do not believe," I replied, "that we should ennoble something inherently bad. And the woman who gets caught in this parliamentary machinery will not ennoble it; instead it will dishonor her. I do not want to leave something to woman that I intend to take away from men." My opponents believed that we would never win women for our movement. But we gained more women than all the other parties put together, and I know we would have won over the very last German woman if she had only had the opportunity to study the parliament and the degrading function of the women involved in it.

We have therefore included women in the struggle of the national community as nature and providence intended. Our women's movement is for us not a movement that inscribes on its banner a program of fighting against man, but instead it is a movement that embraces in its program the common struggle of woman together with man. For we have strengthened the new National Socialist *Volksgemeinschaft* precisely because millions of women became the most loyal, fanatical comrades-in-arms; women fighting for life together in the service of the common

preservation of life; women fighters who in this struggle do not set their
gaze on rights with which a Jewish intellectualism bedazzles them, but
on duties which nature imposes on all of us in common. . . .

You, my party comrades, stand here as leaders, organizers, and
helpers in this struggle. You have accepted a magnificent responsibility.
What we want to create in our nation as a whole is what you must establish and firmly support in the inner world. You must provide the inner
psychological and emotional stability! You must complement man in this
struggle that we are leading for our people's freedom, equality, honor,
and peace, so that we can look to the future as fighters for our people!

Then strife and discord can never break out between the sexes;
instead they will go through life hand in hand fighting together, just
the way providence intended, and for the purpose that both sexes were
created. Then the blessing of such work carried out together can not
fail to appear. Then no insane struggle will flare up over theories, and
man and woman will not quarrel because of false ideas; instead the
blessing of the Almighty will accompany their joint fight for survival!

23

"Healthy Parents—Healthy Children!" Poster
ca. 1934

*The Nazis sought to replace a Marxist ideology of class struggle and a lib-
eral ideology of individualism with an ideology of race that united some—
Aryans—while excluding others. The bases of Nazi racial science seem
preposterous today, but Nazi concepts of racial difference profoundly influenced law, public policy, and popular attitudes. Nazi scientists also determined race by facial characteristics—the curve of the nose, the shape of
the ear—and hair and eye color. Those deemed fit had the national
responsibility to reproduce the race. Those deemed unfit should not (see
Document 26). This poster by Franz Würbel promotes the properly Aryan
family with its "healthy parents" and "healthy children." Note the family's
size and appearance, including the young boy wearing the uniform of a
Nazi youth organization.*

Deutsches Historisches Museum Picture Archive, Berlin.

Gesunde Eltern — gesunde Kinder!

Lest die bevölkerungspolitischen Aufklärungsschriften der N.S.Volkswohlfahrt!

Die Broschüre „Gesunde Eltern — gesunde Kinder!" enthält den Wortlaut des
Gesetzes zur Bekämpfung erbkranken Nachwuchses und seiner Begründung.

Zu beziehen durch die Ortsgruppen der N.S.D.A.P. und alle Postschalter / Preis 10 Pfennig   N.S. Volkswohlfahrt - Reichsführung: Berlin NW, Reichstag

24

JUTTA RÜDIGER

On the League of German Girls

1939

The Hitler Youth (Hitlerjugend) was entrusted with coordinating all activities for young people. By the time membership was made mandatory for all youths ages ten and older in March 1939, 8.7 million young people, in Germany, Austria, and the Sudetenland, had joined the organization. Jews and others deemed undesirable were excluded. For some, participation in the group was an excuse to escape parental control and engage in outdoor activities. For others, it was the gateway to the Nazi party. The Hitler Youth was divided by gender. Jutta Rüdiger (1910–2001), an official in the national office of the League of German Girls (Bund deutscher Mädel), explains the official party line on the female section of the organization in this document.

The League of German Maidens, today the largest association of girls in the world, can only be understood in terms of National Socialism. The old youth movement, whether we are talking now of the movement for boys or girls, arose at the turn of the century from a form of rebellion; rebellion against the narrow, bourgeois, petty world, against the materialistic spirit of the times. But just as the times themselves were uncreative and without a style of their own, so the youth movement itself had no ideas of its own.

Worthwhile individuals often found themselves gathered together. They forgot, however, that opposition must never become the primary object, but that only a powerful idea can overcome the old, and create new values. Hence, they often lost themselves in romantic daydreams and discussions beside the camp fire....

From an essay by Jutta Rüdiger, on the League of German Girls, in *The Racial State: Germany, 1933–1945*, by Michael Burleigh and Wolfgang Wippermann (Cambridge, U.K.: Cambridge University Press, 1991), 235–36.

The Hitler Youth was the first and only youth movement which recognised that the death of two million soldiers in the World War signified a responsibility: namely the idea of serving Germany through deeds.

They knew that youth does not have the right to criticise and oppose, but rather that they bear the responsibility of the future of our nation. . . .

Already in the time of struggle, the differences between them and the old youth associations became apparent, as was also the case with girls. Here the idea was there, the idea of Germany, which by necessity put them under its spell. . . .

The fact that the Hitler Youth is the most powerful youth organisation in the world today can only be understood if we acknowledge that Adolf Hitler is our starting point. Today, we all know that men and women, and boys and girls make up the nation, and that each has to carry out his duty to the nation according to his station. Boys will be raised as political soldiers, and girls as brave and strong women, who will be the comrades of these political soldiers—and who will go on to live in their families as women and mothers, and help shape our National Socialist world view—and to raise a new generation which is hard and proud.

Therefore, we want to shape girls who are politically conscious. That does not mean women who debate or discuss things in parliament, but girls and women, who know about the necessities of life in the German nation, and act accordingly.

25

PETER GAY

A Jewish Teenager Remembers the 1936 Berlin Olympics

1998

Germany won the right to host the 1936 Olympics before the Nazis came to power, but the Nazis used the event to put on a show for the rest of the world. They went to great lengths to portray a peaceful, prosperous, racially fit Germany. Celebrations of Aryan prowess were directly challenged, however, by Jesse Owens, an African American who won four gold medals in track and field. Peter Gay, born Peter Fröhlich in 1923, recalls not the squeaky-clean Berlin created by the Nazis, but the victorious Americans. Gay, a Jew, escaped Hitler's Germany, reaching America via Cuba in 1940. In 1998, he wrote this account of how the 1936 Olympics affected him.

For me, by far the most formidable adventure of the year, breathlessly anticipated and just as breathlessly enjoyed, were the Olympic Games. . . . There was so much else to think about in 1936: the Nazi regime had unilaterally nullified portions of the Versailles treaty by starting to rearm and by reoccupying the Rhineland; treaties with Italy and Japan, creating the Axis, came later in the year. But to omit or drastically abridge my Olympic week would be to distort the oscillating balance of the experiences that those trying years deposited in my private history.

My father shone. Exceedingly well informed about sports, he had bought two tickets in 1932 on one of his business trips to Budapest, well before Berlin's Olympic stadium had even been built. Much, of course, had changed in Germany between the time of his purchase of the tickets and the event, but the tickets held good. It turned out to be a move even shrewder than my father could have imagined. Getting ahead of the mob of ticket buyers was canny enough; placing us

From Peter Gay, *My German Question: Growing Up in Nazi Berlin* (New Haven, Conn.: Yale University Press, 1998), 78–80.

among a small cadre of colorful, noisy Hungarian fans was cannier still. It meant that my father and I could simply blend in with our surroundings so that we did not have to give the Nazi salute when the Führer appeared or a German was awarded a gold medal. (The ceremony of handing out the medals took place right in the stadium and called for the playing of the winner's national anthem, of which the Nazis had not one but two.)

Conversely, we were safe in supporting the Americans passionately, and we did. Fortunately, they gave us many opportunities to have their hymn roll over the assembled masses, standing quietly or singing along. "O say, can you see . . ." were words whose meaning I could barely guess at . . . , but I thought nothing more satisfying than to salute them by solemnly standing up with all the others.

It was a memorable week, and I want to give full weight to the adjective: I remember most of it. The occasional sight of Hitler was a nauseating byproduct. Since we sat almost directly opposite the prestige boxes, on the other side of the big oval, we were doomed to notice all the so-called German dignitaries. When Göring appeared he was hailed with shouts of "Hermann! Hermann!" His bulk, his rows of medals, and his all-too-naked self-importance made him a figure of affectionate fun, a reputation the regime fostered precisely because the real Göring was a thief and a murderer like all his comrades. Fortunately, there was constant activity on the field. . . .

The hero of the Olympics, and not only my father's and mine, was Jesse Owens. As so often in earlier Olympic Games, the Americans were favored in the sprints, and they did not let us down. But Owens was a revelation. His style of running seemed supremely effortless, in fact elegant. He took home four gold medals, winning each of the events he entered: the 100 meters, the 200 meters, the long jump, and the 4×100-meter relay race. There was talk at the time and later—I cheerfully believed all of it—that Hitler, appalled to see a black man showing himself superior to "Nordics," refused to shake Owens's hand. The story has been carefully researched, and apparently there is nothing in it. But from my father's point of view and my own, this is what *must* have happened—it was *morally* true. The swine who were ruining our lives could not have behaved differently. Whatever did happen, there was no denying that Owens had done his bit to puncture the myth of Aryan superiority.

26

Law for the Prevention
of Hereditarily Diseased Offspring

July 14, 1933

Nazi policy aggressively encouraged racially fit Germans to reproduce. Just as aggressively, it imposed sanctions to prevent those deemed unfit from bringing any children into the world. On the day that the French celebrated the 144th anniversary of the revolution of 1789 and the ideals of liberty, equality, and fraternity, the Nazis passed a law that provided for the sterilization of Germans with hereditary diseases, clearly stating that not all lives should be equally valued and not everyone should have access to the same human rights. The test that determined "mental and hereditary illness" assessed basic math skills but also asked "What type of state do we have at present?" and "What are loyalty, piety, respect, modesty?" A wrong answer to any of these questions could result in a diagnosis of "moral feeble-mindedness." Also subject to sterilization were so-called asocials, male homosexuals, and progeny of German women and black French colonial troops who had occupied parts of western Germany after the First World War.

§1. (i) Anyone who has a hereditary illness can be rendered sterile by a surgical operation if, according to the experience of medical science, there is a strong probability that his/her offspring will suffer from serious hereditary defects of a physical or mental nature.

(ii) Anyone is hereditarily ill within the meaning of this law who suffers from one of the following illnesses: (*a*) Congenital feeble-mindedness. (*b*) Schizophrenia. (*c*) Manic depression. (*d*) Hereditary epilepsy. (*e*) Huntington's chorea. (*f*) Hereditary blindness. (*g*) Hereditary deafness. (*h*) Serious physical deformities.

(iii) In addition, anyone who suffers from chronic alcoholism can be sterilized.

§2. An application for sterilization can legitimately be made by the person to be sterilized. In the case of persons who are either not

From Jeremy Noakes and Geoffrey Pridham, eds., *Nazism, 1919–1945: A Documentary Reader*, vol. 2, *State, Economy, and Society, 1933–1939* (Exeter, U.K.: University of Exeter Press, 2000), 263–64.

legally responsible or have been certified because of mental deficiency or have not yet reached their nineteenth birthday, the legal guardian is so entitled.

§3. Sterilization can also be requested by (i) The Medical Officer. (ii) In the case of inmates of hospitals, or institutions of the incurably ill or penal institutions, the director. . . .

§5. The responsibility for the decision lies with the Hereditary Health Court which has jurisdiction over the district where the person to be sterilized officially resides.

§6. The Hereditary Health Court is to be connected administratively to the Magistrates Court (*Amtsgericht*). It consists of a magistrate as chairman, a medical officer, and a further physician qualified to practise within the German Reich who is particularly familiar with the theory of hereditary health. . . .

§12. If the Court had decided finally in favour of sterilization, the sterilization must be carried out even against the wishes of the person to be sterilized unless that person was solely responsible for the application. The medical officer is responsible for requesting the necessary measures to be taken by the police authority. In so far as other measures prove insufficient the use of force is permissible.

Reasons for the Law: Since the National Uprising public opinion has become increasingly preoccupied with questions of population policy and the continuing decline in the birthrate. However, it is not only the decline in population which is the cause of serious concern but equally the increasingly evident genetic make-up of our people. Whereas the hereditarily healthy families have for the most part adopted a policy of having only one or two children, countless numbers of inferiors and those suffering from hereditary ailments are reproducing unrestrainedly while their sick and asocial offspring are a burden on the community.

27

SS SECURITY SERVICE

Report Assessing Public Response to the Film I Accuse

January 15, 1942

In its drive to eliminate "lives not worth living," the Nazis promoted euthanasia of the terminally ill and the seriously disabled. The program was code-named T-4, short for Tiergartenstrasse 4, the address of the program's headquarters in Berlin. The euthanasia campaign was carried out in secret, usually without the knowledge of the families of those who were killed. Doctors used poison gas to kill these people, then their bodies were burned in crematoria. The T-4 program served as a laboratory in which to perfect techniques that were later used in mass-killing facilities such as Auschwitz. In the document excerpted here, the intelligence wing of the SS, the SD (Sicherheitsdienst, or security service), reports on responses to Ich klage an *(I Accuse), an extremely popular 1941 film that provides a melodramatic defense of euthanasia. (In the movie, a doctor's wife suffers from multiple sclerosis, and he seeks to fulfill her wish to die.) Sensitive to protests from some church leaders, the Nazis officially abandoned the euthanasia program in August 1941. In fact, however, the program continued in secret. The document illustrates how seriously the Nazis took public opinion and the methods they used to assess how the public received their propaganda and policies.*

All the reports to hand indicate that the film *I Accuse* has aroused great interest in all areas of the Reich. In general it can be stated that with the help of extensive word-of-mouth publicity the film has been favourably received and discussed. Characteristic of the interest this film has provoked among the population is the fact that in many towns which had not yet seen it the film was being described—even by unsophisticated people—as one which simply had to be seen. The

From SD (Sicherheitsdienst), "Reports from the Reich," January 15, 1942, in *The Racial State: Germany, 1933–1945*, by Michael Burleigh and Wolfgang Wippermann (Cambridge: Cambridge University Press, 1991), 158–61.

performances were generally enthusiastically received, and the film's content has actively stimulated people to think about it and has provoked lively discussion.

The film *I Accuse* raises two issues. Its main theme is the problem of *death on demand in cases of incurable illnesses*. A secondary theme deals with the question of putting an end to a life which is no longer worth living.

Judging by the reports received from all parts of the Reich, the majority of the German population accepts the film's proposition *in principle, though with some reservations*—that is, that people suffering from serious diseases for which there is no cure should be allowed a quick death sanctioned by law. This conclusion can also be applied to a number of religiously-minded people.

The *attitude of the Church*, both Catholic and Protestant, is one of almost total rejection. There are reports that Catholic priests have used house visits to try to stop individual members of the population from going to see the film on the grounds that it is an inflammatory film directed against the Catholic Church or a State propaganda film designed to justify the killing of people suffering from hereditary illness.

In a number of cases the Catholic clergy has made only an indirect attack on the film, and according to reports has described it as being so good that it could be dangerous and "as tempting as sin." Despite this clear rejection of the film in Catholic circles, it has also been frequently reported that the film has in fact occasioned a conflict of opinion in the Catholic camp, with one faction supporting the principle that a person may be deprived of life if in particularly serious cases a panel of doctors has diagnosed an incurable illness and the administering of death could be considered a blessing for both parties. The other faction, however, still uses the word "murder" in connection with the film.

All reports, even those coming from predominantly Catholic regions of the Reich, refer to the fact that the celebrated statements by Bishop Clemens August of Münster have in many cases been taken as a starting-point in discussions of the film, to the extent that there have been several comments about the film referring to it as an attempt to justify the State's measures now that the Bishop has attacked them. For instance the following comments have been heard:

> The film is quite interesting, but the story's just like the lunatic asylums where they're killing off all the crazy people now.

You can think what you like about this, but who is going to guarantee that there won't be any abuses? As soon as laws like this are introduced it will be easy for the government to have anyone they consider undesirable declared incurable by a commission for any reason at all and eliminate them. And moreover people with enough influence or money to criticise others will soon have somebody declared insane.

In Protestant circles the open rejection of the film is not as strongly expressed. Yet here too people often say that life, which is God-given, can and should only be taken by God.

But we have also heard of *positive* opinions in Church circles. The Superintendent of Bautzen, for instance, said the following: "It will be the State's concern to prevent abuse, to take the responsibility and to ensure that loving kindness is extended to those incurables who are suffering. All this will be easier than the actual act of deliverance. As a Christian I must approve of this film."

As regards *medical circles*, a mostly positive response is reported to the questions raised by the film. Younger doctors in particular, apart from a few bound by religious beliefs, are completely in favour.

Doubts are expressed among older doctors particularly, despite their agreement in principle. In many cases doctors see it as a mistake to publicise the issues openly.

Here and there the question has been raised as to whether medical diagnosis in borderline cases can really be sufficiently accurate to declare a patient incurable. For example, there are frequent cases of seriously ill patients who have been given up by all doctors and have then improved and lived on for years. Such cases are known to every doctor and every hospital. Other doctors mention that in their experience people, especially if they are seriously ill or old, talk only of their wish to die when they have temporarily succumbed to deep despair because of severe pain. However, in the moments when they have been free of pain these patients have shown remarkable spirit and have gone on hoping for recovery until the end. . . .

On the whole the working classes are more favourably disposed to the change in the law suggested by the film than people from intellectual circles. The reason for this, according to our information, is that the socially less privileged classes are by nature more concerned about their own financial obligations. Most people respond to the film's immediate story, with the result that the theme of a long-suffering person being released from his misery is relegated to the background. Only doctors interpret the film in terms of this issue.

The negative attitudes towards the questions raised in the film are by far the minority opinion, and apart from the church's point of view they can hardly be described as fundamentally contrary opinions.

To sum up, from the wealth of material to hand it emerges that in general the practice of euthanasia is approved, *when decided by a committee of several doctors with the agreement of the incurable patient and his relatives.*

The general approval finds its best expression in the words of the Major[1] in the film: "The state, which demands from us the duty to die, must give us the *right* to die."

[1]A member of the jury that determines the doctor's fate in the film. He is in favor of legal euthanasia.

28

HEINRICH HIMMLER

On the Question of Homosexuality

February 18, 1937

Under Paragraph 175 of Germany's criminal code, in force since 1871, male homosexuals were subject to criminal penalties only when the prosecution could prove that they had engaged in "activity similar to sexual intercourse." This was not easy, and the rate of prosecution remained low. The Nazi revision of the law in 1935 made punishable any form of "criminal indecency" that violated "public morality." Lesbians were exempt from criminal prosecution because Nazi legal experts argued that they would not "lastingly withdraw from normal sexual relations, but will be useful as before in terms of population policy." The number of prosecutions of male homosexuals increased dramatically. Until 1933, the annual rate of convictions for violations of Paragraph 175 averaged about 500. From 1933 to 1945, some 50,000 men were charged with violating the law, two-thirds of whom spent time in prison. As many as 15,000 ended up in concentration camps.

From Heinrich Himmler, speech to the SS-Gruppenführer, February 18, 1937, in *The Racial State: Germany, 1933–1945*, by Michael Burleigh and Wolfgang Wippermann (Cambridge: Cambridge University Press, 1991), 192–93.

*Heinrich Himmler (1900–1945), head of the SS, was particularly ven-
omous in his denunciation of homosexual men. In this excerpt from his
1937 remarks to SS leaders, he makes clear that in Nazi Germany, sexuality is not a private affair.*

If you further take into account the facts I have not yet mentioned,
namely that with a static number of women, we have two million men
too few on account of those who fell in the war, then you can well
imagine how this imbalance of two million homosexuals and two million war dead, or in other words a lack of about four million men capable of having sex, has upset the sexual balance sheet of Germany,
and will result in a catastrophe.

I would like to develop a couple of ideas for you on the question of
homosexuality. There are those homosexuals who take the view: what
I do is my business, a purely private matter. However, all things which
take place in the sexual sphere are not the private affair of the individual, but signify the life and death of the nation. . . . The people which
has many children has the candidature for world power and world
domination. A people of good race which has too few children has a
one-way ticket to the grave, for insignificance in fifty or a hundred
years, for burial in two hundred and fifty years. . . .

Therefore we must be absolutely clear that if we continue to have
this burden in Germany, without being able to fight it, then that is the
end of Germany, and the end of the Germanic world. Unfortunately,
we don't have it as easy as our forefathers. The homosexual, whom one
called "Urning,"[1] was drowned in a swamp. The professorial gentle-
men who find these corpses in the peat-bogs are certainly unaware
that in ninety out of a hundred cases, they have a homosexual before
them, who was drowned in a swamp, clothes and all. That wasn't a
punishment, but simply the extinguishing of abnormal life. It had to be
got rid of, just as we pull out weeds, throw them on a heap, and burn
them. It was not a feeling of revenge, simply that those affected had to
go. . . . In the SS, today, we still have about one case of homosexuality
a month. In a whole year, about eight to ten cases occur in the entire
SS. I have now decided upon the following: in each case, these people
will naturally be publicly degraded, expelled, and handed over to the

[1] A word invented in Germany in the second half of the nineteenth century to refer to
men who were physically attracted to men.

courts. Following completion of the punishment imposed by the courts, they will be sent, by my order, to a concentration camp, and they will be shot in the concentration camp, while attempting to escape. I will make that known by order to the unit to which the person so affected belonged. Thereby, I hope finally to have done with persons of this type in the SS, so that at least the good blood, which we have in the SS, and the increasingly healthy blood which we are cultivating for Germany, will be kept pure.

However this does not represent a solution to the problem for the whole of Germany. One must not have any illusions about the following. When I bring a homosexual before the courts and have him locked up, the matter is not settled, because the homosexual comes out of prison just as homosexual as before he went in. Therefore the whole question is not clarified. It is clarified in the sense that this burden has been identified, in contrast to the years before the seizure of power.

29

HEINRICH HIMMLER

Fight against the Gypsy Nuisance

December 8, 1938

For the Nazis, no group threatened "racial purity" more than the Jews, but the Jews were not the only ones targeted for particularly vicious discriminatory treatment. In this 1938 official circular, Himmler identifies Gypsies (Sinti and Roma) as an undesirable group defined by race.

Experience gained in the fight against the Gypsy nuisance, and knowledge derived from race-biological research, have shown that the proper method of attacking the Gypsy problem seems to be to treat it as a matter of race. Experience shows that part-Gypsies play the

From Heinrich Himmler, "Fight against the Gypsy Nuisance," circular, December 8, 1938, in *The Racial State: Germany, 1933–1945*, by Michael Burleigh and Wolfgang Wippermann (Cambridge: Cambridge University Press, 1991), 120–21.

greatest role in Gypsy criminality. On the other hand, it has been shown that efforts to make the Gypsies settle have been unsuccessful, especially in the case of pure Gypsies, on account of their strong compulsion to wander. It has therefore become necessary to distinguish between pure and part-Gypsies in the final solution of the Gypsy question.

To this end, it is necessary to establish the racial affinity of every Gypsy living in Germany and of every vagrant living a Gypsy-like existence.

I therefore decree that all settled and non-settled Gypsies, and also all vagrants living a Gypsy-like existence, are to be registered with the Reich Criminal Police Office–Reich Central Office for the Fight against the Gypsy Nuisance. . . .

Treatment of the Gypsy question is part of the National Socialist task of national regeneration. A solution can only be achieved if the philosophical perspectives of National Socialism are observed. Although the principle that the German nation respects the national identity of alien peoples is also assumed in the fight against the Gypsy Nuisance, nonetheless the aim of measures taken by the State to defend the homogeneity of the German nation must be the physical separation of Gypsydom from the German nation, the prevention of miscegenation, and finally the regulation of the way of life of pure and part-Gypsies. The necessary legal foundation can only be created through a Gypsy Law, which prevents further intermingling of blood, and which regulates all the most pressing questions which go together with the existence of Gypsies in the living space of the German nation.

30

OTTO D. TOLISCHUS AND FREDERICK T. BIRCHALL

Reports on the Introduction of Anti-Semitic Laws

1935

At the annual Nazi party congress in Nuremberg in September 1935, Hitler announced new laws that denied Jews basic rights and citizenship. In subsequent legislation issued in November, a Jew was defined as someone "descended from at least three racially full Jewish grandparents." The new laws also explicitly prohibited sexual relations between Germans and Jews, another indication of the regime's insistence that what happened in private was of extraordinary public significance. Widely publicized in Germany, the Law for the Protection of German Blood and German Honor and the Reich Citizenship Law, the so-called Nuremberg Laws, also were covered in the American press, as these articles from the New York Times *show.*

OTTO D. TOLISCHUS

Reich Adopts Swastika as Nation's Official Flag; Hitler's Reply to "Insult"

September 16, 1935

NUREMBERG, GERMANY, Sept. 15.—National Socialist Germany definitely flung down the gauntlet before the feet of Western liberal opinion tonight when the Reichstag,[1] assembled for a special session here in connection with the "Party Day of Freedom," decreed a series of laws that put Jews beyond the legal and social pale of the German nation. . . .

---

[1]The Reichstag was the German parliament. Starting in March 1933, its members did nothing but enthusiastically approve the policies of Hitler's government.

From Otto D. Tolischus, "Reich Adopts Swastika as Nation's Official Flag; Hitler's Reply to 'Insult,'" *New York Times*, September 16, 1935; Frederick T. Birchall, "Reich Puts Laws on Jews in Force; Trade Untouched," *New York Times*, November 16, 1935.

The new laws provide:

1. German citizenship with full political rights depends on the special grant of a Reich citizenship charter, to be given only to those of German or racially related blood, who have proved by their attitude that they are willing and fit loyally to serve the German people and the Reich.

This deprives Jews of German citizenship but leaves them the status of "State members" (Staatsangehoeriger), and Germans found undeserving of Reich citizenship may likewise be reduced to this status, which, among other disadvantages, entails loss of the vote.

2. Marriages between Jews and citizens of German or racially related blood, as well as extra-marital sexual relations between them, are forbidden and will be punished by penal servitude or imprisonment. Jews must not engage feminine domestic help of German or racially related blood under 45 years old. Jews likewise are forbidden to show the German national flag, but may under protection of the State show the Jewish colors of white and blue. Violations of the last two provisions are punishable by imprisonment up to one year or a fine or both.

3. The Reich, or national, flag is the swastika flag, which is also the flag of commerce to be flown by German merchant ships. But a special war flag is to be fixed by Hitler and the War Minister, which is expected to follow the present black, white and red flag and will probably contain the swastika cross in place of the iron cross for a symbol.

Those laws, which General Goering himself called momentous, were introduced with speeches by Hitler and General Goering and adopted unanimously and with many cheers by the Reichstag, which by like unanimity and cheers rendered itself voiceless at the beginning of the session.

FREDERICK T. BIRCHALL

Reich Puts Laws on Jews in Force; Trade Untouched

November 16, 1935

Hereafter the Reich will recognize only three classes: Germans (of German or related blood), Jews and "Jewish mixtures."

"A person of Jewish mixture," says the new law, "is whoever is descended from one or two racially full Jewish grandparents."

But persons who have only one Jewish grandparent and thus are 25 per cent "non-Aryan" will hereafter be accepted under the new law as German and capable of obtaining Reich citizenship.

On the other hand, Jews are classified as those persons descended from at least three racially full Jewish grandparents. In other words, those 75 per cent Jewish by descent are rated Jews.

Persons 50 per cent Jewish—that is, those who have two racially full Jewish grandparents—are to be classed as Jews, first, if they belonged to a Jewish religious community at the time of the passage of the Nuremberg laws on Sept. 15 last; secondly, if at that time the person was married to a Jew or married one subsequently, and, thirdly, if they are the offspring of a marriage with a three-quarters Jew or a full Jew concluded after the passage of the law or are the illegitimate offspring of either. All other 50 per cent Jews may, however, become Reich citizens. . . .

The second decree, "for the protection of German blood and honor," forbids marriages between Germans and Jews and also between Jews and 25 per cent Jewish mixtures whom the law admits to Reich citizenship. Those persons rated as half-Jewish may marry Germans or "related peoples" only if they obtain the permission of Dr. Frick and Mr. Hess.[1]

Such permission is to be granted only with due regard to characteristics of "body, soul and character." It is explained officially that the period during which the families concerned lived in Germany, what they did in the World War and their political attitude afterward will be factors in the decision.

Marriages between persons rated as 25 per cent Jewish are forbidden entirely. A person 25 per cent Jewish may marry only a German since the object of establishing this class is its assimilation.

In principle every marriage is forbidden, the offspring from which might "endanger the purity of German blood." To contract a specially permitted marriage a certificate will be required and it must show that there is no racial objection to the marriage. If one of the parties to the proposed marriage is a foreigner, the Minister of the Interior will decide whether the marriage is permissible or not.

Extramarital relations between Jews and Germans and between Jews and 25 per cent Jewish persons are forbidden.

Regarding the employment of female domestic help below the age of 45, which is forbidden in Jewish households, a household is classified as Jewish if any male member of it is a Jew. However, if a German servant was employed in that particular establishment before the Nuremberg law was passed, she may remain if she is 35 years old, or older. This somewhat modifies the original decree.

[1]Wilhelm Frick was the minister of the interior, and Rudolf Hess was a prominent Hitler supporter and deputy leader of the Nazi party.

31

MARTA APPEL

Jewish Life after the Nazi Seizure of Power in 1933
1940–1941

*Constituting less than 1 percent of the population in 1933, German Jews
were for Hitler a subversive force of incalculable power, participants in an
international conspiracy that sought to destroy Germany. Soon after taking
power, the Nazis excluded Jews from all forms of state employment—from
bureaucrats, teachers, and professors to postal carriers and railroad
workers—and also from many realms of cultural life. No German—
Jewish or non-Jewish—could have been unaware of the marginalization
of Jews. There were about 525,000 Jews in Germany in 1933, and as
many as 300,000 left the country, but the decision to leave was not easy.
Jews were tied to Germany by language, culture, friends, and family and
stood to lose their homes and livelihoods once they emigrated. In this
excerpt from her memoir, Marta Appel, the wife of a rabbi in Dortmund,
describes the SA boycott of Jewish stores in April 1933 and her family's
growing sense of isolation. Appel left Germany with her family in 1937,
settling in the United States.*

The children had been advised not to come to school on April 1, 1933,
the day of the boycott.[1] Even the principal of the school thought Jewish children's lives were no longer safe. One night they placed big
signs on every store or house owned by Jewish people. In front of our
temple, on every square and corner, billboards were scoffing at us.
Everywhere, and on all occasions, we read and heard that we were
vermin and had caused the ruin of the German people. No Jewish
store was closed on that day; none was willing to show fear in the face
of the boycott. The only building which did not open its door as usual,

[1]The Nazis ordered a national boycott of Jewish businesses for this day, but the initiative did not win widespread support.

From Marta Appel, undated manuscript, in *Jewish Life in Germany: Memoirs from Three
Centuries*, ed. Monika Richarz, trans. Stella P. Rosenfeld and Sidney Rosenfeld (Bloomington: Indiana University Press, 1991), 351–54.

since it was Saturday, was the temple. We did not want this holy place desecrated by any trouble.

I even went downtown that day to see what was going on in the city. There was no cheering crowd as the Nazis had expected, no running and smashing of Jewish businesses. I heard only words of anger and disapproval. People were massed before the Jewish stores to watch the Nazi guards who were posted there to prevent anyone from entering to buy. And there were many courageous enough to enter, although they were called rude names by the Nazi guards, and their pictures were taken to show them as enemies of the German people in the daily papers. Inside the stores, in the offices of the owners, there was another battle proceeding. Nazis were forcing those Jewish men to send wires abroad to foreign businesses, saying that there was no Jewish boycott and that nothing unusual was happening. Accompanied by two Nazi officials, one of the men was taken even to Holland to convince the foreign customers and businessmen there.

Our gentile friends and neighbors, even people whom we had scarcely known before, came to assure us of their friendship and to tell us that these horrors could not last very long. But after some months of a regime of terror, fidelity and friendship had lost their meaning, and fear and treachery had replaced them. For the sake of our gentile friends, we turned our heads so as not to greet them in the streets, for we did not want to bring upon them the danger of imprisonment for being considered a friend of Jews.

With each day of the Nazi regime, the abyss between us and our fellow citizens grew larger. Friends whom we had loved for years did not know us anymore. They suddenly saw that we were different from themselves. Of course we were different, since we were bearing the stigma of Nazi hatred, since we were hunted like deer. Through the prominent position of my husband we were in constant danger. Often we were warned to stay away from home. We were no longer safe, wherever we went.

How much our life changed in those days! Often it seemed to me I could not bear it any longer, but thinking of my children, I knew we had to be strong to make it easier for them. From then on I hated to go out, since on every corner I saw signs that the Jews were the misfortune of the people. Wherever I went, when I had to speak to people in a store I imagined how they would turn against me if they knew I was Jewish. When I was waiting for a streetcar I always thought that the driver would not stop if he knew I was Jewish. Never did anything unpleasant happen to me on the street, but I was expecting it at every

moment, and it was always bothering me. I did not go into a theater or
a movie for a long time before we were forbidden to, since I could not
bear to be among people who hated me so much. Therefore, when,
later on, all those restrictions came, they did not take away from me
anything that I had not already renounced. Nevertheless, it meant a
new shame. Not to go of my own accord was very different from not
being allowed to go. . . .

. . . It required a great deal of inner strength, of love and harmony
among the Jewish families, to make our children strong enough to
bear all that persecution and hatred. . . . My heart was broken when I
saw tears in my younger child's eyes when she had been sent home
from school while all the others had been taken to a show or some
other pleasure. It was not because she was denied going to the show
that my little girl was weeping—she knew her Mommy always could
take her—but because she had to stay apart, as if she were not good
enough to associate with her comrades any longer. It was this that
made it hard and bitter for her. I think that even the Nazi teacher
sometimes felt ashamed when she looked into the sad eyes of my little
girl, since several times, when the class was going out for pleasure,
she phoned not to send her to school. Maybe it was not right to hate
this teacher so much, since everything she did had been upon orders,
but it was she who brought so much bitterness to my child, and never
can I forget it.

Almost every lesson began to be a torture for Jewish children.
There was not one subject anymore which was not used to bring up
the Jewish question. And in the presence of Jewish children the teachers denounced all the Jews, without exception, as scoundrels and as
the most destructive force in every country where they were living.
My children were not permitted to leave the room during such a talk;
they were compelled to stay and to listen; they had to feel all the other
children's eyes looking and staring at them, the examples of an outcast race.

Every day they had to face another degrading and offensive incident. As Mother's Day came near, the children were practicing songs
at school to celebrate that day. Every year on that occasion the whole
school gathered in a joint festival. It was the day before when my girls
were ordered to see the music teacher. "You have to be present for the
festival," the teacher told them, "but since you are Jewish, you are not
allowed to join in the songs." "Why can't we sing?" my children
protested with tears in their eyes. "We have a mother too, and we wish
to sing for her." But it seemed the teacher did not want to understand

the children's feelings. Curtly she rebuked their protest. "I know you have a mother," she said haughtily, "but she is only a Jewish mother." At that the girls had no reply; there was no use to speak any longer to the teacher, but seldom had they been so much disturbed as when they came from school that day, when someone had tried to condemn their mother.

The only hope we had was that this terror would not last very long. The day could not be far off when this nightmare would cease to hound the German people. How could anybody be happy in a land where "freedom" was an extinct word, where nobody knew that the next day he would not be taken to jail, possibly tortured to death. The Jewish people were not the only ones afraid of a loud spoken word; many others, too, were trembling for fear that somebody might listen even to their thoughts.

32

INGE DEUTSCHKRON

Growing Up Jewish in 1930s Germany

1978

Inge Deutschkron was born in 1922. Her father, a schoolteacher, was dismissed from public service in 1933. He was a Jew and a Social Democrat, and the Nazis persecuted him and his family for both reasons. He was able to escape to England, but his hopes that his daughter and wife would be able to join him were not fulfilled, and Inge and her mother survived the war in Germany. Inge watched as friends and family members were deported, and on the advice of friends, she went underground in 1943 and spent the remainder of the war in hiding. Her memoir, Outcast, *originally published in German in 1978, is an extraordinary account of her survival under National Socialism. In this excerpt, she offers poignant testimony of the incalculable small ways in which anti-Semitism entered the lives of German Jewish young people.*

From Inge Deutschkron, *Outcast: A Jewish Girl in Wartime Berlin*, trans. Jean Steinberg (New York: Fromm International, 1989), 26–29.

In looking back at those days, I am struck by the fact that we children never discussed our situation. When one of us said good-bye because she was emigrating, we of course envied her, not because she was exchanging our insecure existence for greater security but because of the adventure awaiting her. Neither we nor many of our parents seemed to realize that with each passing day our life was becoming more dangerous. We knew that people were being arrested, and when a girl was absent from school for a few days, we would whisper among ourselves that someone in her family had probably been arrested. Then one of us would go to that girl's house to find out what was wrong, and when she returned to school we would instinctively shun her, as though she were marked. But after a few days we'd get used to her misfortune and readmit her to our circle. Perhaps we also sensed that the same thing could happen to any of us.

That is how we found out about the first wave of mass arrests in June 1938, in which fifteen hundred Jews were swept up. They were people with "prior records," those officially designated as "asocial, parasitic elements." A cousin of mine who once had been fined for being involved in an automobile accident was among those arrested. I suppose the reference to the victims' "prior record" was supposed to still any doubt about the reasons for their arrest. Although indignant about the blatant illegality of the action, we were not directly affected by it.

Another, seemingly innocuous, incident hit me much harder. It happened at a photo studio. Like any other sixteen-year-old I was vain, and so when the photographer told me to push my hair back behind my left ear I became angry and tearful. There was nothing extraordinary about his suggestion; he had no ulterior motive. Still I felt humiliated, as though I'd been struck. However, I prided myself on my self-control and was determined not to show how upset I was. Yet I knew even then that despite my best effort the picture would show me looking bitter, defiant, and tearful. My reaction was triggered by an absurd Nazi racial theory postulating that Jews' left ears were indicative of their Semitic descent. That is why passport photos of Jews had to show the left ear. On July 23, 1938, it was decreed that all Jews past the age of fifteen had to carry an identity card with a photograph. And lest there was any doubt about the racial classification of the passport's owner, both its cover and inner pages were stamped with a large "J."

Going home from school on the underground or bus, I would try to get close enough to other passengers to compare their left ears with mine. I couldn't see any difference. My ear, which I examined closely in the mirror hundreds of times, looked exactly like the ears of the Aryans in Berlin.

I didn't tell my parents about the incident at the photographer's; I was afraid they'd laugh at me. A story was then making the rounds among Jews about a man at a Nazi rally who was asked to come up to the podium to show what the ear of a pure Aryan looked like. Naturally the Nazi speaker didn't know that his model Aryan was a Jew, and of course the man didn't enlighten him, and so the ear of a Jew was used to demonstrate Aryan purity. The story may or may not have been apocryphal. It didn't matter. Jews loved it because it helped them bear the humiliation of this particular indignity.

33

DAVID H. BUFFUM

Report on Kristallnacht

November 1938

Conditions for Jews worsened markedly in 1938 after Ernst vom Rath, a German foreign service officer in Paris, was shot and killed by Herschel Grynszpan, a Polish Jew angered over the deportation of his parents from Germany. Joseph Goebbels labeled Rath's murder an act of "World Jewry" and sanctioned widespread violence against Jews. In virtually every city in Germany and Austria, from November 9 to 10, Nazis burned down synagogues, defaced Jewish cemeteries, smashed the windows of Jewish businesses, and, for the first time, arrested Jews in large numbers. The event became known as Kristallnacht (Crystal Night), or the "Night of Broken Glass." In the document excerpted here, David Buffum, the American consul in Leipzig, provides a detailed account of the violence against Jews in that city. It was part of the evidence presented at the postwar Nuremberg trials of Nazi war criminals.

From David H. Buffum, "Antisemitic Onslaught in Germany as Seen from Leipzig," doc. L-202, in Office of the United States Chief of Counsel for Prosecution of Axis Criminality, *Nazi Conspiracy and Aggression* (Washington, D.C.: U.S. Government Printing Office, 1946), 7:1037–41.

The macabre circumstances that form the subject matter of this report had a fittingly gruesome prelude in Leipzig a few hours before they occurred in the form of rites held on one of the principal squares of the city on the night of November 9, 1938 in commemoration of fallen martyrs to the Nazi cause prior to the political take-over in 1933.[1] To such end apparently anything in the corpse category that could be remotely associated with Nazi martyrdom, had been exhumed. At least five year old remains of those who had been considered rowdyish violators of the law and order at the time, had been placed in extravagant coffins; arranged around a colossal, flaming urn on the Altermarkt for purposes of display, and ultimately conveyed amid marching troops, flaring torches and funeral music to the "Ehrenhain," Leipzig's National Socialist burial plot. For this propagandistic ceremony the entire market place had been surrounded with wooden lattice work about ten yards high. This was covered with white cloth to form the background for black swastikas at least five yards high and broad. Flame-spurting urns and gigantic banners completed a Wagnerian[2] ensemble as to pomposity of stage setting; but it can not be truthfully reported that the ceremony aroused anything akin to awe among the crowds who witnessed it. Judging from a few very guardedly whispered comments, the populace was far more concerned over the wanton waste of materials in these days when textiles of any kind are exceedingly scarce and expensive, rather than being actuated by any particularly reverent emotions. On the other hand for obvious reasons, there were no open manifestations of disapproval. The populace was destined to be much more perturbed the following morning during the course of the most violent debacle the city had probably ever witnessed.

The shattering of shop windows, looting of stores and dwellings of Jews which began in the early hours of November 10, 1938, was hailed subsequently in the Nazi press as "a spontaneous wave of righteous indignation throughout Germany, as a result of the cowardly Jewish murder of Third Secretary von Rath in the German Embassy at Paris." So far as a very high percentage of the German populace is concerned, a state of popular indignation that would spontaneously lead to such excesses, can be considered as nonexistent. On the contrary, in

[1] Buffum suggests a relationship between the outbreak of Kristallnacht (November 9–10) and an event to commemorate the Nazis who had been killed before Hitler came to power.

[2] A reference to Richard Wagner, the famous nineteenth-century German opera composer.

viewing the ruins and attendant measures employed, all of the local crowds observed were obviously benumbed over what had happened and aghast over the unprecedented fury of Nazi acts that had been or were taking place with bewildering rapidity throughout their city. The whole lamentable affair was organized in such a sinister fashion, as to lend credence to the theory that the execution of it had involved studied preparation. It has been ascertained by this office that the plan of "spontaneous indignation" leaked out in Leipzig several hours before news of the death of Third Secretary von Rath had been broadcasted at 10 P.M. November 10, 1938. . . .

At 3 A.M. November 10, 1938 was unleashed a barrage of Nazi ferocity as had had no equal hitherto in Germany, or very likely anywhere else in the world. . . . Jewish dwellings were smashed into and contents demolished or looted. In one of the Jewish sections an eighteen year old boy was hurled from a three story window to land with both legs broken on a street littered with burning beds and other household furniture and effects from his family's and other apartments. This information was supplied by an attending physician. It is reported from another quarter that among domestic effects thrown out of a Jewish dwelling, a small dog descended four flights to a broken spine on a cluttered street. Although apparently centered in poor districts, the raid was not confined to the humble classes. One apartment of exceptionally refined occupants known to this office, was violently ransacked, presumably in a search for valuables that was not in vain, and one of the marauders thrust a cane through a priceless medieval painting portraying a biblical scene. Another apartment of the same category is known to have been turned upside down in the frenzied course of whatever the invaders were after. Reported loss of looting of cash, silver, jewelry, and otherwise easily convertible articles, have been frequent.

Jewish shop windows by the hundreds were systematically and wantonly smashed throughout the entire city at a loss estimated at several millions of marks. . . . The spectators who viewed the wreckage when daylight had arrived were mostly in such a bewildered mood, that there was no danger of impulsive acts, and the perpetrators probably were too busy in carrying out their schedule to take off a whole lot of time for personal profit. At all events, the main streets of the city were a positive litter of shattered plate glass. According to a reliable testimony, the debacle was executed by S.S. men and Storm Troopers not in uniform, each group having been provided with hammers, axes, crowbars and incendiary bombs.

Three synagogues in Leipzig were fired simultaneously by incendiary bombs and all sacred objects and records desecrated or destroyed, in most instances hurled through the windows and burned in the streets. No attempts whatsoever were made to quench the fires, functions of the fire brigade having been confined to playing water on adjoining buildings. All of the synagogues were irreparably gutted by flames, and the walls of the two that are in the close proximity of the consulate are now being razed. The blackened frames have been centers of attraction during the past week of terror for eloquently silent and bewildered crowds. One of the largest clothing stores in the heart of the city was destroyed by flames from incendiary bombs, only the charred walls and gutted roof having been left standing. As was the case with the synagogues, no attempts on the part of the fire brigade were made to extinguish the fire, although apparently there was a certain amount of apprehension for adjacent property, for the walls of a coffee house next door were covered with asbestos and sprayed by the doughty firemen. It is extremely difficult to believe, but the owners of the clothing store were actually charged with setting the fire and on that basis were dragged from their beds at 6 A.M. and clapped into prison.

Tactics which closely approached the ghoulish took place at the Jewish cemetery where the temple was fired together with a building occupied by caretakers, tombstones uprooted and graves violated. Eye witnesses considered reliable report that ten corpses were left unburied at this cemetery for a week's time because all grave diggers and cemetery attendants had been arrested.

Ferocious as was the violation of property, the most hideous phase of the so-called "spontaneous" action, has been the wholesale arrest and transportation to concentration camps of male German Jews between the ages of sixteen and sixty, as well as Jewish men without citizenship. This has been taking place daily since the night of horror. This office has no way of accurately checking the numbers of such arrests, but there is very little question that they have gone into several thousands in Leipzig alone. Having demolished dwellings and hurled most of the moveable effects to the streets, the insatiably sadistic perpetrators threw many of the trembling inmates into a small stream that flows through the Zoological Park, commanding horrified spectators to spit at them, defile them with mud and jeer at their plight. The latter incident has been repeatedly corroborated by German witnesses who were nauseated in telling the tale. The slightest manifestation of sympathy evoked a positive fury on the part of the perpetrators, and the crowd was powerless to do anything but turn horror-stricken eyes from the scene of abuse, or leave the vicinity. These tactics were carried out the entire morning of November 10th without police intervention and they were applied to men, women and children.

There is much evidence of physical violence, including several deaths. At least half a dozen cases have been personally observed, victims with bloody, badly bruised faces having fled to this office, believing that as refugees their desire to emigrate could be expedited here. As a matter of fact this consulate has been a bedlam of humanity for the past ten days, most of these visitors being desperate women, as their husbands and sons had been taken off to concentration camps.

Similarly violent procedure was applied throughout this consular district, the amount of havoc wrought depending upon the number of Jewish establishments or persons involved. It is understood that in many of the smaller communities even more relentless methods were employed than was the case in the cities. Reports have been received from Weissenfels to the effect that the few Jewish families there are experiencing great difficulty in purchasing food. It is reported that three Aryan professors of the University of Jena have been arrested and taken off to concentration camps because they had voiced disapproval of this insidious drive against mankind.

3

Germany Goes to War

34

ADOLF HITLER

Speech before the Reichstag

September 1, 1939

In the second half of the 1930s, Hitler repeatedly tested the international community's willingness to challenge his plans for expansion of the territory under German control. He confronted no opposition to his aggressive moves to rearm Germany, remilitarize the Rhineland, annex Austria, and occupy the Sudetenland and the rest of Czechoslovakia. When the Wehrmacht, the German army, invaded Poland in September 1939, however, Britain and France declared war on Germany. The Second World War had begun. In his speech to the German parliament excerpted here, Hitler charges that the Poles attacked first, provoking the German response, a fabrication he used to justify German aggression.

For months we have been tormented by a problem once imposed upon us by the Dictate of Versailles and which, in its deterioration and corruption, had now become utterly intolerable. Danzig is a German City. The Corridor was and is German. All these territories owe their cultural development exclusively to the German people, without whom absolute barbarism would reign in these Eastern territories.... As usual, I have tried to change this intolerable state of affairs through

---

From Adolf Hitler, speech before the Reichstag, September 1, 1939, doc. 2322-PS, in Office of the United States Chief of Counsel for Prosecution of Axis Criminality, *Nazi Conspiracy and Aggression* (Washington, D.C.: U.S. Government Printing Office, 1946), 4:1026, 1031–32.

proposals for a peaceful revision. . . . There was ample opportunity for fifteen years before National Socialism assumed power to carry through revisions by means of a peaceful understanding. This was not done. . . .

Last night for the first time regular soldiers of the Polish Army fired shots on our territory. Since 5:45 A.M. we have been returning their fire. From now on, every bomb will be answered by another bomb. Whoever fights with poison gas will be fought with poison gas. Whoever disregards the rules of human warfare can but expect us to do the same.

I will carry on this fight, no matter against whom, until such time as the safety of the Reich and its rights are secured!

For more than 6 years now I have been engaged in building up the German armed forces. During this period more than 90 billion Reichsmark were spent building up the Wehrmacht. Today, ours are the best equipped armed forces in the world and they are far superior to those of 1914. My confidence in them can never be shaken.

If I call upon the Wehrmacht and if I ask sacrifices of the German people and, if necessary, unlimited sacrifices, then I am in the right to do so, for I myself am just as ready today as I was in the past to make every personal sacrifice. I don't ask anything of any German which I myself was not prepared to do at any moment for more than four years. There shall not be any deprivations for Germans in which I myself shall not immediately share. From this moment on my whole life shall belong more than ever to my people. I now want to be nothing but the first soldier of the German Reich.

Thus I have put on once again the coat which has always been the most sacred and dearest to me. I shall not put it aside until after victory—or I shall not live to see the end. . . .

As a National Socialist and a German soldier I enter upon this fight with a stout heart! My whole life has been but one continuous struggle for my people, for its resurrection, for Germany, and this whole struggle has been inspired by one single conviction: faith in this people!

One word I have never known: capitulation. . . .

As for the rest of the world, I can only assure them that a November 1918 shall never occur again in German history.

I ask of every German what I myself am prepared to do at any moment: to be ready to pay with his life for his people and for his country.

Whoever believes to have a chance to evade this patriotic duty directly or indirectly, shall perish. We will have nothing to do with traitors. We all are acting only in accordance with our old principle: our own life matters nothing, all that matters is that our people, that Germany shall live. . . .

I also expect every German woman to take her place with unflinching discipline in this great fighting community.

German youth, needless to say, will do with heart and soul what is expected and demanded of it by the nation and by the National Socialist State.

If we form this community, forged together, ready for everything, determined never to capitulate, then our strong will shall master every emergency.

I conclude with the words with which I once started my fight for power in the Reich. At that time I said: "If our will is so strong that it cannot be broken through any distress, then our will and our German state will be able to master and subjugate distress."

Germany—Sieg Heil!

35

REICH COMMISSIONER FOR THE STRENGTHENING OF THE NATIONAL CHARACTER OF THE GERMAN PEOPLE

On the Re-Germanization of Lost German Blood
December 1940

The Germans invaded Poland in 1939, quickly incorporating the western part of the country directly into the Greater German Reich and leaving the rest under the control of the military. Although Polish Jews were subjected to especially harsh treatment, the German occupiers treated all Poles as subhuman; at best they were seen as a slave labor force. The Nazis cleared out the indigenous population in some areas, replacing Poles with ethnic Germans from other parts of eastern Europe. Although many Poles were killed or forcibly removed, others whom the Nazis believed

From Reich Commissioner for the Strengthening of the National Character of the German People, "Commitment of Manpower Doctrines-Orders-Directives," doc. 2915-PS, in Office of the United States Chief of Counsel for Prosecution of Axis Criminality, *Nazi Conspiracy and Aggression* (Washington, D.C.: U.S. Government Printing Office, 1946), 5:581–82.

to have some "German blood" were targeted for "Germanization," so that this "lost German blood" could benefit the Reich. Both aspects of Nazi racial policy are outlined in this directive from the Reich Commissioner for the Strengthening of the National Character of the German People, showing that from the very start, the war in the east was a race war.

The removal of foreign races from the incorporated Eastern Territories is one of the most essential goals to be accomplished in the German East. This is the chief *national political* task, which has to be executed in the incorporated eastern territories by the "Reichsfuehrer SS," Reich Commissioner for the strengthening of the national character of the German people. In solving this question, which is most closely connected with the ethno-indigenous problem in the eastern territories the racial selection is of the utmost and actually decisive importance, next to the aspects of language, education and confession. As necessary as it is, in the interest of a permanent solution for the German eastern territories, that the elements there of forcign descent should not be allowed to have or to take up their permanent residence there, so it is indispensable too, that persons of German blood in these territories must be regained for the German nation, even if those of German blood are Polonized as far as their confession and language is concerned. Just from these people of German blood, the former Polish State obtained those leaders, who eventually showed a violent hostile attitude against their own German People, be it through delusion, be it through a desired or unconscious misconception of their ties of blood.

Therefore, it is an absolute *national political* necessity to comb out those of German blood in the incorporated eastern territories and later also in the general government and to return the lost German blood to its own German people. It is, perhaps of secondary importance, what kind of measures are to be taken against renegades. It is critical that at least their children do not devolve anymore to the Poles, but are brought up in a German environment. . . .

Thus, there are the following two primary reasons, which makes the regaining of lost German blood an urgent necessity.

1. Prevention of a further increase of the Polish intelligentsia, through families of German descent even if they are Polonized.

2. Increase of the population by racial elements desirable for the German nation, and the acquisition of ethno-biologically unobjectionable forces for the German reconstruction of agriculture and industry.

36

MELITA MASCHMANN

A German Colonizer of Poland in 1939 or 1940
1963

*By the late 1930s, Melita Maschmann (see Document 9) had risen to a
position of prominence in the League of German Girls (see Document
24). After the invasion of Poland, she went to Posen, a city in that part of
Poland that was directly annexed by Germany. She saw herself as a colonizer, eager to participate in the project of saving Poland from the Poles.*

During the first weeks at Posen an image surfaced in my memory and
from then on stuck in my mind. I must have been still at primary
school the day I pulled a map out of our letter box which pleased me
because of its gaiety. The countries of Europe stood out from one
another in bright colours and on each country sat, crawled or stood a
naked baby. I showed the map to my father because I wanted to know
the significance of the babies. He explained to me that each of these
children was a symbol of the birthrate of the country. The German
families had on the average far less children than, say, Polish families.
That was why only a frightened little girl sat on the patch of blue that
meant Germany. On the yellow patch, just next door to the right, a
sturdy little boy was crawling on all fours aggressively in the direction
of the German frontier.

"Look at the boy," said my father. "He is bursting with health and
strength. One day he will overrun the little girl."

The picture map stuck in my memory. It kept alive in me the feeling that the Poles were a menace to the German nation.

Later in "racial science" classes in the upper school the emotional
lesson was "scientifically" reinforced. [Previously] we compared the
birth rates of the Slavonic nations with those of the German nation
and were instructed about the "average qualities of the east European
races." Amongst them, so we heard, the intellectual and particularly

From Melita Maschmann, *Account Rendered: A Dossier on My Former Self*, trans. Geoffrey Strachan (London: Abelard-Schuman, 1964), 66.

the creative element came to the fore much more rarely. The noble, refined and intellectual qualities were everywhere in danger of being suppressed by the brutality of the primitive. That was why the Nordic nations were threatened with annihilation by the biological superiority of the Slavs. Primed with these views I came to the region which had been for generations a battlefield in the nationalist struggle between Poles and Germans. What I saw and heard seemed to confirm the National Socialist theories: the foreign nation seemed to consist only of manual workers, poor peasants and lower middle class townspeople, and the few Polish families I had a chance to study had substantially more children than corresponding German families.

37

KARL FUCHS

A German Soldier's Letters from France

1940

Karl Fuchs was born on March 18, 1917, the son of a schoolteacher in a small town in southern Germany; his father joined the Nazi party in 1923. Karl had planned to become a schoolteacher, too, but in October 1939, shortly after the German invasion of Poland, he joined the army. As a member of a tank unit, he participated in the German occupation of France in 1940. Karl's correspondence with his wife and loved ones gives us some insights into how German soldiers experienced the war. Mädi is the nickname Fuchs gave to his wife, Helene, whom he married in 1940. His own nickname was Korri. The couple had a son, Horst, in 1941. Fuchs was killed on the eastern front on November 21, 1941 (see Document 39). His letters were translated into English more than forty years later by his son.

From Horst Fuchs Richardson, ed., *Sieg Heil! War Letters of Tank Gunner Karl Fuchs, 1937–1941*, trans. Horst Fuchs Richardson (Hamden, Conn.: Archon Books, 1987), 68–69, 76–77.

15 JULY 1940
Dear Mädi,

Today I bought this exquisite stationery in Versailles for a reasonable price. We were driven to the French Potsdam today in order to visit the château and the park of Versailles. It was a pity that all the rooms had been emptied of all artifacts, but the French government had removed them for safe keeping. . . .

When we entered the sleeping quarters of the powerful Sun King, King Louis XIV, we could almost breathe the air of numbing sultriness of the time. Here in these quarters you could imagine what decadent debauchery this most famous French king was engaged in with that Pompadour woman. This is the air that France still breathes today. Life seems to be devoted to passion alone.

Later my soldier-friends and I went to a "bookstore" in Versailles. You can't imagine what junk and pornography we saw! There were nothing but magazines full of erotic pictures. The shopkeeper kept saying, "Oh messieurs, très bien," in order to get us to buy some of these books. We, however, had only one answer: "No, monsieur, très mal." You can truly see that in the areas of cleanliness and morality, the French people have skidded to a new low. Such an incident is simply unthinkable and impossible in our German Fatherland. When a society is capable of reducing the feminine beauty to such a level, then this society has lost its right to be called a "grande nation." Yes, this society has lost not only its vitality but also its morality.

Love, Korri

1 SEPTEMBER 1940
Dear Mädi,

. . . The September sun is scorching hot and the sky is a deep blue. The air, however, is filled with the thunder and roar of German bombers, Stukas and fighter planes. All are headed towards England, the archenemy. Only a little while ago some of us were talking about receiving our marching orders to move over there. We have no choice but to wait, even though it is very difficult for us. Apparently the time is not yet ripe to reap the harvest which the German air heroes have sown. The time will come, though, and it will be a pitiless and dreadful time for England.

Yesterday we actually visited Paris. You have to admit that it's a grandiose city with its wonderful boulevards with beautiful views. . . .

Life itself in Paris is back to normal. I must say, though, the most terrible sights are the Negroes who walk arm-in-arm with white

French women and who sit with them in the street cafes. I just can't approve of that!

In the evening we drove back to the base in our trucks because none of us were allowed to stay and go shopping in Paris. We're prohibited from walking alone through Paris. One more nice thing is that in front of the headquarters of the German army in France there were two guards and around them approximately a hundred Frenchmen. They stood there and just stared at the guards. Apparently they had never seen anything like this before—I mean, they had seen guards but not this kind of guard. The two Germans, who looked like they were cast in bronze, stood there with rifles ready. Nothing moved, not a muscle or an eyelid! It was a wonderful picture of genuine German soldiership. My comrades and I felt proud when we saw them.

Well, so much for Paris.

Love and kisses, Korri

38

FIELD MARSHAL WALTER VON REICHENAU

Conduct of Troops in Eastern Territories
October 10, 1941

On June 22, 1941, the Nazis invaded the Soviet Union with a force of more than three million troops. In the struggle to destroy the heartland of "Judeo-Bolshevism," there was no doubt that conventional rules of warfare were suspended. Even before the war began, secret orders to German military leaders instructed them to pay no attention to international law in the fight against Bolshevism. These sentiments were clearly reiterated in the following secret memo by Field Marshal Walter von Reichenau (1884–1942), commander of the German Sixth Army, in October 1941. Reichenau's memo only hints at the systematic ill treatment of Soviet prisoners of war. Of some 5.7 million, about 3.3 million would die while incarcerated.

From Field Marshal Walter von Reichenau, memo, doc. UK-81, in Office of the United States Chief of Counsel for Prosecution of Axis Criminality, *Nazi Conspiracy and Aggression* (Washington, D.C.: U.S. Government Printing Office, 1946), 8:585–87.

SECRET!

ARMY H.Q., 10.10.41

Army Command 6., Sec. Ia—A.7

Subject: Conduct of Troops in Eastern Territories.

Regarding the conduct of troops towards the bolshevistic system, vague ideas are still prevalent in many cases. The most essential aim of war against the Jewish-bolshevistic system is a complete destruction of their means of power and the elimination of asiatic influence from the European culture. In this connection the troops are facing tasks which exceed the onesided routine of soldiering. The soldier in the eastern territories is not merely a fighter according to the rules of the art of war but also a bearer of ruthless national ideology and the avenger of bestialities which have been inflicted upon German and racially related nations.

Therefore the soldier must have full understanding for the necessity of a severe but just revenge on subhuman Jewry. The Army has to aim at another purpose, i.e., the annihilation of revolts in hinterland which, as experience proves, have always been caused by Jews.

The combating of the enemy behind the front line is still not being taken seriously enough. Treacherous, cruel partisans and unnatural women are still being made prisoners of war and guerilla fighters dressed partly in uniforms or plain clothes and vagabonds are still being treated as proper soldiers, and sent to prisoner of war camps. In fact, captured Russian officers talk even mockingly about Soviet agents moving openly about the roads and very often eating at German field kitchens. Such an attitude of the troops can only be explained by complete thoughtlessness, so it is now high time for the commanders to clarify the meaning of the present struggle.

The feeding of the natives and of prisoners of war who are not working for the Armed Forces from Army kitchens is an equally misunderstood humanitarian act as is the giving of cigarettes and bread. Things which the people at home can spare under great sacrifices and things which are being brought by the Command to the front under great difficulties, should not be given to the enemy by the soldier not even if they originate from booty. It is an important part of our supply.

When retreating the Soviets have often set buildings on fire. The troops should be interested in extinguishing of fires only as far as it is necessary to secure sufficient numbers of billets. Otherwise the disappearance of symbols of the former bolshevistic rule even in the form of buildings is part of the struggle of destruction. Neither historic nor artistic considerations are of any importance in the eastern territories. . . .

... Being far from all political considerations of the future the soldier has to fulfill two tasks:

1. *Complete annihilation of the false bolshevistic doctrine of the Soviet State and its armed forces.*
2. *The pitiless extermination of foreign treachery and cruelty and thus the protection of the lives of military personnel in Russia.*

This is the only way to fulfil our historic task to liberate the German people once forever from the Asiatic-Jewish danger.

> Commander in Chief
> (Signed) von Reichenau
> Field Marshal.

39

KARL FUCHS

A German Soldier's Letters from the Eastern Front
1941

Tank gunner Karl Fuchs (see Document 37) took part in the invasion of the Soviet Union in June 1941. By November, along with the rest of the German army, he was bogged down in the Russian winter. His letters to his wife, infant son, and parents illustrate the harsh conditions that the German army faced and also the extent to which he embraced the virulent anti-Communism that was central to Nazi ideology.

28 JUNE 1941
My dearest wife, my dear little Horsti,
    ... Up to now, all of the troops have had to accomplish quite a bit. The same goes for our machines and tanks. But, nevertheless, we're going to show those Bolshevik bums who's who around here! They fight like

From Horst Fuchs Richardson, ed., *Sieg Heil! War Letters of Tank Gunner Karl Fuchs, 1937–1941*, trans. Horst Fuchs Richardson (Hamden, Conn.: Archon Books, 1987), 115–16, 118–19, 124, 138–39, 144–45, 155–57.

hired hands—not like soldiers, no matter if they are men, women or children on the front lines. They're all no better than a bunch of scoundrels. By now, half of Europe is mobilized. The entry of Spain and Hungary on our side against this Bolshevik archenemy of the world overjoyed us all. Yes, Europe stands under the leadership of our beloved Führer Adolph Hitler, and he'll reshape it for a better future. The entry of all these volunteer armies into this war will cause the war to be over soon.

The impressions that the battles have left on me will be with me forever. Believe me, dearest, when you see me again, you will face quite a different person, a person who has learned the harsh command: "I will survive!" You can't afford to be soft in war; otherwise you will die. No, you must be tough—indeed, you have to be pitiless and relentless. Don't I sound like a different person to you? Deep down in my heart, I remain a good person and my love for you and our son will never diminish. Never! This love will increase as will my longing for you. I kiss you and remain forever

your Korri

5 JULY 1941
My darling wife! My dear boy!
We have fought in battle many days now and we have defeated the enemy wherever we have encountered him. Let me tell you that Russia is nothing but misery, poverty and depravity! That is Bolshevism! . . .

Our losses have been minimal and our success is great. This war will be over soon, because already we are fighting against only fragmented opposition. . . .

Intimate kisses to you, Papi

P.S. Greet your parents and my mother.

17 JULY 1941
Sweet Mädi! My dear son!
. . . Yesterday I participated in my twelfth attack. Some of these attacks were more difficult than others. With twelve attacks under my belt, I have now caught up to the boys who had a head start in France! You can imagine that I'm very proud of this achievement. Recent orders have moved us seasoned veterans to the rear so that others have a chance to engage in battle. That makes sense to us, but it wasn't necessarily right because all of us veterans had become accustomed to battle and were at ease on the front line. These newcomers must first earn their seasoned status. . . .

Mädi, a few words about Russia. All those who today still see any kind of salvation in Bolshevism should be led into this "paradise." To sum it up with one phrase: "It's terrible!" When I get back I will tell you endless horror stories about Russia. Yesterday, for instance, we saw our first women soldiers—Russian women, their hair shorn, in uniform! And these pigs fired on our decent German soldiers from ambush positions.

... In my thoughts I hold you in my arms and kiss your lips and the cheeks of my son.

Your Papi

4 AUGUST 1941

Dear Father,

... The pitiful hordes on the other side are nothing but felons who are driven by alcohol and the threat of pistols pointed at their heads. There is no troop morale and they are at best cannon fodder. You should read the pamphlets that they drop from the sky with better accuracy than their bombs. "Desert! Join the Bolsheviks! You'll be safe with us!" They are nothing but a bunch of assholes! Excuse the expression, but there simply is no other term for them. Having encountered these Bolshevik hordes and having seen how they live has made a lasting impression on me. Everyone, even the last doubter, knows today that the battle against these subhumans, who've been whipped into a frenzy by the Jews, was not only necessary but came in the nick of time. Our Führer has saved Europe from certain chaos.

And so we move on to the final battle and victory. I shake your hand and greet you. Germany, Sieg Heil!

Your loyal son, Karl

22 SEPTEMBER 1941

My dearest Mädi,

... If you only knew under what arduous conditions our victories were fought and won. Sometimes it was incredible, fighting on muddy Russian roads or in rainy weather that seemed to have no end. Time and space are suspended. Once this last battle is over, peace will return to Germany and Europe. We out here on the front carry this belief in our hearts. You back home should have the same belief and hope as we do. Due to this common belief and hope, the front and the homeland are united in the real sense of the word. This point of view should play an important part in the schools today. You as teachers who are able to mold and educate the youth of our great country should, in this difficult and proud time, let our children participate in the heroism of their brothers and fathers. I would give anything if I were able to stand in front of my elementary school students for just one day. . . .

You probably are spending much time with our son. Your entire love must belong to this child since it is our child. But when you are teaching school, you must also share this love and enthusiasm with your pupils. Otherwise you should quit your job. I've become very conscious of the fact that our teaching profession, especially today and after the war, will demand real idealists. You can't do this job well if you do it half-heartedly. . . .

With all my love, Your Korri

15 OCTOBER 1941

My dear Mother,

While a terrible snowstorm is howling outside, my comrades and I are camping in one of these terrible peasant houses. Although it's not much of a home, we managed to clean it up yesterday. Up until now we've always preferred to dig a hole in the ground and maybe pitch a tent. Now, however, it's simply too cold outside. If you could see how these people live here, you would be horrified!

This present abode is in better shape than most. In one corner there is even a structure that looks like a bed. Most Russians don't sleep in beds, but either behind or on top of their stove. I won't describe the other facilities, such as water and sanitation. Suffice it to say that they hardly exist.

Our duty has been to fight and to free the world from this Communist disease. One day, many years hence, the world will thank the Germans and our beloved Führer for our victories here in Russia. Those of us who took part in this liberation battle can look back on those days with pride and infinite joy. That's all for today. I send you my greetings.

Your son, Karl

11 NOVEMBER 1941

My dearest, my little boy,

Today is a very happy day for me. It's almost as if I'm back in my childhood because I remember St. Nicholas Day and all the activities associated with it. Starting with St. Nicholas Day, the anticipation of Christmas grows real. I suppose St. Nick thought of me a distant soldier today since I received so many presents. Dear Mädi, I really want to thank you for all the lovely gifts. Let me tell you what they are so that you know that I received them; first of all, many thanks for the cigarettes. . . . Thank you also for the candy, the toothpaste and the lotion, the woolen gloves and the woolen scarf. I can really use the last two items now.

Yes, here I am again, sitting in one of these God-forsaken, Russian peasant houses supporting my head with my hand and thinking of you, my dear boy and of all those loved ones back home who've been so good to me. And today, our boy is five months old. I suppose that's a birthday of sorts. I can imagine that he has grown big and strong and is a very sweet baby.

All of us out here, all my comrades, continuously ask the all important question—when, when are we going to be able to go home? I still can't give you a definitive answer to that question. When I do return from these battles, I will probably come empty-handed, but my heart will be full of endless love for you and that is probably worth more than any present.

A few days ago it really started to get cold around here. It's a gripping cold and not comparable to anything that we might experience at home. Yes, we really have to bite the bullet now but we will survive this as well.

I love you forever—you alone and Horsti.

Your Korri

2 DECEMBER 1941

My dear Mrs. Fuchs,

As leader of the unit to which your husband, Sergeant Karl Fuchs, was assigned, I have the sad duty to inform you that your husband was killed on the field of battle on 21 November 1941.

His heroic death occurred when he was fighting bravely for Greater Germany in the front lines during a heavy battle with Russian tanks. The entire company and I would like to extend our deepest sympathies to you for the terrible loss which has befallen you.

We commiserate and are saddened that fate did not allow Karl to see his little daughter[1] of whom he was so proud. Be assured, however, that we will never forget your husband who was one of our best and bravest tank commanders and who always fought in an exemplary fashion against the enemy.

[1] Fuchs had a son, not a daughter.

We have prepared a dignified resting place for him near the city of Klin, north of Moscow. I hope it will be a small consolation for you when I tell you that your husband gave his life so that our Fatherland may live. I greet you with sincere compassion.

Lieutenant Reinhardt,
Company Commander

40

"Total War" Cover Illustration

1943

This image served as the cover illustration for a pamphlet about Germany's "total war" proclaimed by Propaganda Minister Joseph Goebbels after the defeat of the German army at Stalingrad in February 1943. Within Germany, that defeat triggered a dramatic shift in public opinion about the war and an acknowledgment that things were going quickly from bad to worse. In a famous speech before the party faithful in Berlin shortly after the German surrender at Stalingrad, Goebbels exhorted his listeners to ever more valiant efforts and greater self-sacrifice. The illustration quotes from Goebbels's speech: "Now, Nation, Rise and Storm, Erupt!" Note how the artist, not identified here, underscored Goebbels's claims that there was no separation between the military front and the home front.

Deutsches Historisches Museum Picture Archive, Berlin.

41

KÄTHE RICKEN

Life under the Bombs

1943

British and American forces did not open a second front on the ground in the west until June 1944. But long before then, they initiated a strategic bombing campaign that aimed at destroying German industrial plants, disrupting civilian life, and undermining morale on the home front. By the end of the war, bombs had killed about 400,000 Germans, mostly civilians, and in many big cities they had destroyed 70 percent of homes. The bombing campaign intensified in 1943, and Operation Gomorrah—the bombing of Hamburg in late July and early August—demonstrated the massive destruction that incendiary bombs, intended to create firestorms and level working-class housing, could cause. The attacks killed 41,000 and left 900,000 homeless. Survival "under the bombs" was a defining characteristic of the war in all major German cities. Käthe Ricken, a young mother whose husband was away at the front, kept a diary during the war. Here she describes her experience of the firebombing of Hamburg; Christmas with her son, Wolfgang; and life in the months before the German surrender.

---

25 JULY 1943

How terrified I was in our little cellar last night. I sat there, cowering, with my head tucked down between my shoulders. We all prayed out loud together with our landlord. The whole world was shaking like in an earthquake. You could actually feel our house moving up and down. Every bomb made a hissing and whistling noise as it fell. Then there would be a bang, followed by a rumbling sound. How often we thought: "This one's for us!" Frau Stuhr wanted us to put the candle out. She thought that the light might escape outside. That feeble gleam! If only she knew! Some of the men who had gone outside to

---

From Käthe Ricken, diary, in *War Wives: A Second World War Anthology*, by Colin Townsend and Eileen Townsend (London: Grafton Books, 1989), 274–76.

126

see how bad things were told us that the whole of Hamburg was blazing like a torch. I held little Wolfgang close and just prayed to get out of that hell-hole alive. Even if it meant being a poor suffering beggar for the rest of my days!

27 JULY 1943

Can't go on living here in the flat. No water, no gas, no electricity. There are no houses left and no shops. How am I going to look after Wolfgang? He's got a little brother or sister coming, too! Escape was the only way. The streets were full of dead bodies. There were mothers with children in their arms, shrivelled by the heat into mummies. They had obviously had to get out of their burning cellar, but death found them just as surely out in the streets. Before we went out, I wrapped a piece of clothing loosely around Wolfgang, leaving him just enough room to breathe.

CHRISTMAS 1943

We have been given a little room out in the suburbs, but will have to share it with others. All the upheaval has given Wolfgang diarrhoea. Have to fetch water from a long way off. I can't cook or wash, so the nappies can't be kept clean. I threw them in a nearby stream just to be rid of the smell. Now I'm having to cut up my own underwear for nappies. We have hardly had any bread again these last few days. Wolfgang keeps pleading and pleading for more. Will we ever see the day again when I can push a piece of chocolate into their little mouths? I asked Wolfgang what he would like Father Christmas to bring him. He said, "Bread."

JANUARY 1945

The children have stayed in bed for most of this month, just to keep warm. It has been so cold that the milk on the kitchen table keeps freezing. The food hand-outs are getting smaller and smaller, and our hunger greater. I'm now expecting my third baby. Someone said that they were giving out special allocations of soup for small children. So today I got them dressed up warm—as warm as I can with the few clothes we have left—and we left the cold flat and went out to the even colder street. The children soon forgot the pain of the cold with all the excitement of getting some warm soup. We walked miles and when we arrived we were chilled to the bone. The soup was all finished. What could I say to the children to console them? They were so heart-broken. I hadn't got a thing in the cupboard here. "I'll just have to make something out of nothing," I said to myself, half determined, half despairing.

"Mummy, why don't you make yourself something to eat and then you can come to bed and keep warm?" little Wolfgang said to me. If only! Once home, I breathed on their little hands and feet, then rubbed them between my hands. Then I told them all the cheerful things I could think of, and especially about how lovely everything was going to be when all this was over.

4

The Persecution of the Jews and the Final Solution

42

VICTOR KLEMPERER

Reflections on the Meanings of the Yellow Star for Jews in Germany in 1941

1947

Victor Klemperer (1881–1960) was a rabbi's son who converted from Judaism to Christianity and married a Protestant. To the Nazis, however, his religion made no difference. He managed to stay off the deportation lists until mid-February 1945. The Allied bombing of Dresden on the night of February 13 destroyed much of the city and killed tens of thousands of civilians, but it saved Klemperer and other Jews when the documents proving their Jewish heritage went up in flames. Klemperer, a scholar of Romance languages and literature, was fascinated by the Nazis' use of symbols and language. In a book first published in 1947, he collected his reflections on how the Nazis had perverted language, drawing heavily on observations from the diaries he had kept throughout the Nazi years. In this excerpt, he describes what it meant for German Jews to wear the yellow star, the six-pointed Star of David inscribed with "Jude" (Jew).

From Victor Klemperer, *The Language of the Third Reich: LTI—Lingua Tertii Imperii; A Philologist's Notebook*, trans. Martin Brady (London: Continuum, 2006), 166–69.

Today I ask myself again the same question I have asked myself and all kinds of people hundreds of times; which was the worst day for the Jews during those twelve years of hell?

I always, without exception, received the same answer from myself and others: 19 September 1941. From that day on it was compulsory to wear the Jewish star, the six-pointed Star of David, the yellow piece of cloth which today still stands for plague and quarantine, and which in the Middle Ages was the colour used to identify the Jews, the colour of envy and gall which has entered the bloodstream; the yellow piece of cloth with "Jew" printed on it in black, the word framed by the lines of the two telescoped triangles, a word consisting of thick block capitals, which are separated and given broad, exaggerated horizontal lines to effect the appearance of the Hebrew script.

The description is too long? But no, on the contrary! I simply lack the ability to pen precise, vivid descriptions. Many was the time, when it came to sewing a new star onto a new piece of clothing (or rather an old one from the Jewish clothing store), a jacket or a work coat, many was the time that I would examine the cloth in minute detail, the individual specks of the yellow fabric, the irregularities of the black imprint—and all of these individual segments would not have been sufficient, had I wanted to pin an agonizing experience with the star on each and every one of them.

A man who looks upright and good-humoured comes towards me leading a young boy carefully by the hand. He stops one step away from me: "Look at him, my little Horst!—He is to blame for everything!" . . . A well-groomed man with a white beard crosses the road, greets me solemnly and holds out his hand: "You don't know me, but I must tell you that I utterly condemn these measures." . . . I want to get onto the tram: I am only allowed to use the front platform and then, only if I am travelling to the factory, and only if the factory is more than 6 kilometres from my flat, and only if the front platform is securely separated from the inside of the tram; I want to get on, it's late, and if I don't arrive punctually at work the boss can report me to the Gestapo. Someone drags me back from behind: "Go on foot, it's much healthier for you!" An SS officer, smirking, not brutal, just having a bit of fun as if he were teasing a dog. . . . My wife says: "It's a nice day and for once I haven't got any shopping to do today, I don't have to join any queues—I'll come some of the way with you!"—"Out of the question! Am I to stand in the street and watch you being insulted because of me? What's more: who knows whether someone you don't even know will get suspicious, and then when you are getting rid of my manuscripts you'll accidentally bump into them!" . . . A removal man who is friendly towards me following two moves—good people with more than a whiff of the KPD[1]—is suddenly standing in front of me in the Freiberger Strasse, takes my hand in both of his paws and whispers in a tone which must be audible on the other side of the road: "Well, Herr Professor, don't let it get you down! These wretched brothers of ours will soon have reached rock bottom!" This is meant to comfort me, and it certainly warms the heart; but if the wrong person hears it over there, my consoler will end up in prison and it will cost me my life, via Auschwitz. . . . A passing car brakes on an empty road and a stranger pokes his head out: "You still alive, you wretched pig? You should be run over, across your belly! . . . "

No, the individual segments would not be sufficient to note down all the bitterness caused by the Jewish star. . . .

. . . It is true, I was already cut off from the multitude in 1933, and indeed so was the whole of Germany from that point; but all the same: as soon as I had left the flat behind me, and the street in which everyone knew me, I could submerge myself in the great flow, not without fear, of course, because at any moment anyone with malicious intent could recognize and insult me, but it was nevertheless a submersion; now, however, I was recognizable to everyone all the time, and being recognizable isolated and outlawed me; the reason given for the measure was that the Jews had to be segregated, given that their cruelty had been proved beyond doubt in Russia.

Now, for the first time, the ghettoization was complete: prior to this point, the word "Ghetto" only cropped up on postmarks bearing such addresses as "Litzmannstadt Ghetto"—it was reserved exclusively for conquered lands abroad. In Germany there were isolated Jews' Houses into which the Jews were crowded together, and which from time to time were provided with a sign on the outside bearing the name *"Judenhaus* (Jews' House)." But these houses were situated in Aryan districts, and were themselves not occupied exclusively by Jews; it was for this reason that one sometimes saw the declaration on other houses "This House is Free of Jews (*judenrein*)." This sentence clung to a number of walls in thick black letters until the walls themselves were destroyed in the bombing raids, whilst the signs proclaiming "Fully Aryan Shop (*rein arisches Geschäft*)," the hostile "Jewish Shop!" daubings on display windows, together with the verb *"arisieren* (to aryanize)" and the pleading words on the shop door "Entirely Aryanized Business!" very

[1] The German Communist party.

soon disappeared, because there were no more Jewish shops, and nothing left that could be aryanized.

Now that the Jewish star had been introduced, it made no difference whether the Jews' Houses were scattered or gathered together into their own district, because every star-bearing Jew carried his own Ghetto with him like a snail with its shell. And it was irrelevant whether or not Aryans lived in his house together with the Jews, because the star had to be stuck above his name on the door. If his wife was Aryan she had to put her name away from the star and add the word "Aryan."

And soon other notices began to appear here and there on the doors leading off the corridors, Medusa-like notices: "The Jew Weil lived here." At which point the postwoman knew she didn't have to worry about his address; the letter was returned to sender with the euphemistic remark "addressee gone away." The result being that "gone away (*abgewandert*)," with its dreadful special meaning, definitely belongs in the lexicon of the LTI,[2] in the Jewish section.

[2] *Lingua Tertii Imperii* — language of the Third Reich.

43

JEWISH CULTURAL ASSOCIATION OF WÜRTTEMBERG

On Deportation
November 17, 1941

The Nazis forced Jewish organizations to coordinate the deportation of Jews from Germany. This directive from November 1941, a month after the deportations began, suggests why many Jews could not have anticipated that deportation might quite likely end in death. German Jews had no access to any information that would have allowed them to know their fate, and the explicit instructions that Jews received indicate that

Jewish Cultural Association of Württemberg, circular, November 17, 1941, from Jeremy Noakes and Geoffrey Pridham, eds., *Nazism, 1919–1945: A Documentary Reader*, vol. 3, *Foreign Policy, War, and Racial Extermination* (Exeter, U.K.: University of Exeter Press, 2000), 523–24.

Jewish leaders believed that their communities were being shipped to labor, not death, camps. The possessions they painstakingly packed would ultimately be expropriated by the Nazis.

Re: Evacuation.

On the orders of the Secret State Police regional headquarters in Stuttgart we are obliged to inform you that you and the children mentioned above have been assigned to an evacuation transport to the East. At the same time, you, together with the above-mentioned children who have been assigned to the transport, are hereby obliged to hold yourselves in readiness from Wednesday 26 November 1941 onwards in your present abode and not to leave it even temporarily without the express permission of the authorities.

Employment, even in important plants, does not provide exemption from the evacuation. Any attempt to resist the evacuation or to avoid it is pointless and may have serious repercussions for the person concerned.

The enclosed declarations of assets must be filled in carefully for each member of the family involved, including each child, and delivered to the local police authority within three days.

Enclosed is a list of the most essential items to be brought with you. Each participant in the transport is entitled to take with them up to 50kg of luggage whether in the form of suitcases, rucksacks or shoulder bags. You are recommended to carry a large part of the luggage in a rucksack. It must be assumed that the members of the transport will have to carry their own luggage for part of the time. Suitcases, rucksacks, and travel rugs should be marked with the transport number noted above without fail; in addition, you are strongly advised to add your full name. If possible use indelible ink, otherwise use fixed tags.

In addition, you are advised to put on warm underwear, warm clothing, the strongest possible boots and shoes, galoshes, coats and caps rather than hats.

Apart from hand luggage, it will probably be possible to take with you in addition mattresses, some bedding, some kitchen equipment—but without kitchen furniture—cooking materials, tins of food, first aid materials, sewing equipment, needles, all tools and gardening equipment. Some stoves with chimneys and sewing machines, preferably portable ones, will probably be able to be taken. Spades, shovels and such like as well as building tools are particularly important.

We request that you get such objects ready in your flat and if possible pack them up, with sharp tools covered with protective packing, and mark these things clearly too, particularly mattresses, with the transport number, if necessary with a cardboard label. These objects should be mentioned on the form but with a note "are being taken with me."

With the delivery of this letter you have been officially banned from disposing of your property. Thus you are no longer permitted to sell, give away, lend, pawn or in any way dispose of any of your property.

Every member of the transport will receive RM[1] 50 in Reich credit notes and two food parcels worth RM 7.65, of which one contains food for consuming on the journey, while the second parcel with flour, pulses[2] etc., will be carried as luggage.

You should pay the required sum of RM 57.65 per person immediately to the Jewish Cultural Association of Württemberg, Stuttgatt, Hospitalstrasse 36 or to the special W account of the Württemberg branch of the Reich Association of German Jews at the Gymnasialstrasse branch of the Deutsche Bank.

If you are unable to pay the amount, inform the Jewish Cultural Association immediately. . . .

Prior to your departure, you must return your ration cards for the period after 1 December to the local office in return for a receipt.

Finally, we ask you not to delay; the efforts of our members, particularly in the employment field, entitle us to hope that this new and most difficult task can be mastered as well.

Jewish Cultural Association Württemberg
Ernst Israel Moos   Theodor Israel Rothschild
Alfred Israel Fackenheim

---

[1] RM is the abbreviation for Reichsmark, German currency.
[2] Pulses includes vegetables like peas, beans, and lentils.

44

RIA BRÖRING

A German Woman's Account of
Jewish Deportations

April 23, 1942

Ria Bröring, a native of Düsseldorf, was seventeen when the war started. She kept a diary throughout the war. Bröring helped distribute a statement issued by a leading Catholic bishop denouncing the euthanasia campaign (see Document 27) and engaged in other oppositional activity that led to her arrest and interrogation by the Gestapo. Near the end of the war, she was conscripted to operate the huge searchlights that helped those firing antiaircraft guns find their marks. In this diary entry, Bröring provides evidence of the ways in which non-Jewish Germans unavoidably became aware of what was happening to Jews.

THURSDAY, 23 APRIL 1942

Once again there are huge columns of Jews passing our house. The suffering of these poor tottering figures is indescribable. They stop to rest outside our house. They just flop down in the roadway. Many are so exhausted they can't get up again. Often they are too weary to carry their bundles any further, and just leave them lying in the road. Mothers comfort crying children. Old men are helped along by sons and daughters. Sheer misery stares out of the eyes of every one of them. Is it not an appalling injustice to rob these people of their last possessions and then finally of their homeland? Who is going to take responsibility for such guilt and wickedness? A price will have to be paid in the long run. I heard a German woman in the street say, "Pray God we never have to answer for this." If only we knew what was going to happen to these Jews. The rumour here is that they are taken off to Poland and then killed—that is if they haven't already died from hunger and the hardships of the journey. How can people who do that to them be called human beings? No, those responsible for this are nothing but animals.

From Ria Bröring, diary, in *War Wives: A Second World War Anthology*, by Colin Townsend and Eileen Townsend (London: Grafton Books, 1989), 87–88.

45

HERMANN FRIEDRICH GRAEBE

Description of a Mass Execution of Jews in Ukraine in 1942

1945

Hermann Graebe (1900–1986) was a German engineer. In October 1942, Graebe visited a site in Ukraine, a part of the Soviet Union occupied by the German army, where his company was engaged in construction projects. There he witnessed the mass murder of Jews by SS forces working with Ukrainian collaborators. Graebe's testimony was part of the documentation used in the trials of Nazi leaders at Nuremberg after the war.

I, Hermann Friedrich Graebe, declare under oath:

From September 1941 until January 1944 I was manager and engineer-in-charge of a branch office in Sdolbunow, Ukraine, of the Solingen building firm of Josef Jung. In this capacity it was my job to visit the building sites of the firm. Under contract to an Army Construction Office, the firm had orders to erect grain storage buildings on the former airport of Dubno, Ukraine.

On 5 October 1942, when I visited the building office at Dubno, my foreman Hubert Moennikes of 21 Aussenmuehlenweg, Hamburg–Haarburg, told me that in the vicinity of the site, Jews from Dubno had been shot in three large pits, each about 30 meters long and 3 meters deep. About 1500 persons had been killed daily. All of the 5000 Jews who had still been living in Dubno before the pogrom were to be liquidated. As the shootings had taken place in his presence he was still much upset.

Thereupon I drove to the site, accompanied by Moennikes and saw near it great mounds of earth, about 30 meters long and 2 meters high. Several trucks stood in front of the mounds. Armed Ukrainian

Hermann Friedrich Graebe, statement, doc. 2992-PS, in Office of the United States Chief of Counsel for Prosecution of Axis Criminality, *Nazi Conspiracy and Aggression* (Washington, D.C.: U.S. Government Printing Office, 1946), 5:696–99.

militia drove the people off the trucks under the supervision of an SS-man. The militia men acted as guards on the trucks and drove them to and from the pit. All these people had the regulation yellow patches on the front and back of their clothes, and thus could be recognized as Jews.

Moennikes and I went directly to the pits. Nobody bothered us. Now I heard rifle shots in quick succession, from behind one of the earth mounds. The people who had got off the trucks—men, women, and children of all ages—had to undress upon the order of an SS-man, who carried a riding or dog whip. They had to put down their clothes in fixed places, sorted according to shoes, top clothing and underclothing. I saw a heap of shoes of about 800 to 1000 pairs, great piles of under-linen and clothing. Without screaming or weeping these people undressed, stood around in family groups, kissed each other, said farewells and waited for a sign from another SS-man, who stood near the pit, also with a whip in his hand. During the 15 minutes that I stood near the pit I heard no complaint or plea for mercy. I watched a family of about 8 persons, a man and woman, both about 50 with their children of about 1, 8 and 10, and two grown-up daughters of about 20 to 24. An old woman with snow-white hair was holding the one-year-old child in her arms and singing to it, and tickling it. The child was cooing with delight. The couple were looking on with tears in their eyes. The father was holding the hand of a boy about 10 years old and speaking to him softly; the boy was fighting his tears. The father pointed toward the sky, stroked his head, and seemed to explain something to him. At that moment the SS-man at the pit shouted something to his comrade. The latter counted off about 20 persons and instructed them to go behind the earth mound. Among them was the family, which I have mentioned. I well remember a girl, slim and with black hair, who, as she passed close to me, pointed to herself and said, "23." I walked around the mound, and found myself confronted by a tremendous grave. People were closely wedged together and lying on top of each other so that only their heads were visible. Nearly all had blood running over their shoulders from their heads. Some of the people shot were still moving. Some were lifting their arms and turning their heads to show that they were still alive. The pit was already 2/3 full. I estimated that it already contained about 1000 people. I looked for the man who did the shooting. He was an SS-man, who sat at the edge of the narrow end of the pit, his feet dangling into the pit. He had a tommy gun on his knees and was smoking a cigarette. The people, completely naked, went down some steps which were cut in the clay wall of the pit and clambered over the heads of the people lying there, to the place to which the SS-man directed them. They lay down in front of the dead or injured people; some caressed those who were still alive and spoke to them in a low voice. Then I heard a series of shots. I looked into the pit and saw that the bodies were twitching or the heads lying already motionless on top of the bodies that lay before them. Blood was running from their necks. I was surprised that I was not ordered away, but I saw that there were two or three postmen in uniform nearby. The next batch was approaching already. They went down into the pit, lined themselves up against the previous victims and were shot. When I walked back, round the mound I noticed another truckload of people which had just arrived. This time it included sick and infirm people. An old, very thin woman with terribly thin legs was undressed by others who were already naked, while two people held her up. The woman appeared to be paralyzed. The naked people carried the woman around the mound. I left with Moennikes and drove in my car back to Dubno.

On the morning of the next day, when I again visited the site, I saw about 30 naked people lying near the pit—about 30 to 50 meters away from it. Some of them were still alive; they looked straight in front of them with a fixed stare and seemed to notice neither the chilliness of the morning nor the workers of my firm who stood around. A girl of about 20 spoke to me and asked me to give her clothes, and help her escape. At that moment we heard a fast car approach and I noticed that it was an SS-detail. I moved away to my site. 10 minutes later we heard shots from the vicinity of the pit. The Jews still alive had been ordered to throw the corpses into the pit—then they had themselves to lie down in this to be shot in the neck.

I make the above statement at Wiesbaden, Germany, on 10th November 1945. I swear before God that this is the absolute truth.

46

HEINRICH HIMMLER

Speech to SS Officers in Posen

October 4, 1943

The SS controlled the killing squads that accompanied the German army as it moved farther into the Soviet Union. SS units also were in charge of the Nazi ghetto system and the network of concentration camps and extermination facilities. In the following excerpts from an address to senior SS officers in Posen, a city in German-occupied Poland (see Document 36), Himmler praises his men and acknowledges that mass murder is hard work, a difficult duty carried out "for the love of our people."

I also want to talk to you, quite frankly, on a very grave matter. Among ourselves it should be mentioned quite frankly, and yet we will never speak of it publicly. Just as we did not hesitate on June 30th, 1934[1] to do the duty we were bidden, and stand comrades who had lapsed, up against the wall and shoot them, so we have never spoken about it and will never speak of it. It was that tact which is a matter of course and which I am glad to say, is inherent in us, that made us never discuss it among ourselves, never to speak of it. It appalled everyone, and yet everyone was certain that he would do it the next time if such orders are issued and if it is necessary.

I mean the clearing out of the Jews, the extermination of the Jewish race. It's one of those things it is easy to talk about—"The Jewish race is being exterminated," says one party member, "that's quite clear, it's in our program—elimination of the Jews, and we're doing it, exterminating them." And then they come, 80 million worthy Germans, and each one has his decent Jew. Of course the others are vermin,

---

[1]Date on which the SS assassinated SA leader Ernst Röhm and his followers (see Document 21).

From Heinrich Himmler, speech to SS officers, Posen, October 4, 1943, doc. 1919-PS, in Office of the United States Chief of Counsel for Prosecution of Axis Criminality, *Nazi Conspiracy and Aggression* (Washington, D.C.: U.S. Government Printing Office, 1946), 563–64.

but this one is an A-1 Jew. Not one of all those who talk this way has witnessed it, not one of them has been through it. Most of *you* must know what it means when 100 corpses are lying side by side, or 500 or 1000. To have stuck it out and at the same time—apart from exceptions caused by human weakness—to have remained decent fellows, that is what has made us hard. This is a page of glory in our history which has never been written and is never to be written, for we know how difficult we should have made it for ourselves, if—with the bombing raids, the burdens and the deprivations of war—we still had Jews today in every town as secret saboteurs, agitators and trouble-mongers. We would now probably have reached the 1916/17 stage when the Jews were still in the German national body.

We have taken from them what wealth they had. I have issued a strict order ... that this wealth should, as a matter of course, be handed over to the Reich without reserve. We have taken none of it for ourselves. Individual men who have lapsed will be punished in accordance with an order I issued at the beginning, which gave this warning; Whoever takes so much as a mark of it, is a dead man. A number of SS men—there are not very many of them—have fallen short, and they will die, without mercy. We had the moral right, we had the duty to our people, to destroy this people which wanted to destroy us. But we have not the right to enrich ourselves with so much as a fur, a watch, a mark, or a cigarette or anything else. Because we have exterminated a bacterium we do not want, in the end, to be infected by the bacterium and die of it. I will not see so much as a small area of sepsis appear here or gain a hold. Wherever it may form, we will cauterize it. Altogether however, we can say, that we have fulfilled this most difficult duty for the love of our people. And our spirit, our soul, our character has not suffered injury from it.

47

CHAIM KAPLAN

In the Warsaw Ghetto
1939–1942

After the invasion of Poland in September 1939, the Nazis entered a new phase in their anti-Semitic policy, forcibly moving Jews from all over Poland into ghettos, sealed-off areas in which only Jews lived. The most famous ghetto was in Warsaw. German authorities established the boundaries of the Warsaw ghetto in October 1940, and a month later they closed it off, isolating it from the rest of the city. Mass deportations began in July 1942. Some Jews who remained in the ghetto openly fought back, and only in May 1943 did the Nazis completely crush armed Jewish resistance, liquidating the ghetto. Chaim Kaplan (1880–1942/43?), a resident of Warsaw and the founder of a Hebrew elementary school, kept a diary in Hebrew both before and during the war. Before he was deported to a killing facility, probably Treblinka, he gave his diary to a friend, who smuggled it out of the ghetto. Kaplan did not survive the Holocaust, but his diary did.

DECEMBER 1, 1939

The liquidation of Polish Jewry is in full force, but it is not proceeding everywhere at a uniform rate. It is a mistake to think that the conqueror excels in logic and orderliness. We see quite the opposite of this. Everything that is done by those who carry out his exalted will bears the imprint of confusion and illogic. The Nazis are consistent and systematic only with regard to the central concepts behind their action—that is, the concept of authoritarianism and harshness; and in relation to the Jews—the concept of complete extermination and destruction. . . .

From *Scroll of Agony: The Warsaw Diary of Chaim A. Kaplan*, trans. and ed. Abraham I. Katsh (Bloomington: Indiana University Press, 1999), 80, 93–94, 129–31, 152–54, 234–35, 242–43, 332–33, 336–37, 348, 383–85, 396–97.

DECEMBER 30, 1939

In his press the conqueror admits that up to 50,000 refugees have entered the capital. But as usual he lies. More than 100,000 Jews have actually come to Warsaw. Piled high with belongings and babies, their carts form long lines along the city streets. No organized help has been given them. Each one helps himself in his own way and on his own initiative. Some move in with a relative, a friend, or a distant acquaintance. The poor ones fill the synagogues, which have become refugee centers. One cannot describe the crowded conditions, the congestion and filth in these shelters. . . .

MARCH 10, 1940

The gigantic catastrophe which has descended on Polish Jewry has no parallel, even in the darkest periods of Jewish history. First, in the depth of the hatred. This is not just hatred whose source is in a party platform, and which was invented for political purposes. It is a hatred of emotion, whose source is some psychopathic malady. In its outward manifestations it functions as physiological hatred, which imagines the object of hatred to be unclean in body, a leper who has no place within the camp.

The masses have absorbed this sort of qualitative hatred. Their limited understanding cannot grasp ideological hatred; psychology is beyond them and they are incapable of understanding it. They have absorbed their masters' teachings in a concrete, corporeal form. The Jew is filthy; the Jew is a swindler and an evildoer; the Jew is the enemy of Germany, who undermines its existence; the Jew was the prime mover in the Versailles Treaty, which reduced Germany to nothing; the Jew is Satan, who sows dissension between one nation and another, arousing them to bloodshed in order to profit from their destruction. These are easily understood concepts whose effect in day-to-day life can be felt immediately. . . .

It is our good fortune that the conquerors have failed to consider the nature and strength of Polish Jewry, and this has kept us alive. Logically we should be dead. According to the laws of nature, we ought to have been completely annihilated. How can an entire community feed itself when it has no place in life? There is no occupation, no activity which is not limited, circumscribed for us.

But here again we do not conform to the laws of nature. A certain invisible power is embedded in us, and it is this secret which keeps us alive and preserves us in spite of all the laws of nature: if it is impossible to live by what is permitted, we live from what is forbidden. . . .

We are left naked, but as long as this secret power is still within us we do not give up hope. And the strength of this power lies in the indigenous nature of Polish Jewry, which is rooted in our eternal tradition that commands us to live. . . .

MAY 15, 1940
. . . The children of our poor, with whom the streets of Warsaw are filled at all hours of the day, are not afraid even of the despotic conquerors. They remain as always—lively and mischievous. Their poverty and oppression serves to shield them from robberies and confiscations. No one will harm them. Even the conquerors' eye overlooks them: Let the Jewish weeds pine away in their iniquity. But these weeds watch every act of the conquerors and imitate the Nazis' manner of speech and their cruelty most successfully. For them this is nothing but good material for games and amusements. Childhood does much.

Once there came into the ghetto a certain Nazi from a province where the Jews are required to greet every Nazi soldier they encountered, removing their hats as they do. There is no such practice in Warsaw, but the "honored guest" wanted to be strict and force the rules of his place of origin on us. A great uproar arose suddenly in Jewish Karmelicka Street: Some psychopathic Nazi is demanding that every passerby take his hat off in his honor. Many fled, many hid, many were caught for their transgression and beaten, and many were bursting with laughter. The little "wise guys," the true lords of the street, noticed what was going on and found great amusement in actually obeying the Nazi, and showing him great respect in a manner calculated to make a laughingstock out of the "great lord" in the eyes of all the passersby. They ran up to greet him a hundred and one times, taking off their hats in his honor. They gathered in great numbers, with an artificial look of awe on their faces, and wouldn't stop taking off their hats. Some did this with straight faces, while their friends stood behind them and laughed. Then these would leave, and others would approach, bowing before the Nazi with bare heads. There was no end to the laughter. Every one of the mischievous youths so directed his path as to appear before the Nazi several times, bowing before him in deepest respect. That wasn't all. Riffraff gathered for the fun, and they all made a noisy demonstration in honor of the Nazi with a resounding cheer.

This is Jewish revenge!

DECEMBER 26, 1940
Hanukkah in the ghetto. Never before in Jewish Warsaw were there as many Hanukkah celebrations as in this year of the wall. But because

of the sword that hovers over our heads, they are not conducted among festive crowds, publicly displaying their joy. Polish Jews are stubborn: the enemy makes laws but they don't obey them. That is the secret of our survival. We behaved in this manner even in the days when we were not imprisoned within the ghetto walls, when the cursed Nazis filled our streets and watched our every move. Since the ghetto was created we have had some respite from overt and covert spies, and so Hanukkah parties were held in nearly every courtyard, even in rooms which face the street; the blinds were drawn, and that was sufficient.

How much joy, how much of a feeling of national kinship there was in these Hanukkah parties! After sixteen months of Nazi occupation, we came to life again. . . .

FEBRUARY 15, 1941

Jewish children learn in secret. In back rooms, on long benches near a table, little schoolchildren sit and learn what it's like to be Marranos. Before the ghetto was created, when the Nazis were common in our streets, we trembled at the sound of every driven leaf; our hearts turned to water at the sound of any knock on the door. But with the creation of the ghetto, the situation improved somewhat. The Jewish teachers engage in their teaching with confidence that they and their pupils are in relatively little danger. . . . We arc allowed to feed, direct, and train them; but to educate them is forbidden. But since training is permitted, we allow ourselves education as well. In time of danger the children learn to hide their books. Jewish children are clever—when they set off to acquire forbidden learning they hide their books and notebooks between their trousers and their stomachs, then button their jackets and coats. This is a tried-and-true method, a kind of smuggling that is not readily detected.

In the very midst of the infected ghetto stands a varied group of people. It is apparent that no calamity has occurred; on the contrary, their faces reflect surprise and satisfaction at some exotic pleasure. What is the novelty today? The Jews of the ghetto have made a circle around two Nazi officers, and the two faces are friendly. God in Heaven! Have the laws of nature changed?

I guessed that there was no danger, and so I too approached. Nearby I noticed little Jewish children surrounding the Nazis and nearly embracing them. Every so often the Nazis popped candies into their mouths. I was stunned. Was this a dream? Almost against my will I remained in the stream of traffic. I could not understand the explanation of the scene before me and I wanted to linger, although I'm not the kind to hang around street corners. One of the Nazis was lean, the other fat and paunchy. Suddenly I noticed that the fat one was holding a camera. As his companion fed a candy to a Jewish child, he would focus his camera for a picture. The riddle was answered. There is no Nazi without politics. Apparently they need pictures showing friendship to Jewish children for propaganda, to deceive mankind. Anything goes.

MAY 16, 1942

Life in the ghetto is stagnant and frozen. There are walls around us; we have no space, no freedom of action. Whatever we do we do illegally; legally we don't even have permission to exist. Our sources of livelihood are all tenuous and temporary, based on chance. As many as sixty per cent are starving in the full sense of the word. Up to thirty per cent are in a state of terrible deprivation and hunger, even though it is not apparent from without; only ten per cent are exceptions, making their living from the misfortunes of Israel. These are the smugglers, the bakers, the traders in produce, and the functionaries of the *Judenrat*[1] and those who revolve around it. Our lives—if this can be called living—have taken on their inert, monotonous forms and no changes occur in them. The only ones who bring some activity into the sordid life of the ghetto are the killer and his friend death—the killer with his decrees which are renewed from time to time, and death with his scythe. Today one person died; tomorrow another. When their names are mentioned people wake up for a moment and sigh out of fear for what may befall them tomorrow, then life returns to its usual course. The same is true with a new decree. When a new decree is made it stuns the soul for a moment. Thousands of families fall victim to its cruelty and barbarism, but in the end we "make friends" with it too. . . .

JUNE 9, 1942

The Jewish section of Warsaw has become a city of slaughter.

We have endured three more nights of butchery, and we have almost become accustomed even to this. It is impossible to determine the exact number of victims; the opinions range from 21 up to 115. No matter. The executioner was kept busy enough. Some tens of Jews

---

[1] Jewish Council, consisting of prominent individuals charged by the Nazis with overseeing everyday life in the ghetto.

died a dog's death, in the German manner, and the murderers continue to come with lists in their hands. Moreover, as a byproduct of their job, they also kill others who are not even on the list. A Jewish porter was killed because he answered no when the murderers asked him if he had seen anyone escape. He was immediately shot down on suspicion of sympathizing with the escapee. It is standard procedure with the murderers to take relatives and neighbors in place of an absent victim. . . .

JULY 26, 1942

. . . Some of my friends and acquaintances who know the secret of my diary urge me, in their despair, to stop writing. "Why? For what purpose? Will you live to see it published? Will these words of yours reach the ears of future generations? How? If you are deported you won't be able to take it with you because the Nazis will watch your every move, and even if you succeed in hiding it when you leave Warsaw, you will undoubtedly die on the way, for your strength is ebbing. And if you don't die from lack of strength, you will die by the Nazi sword. For not a single deportee will be able to hold out to the end of the war."

And yet in spite of it all I refuse to listen to them. I feel that continuing this diary to the very end of my physical and spiritual strength is a historical mission which must not be abandoned. My mind is still clear, my need to record unstilled, though it is now five days since any real food has passed my lips. Therefore I will not silence my diary! . . .

The first victim of the deportation decree was the President, Adam Czerniakow,[2] who committed suicide by poison in the *Judenrat* building. He perpetuated his name by his death more than by his life. His end proves conclusively that he worked and strove for the good of his people; that he wanted its welfare and continuity even though not everything done in his name was praiseworthy. . . .

The president, who had a spark of purity in his heart, found the only way out worthy of himself. Suicide! In the end the Nazis would have killed him anyhow, as is their custom in the areas from which they expel the Jewish population; nor would the president have been the last to be shot. From the moment of his refusal to sign the expulsion order he was a saboteur in the eyes of the Nazis and thus doomed to death. With a president one must be very exacting. In any event, he did well to anticipate the Nazis. . . .

[2]Head of the *Judenrat*. In July 1942, after being ordered to organize the first mass deportation from the ghetto, he committed suicide.

AUGUST 2, 1942

Jewish Warsaw is in its death throes. A whole community is going to its death! The appalling events follow one another so abundantly that it is beyond the power of a writer of impressions to collect, arrange, and classify them; particularly when he himself is caught in their vise— fearful of his own fate for the next hour, scheduled for deportation, tormented by hunger, his whole being filled with the fear and dread which accompanies the expulsion. And let this be known: From the beginning of the world, since the time when man first had dominion over another man to do him harm, there has never been so cruel and barbaric an expulsion as this one. From hour to hour, even from minute to minute, Jewish Warsaw is being demolished and destroyed, reduced and decreased. Since the day the exile was decreed, ruin and destruction, exile and wandering, bereavement and widowhood have befallen us in all their fury. . . .

We have no information about the fate of those who have been expelled. When one falls into the hands of the Nazis he falls into the abyss. The very fact that the deportees make no contact with their families by letters bodes evil. Nothing that is related—and many things are related—is based on exact information. One person says that a certain family has received news of one of its members who was deported, that he arrived in the place intended for him alive and well—but he doesn't name the place nor give his address, and he doesn't ask them to write to him. Certain other unconfirmed reports are widespread, but no one knows their source nor lends much credence to them. Nevertheless, there is some local information about one segment of the deportees—the sick, the aged, the crippled and the other invalids, the weak ones who need the care and help of other people. They have returned to the city, not to the living but rather to the dead—to the cemetery. There they have found rest for their oppressed souls, and there they attain eternal peace. I have not yet verified this information myself. I record it as I heard it from the rumor.

48

HIRSH GLICK

Jewish Partisan Song

1943

Throughout the parts of Europe occupied by the Nazis, Jews and others organized resistance to German forces. Called partisans, they were not part of any regular army. Hirsh Glick (1922–1944) lived in Vilna, the capital of Lithuania. He wrote poems in Hebrew and Yiddish, the language spoken by many eastern European Jews. When the Germans marched into Vilna in 1941, Glick was sent to a labor camp. In 1943, he was transferred to the Jewish ghetto in Vilna, where he joined a partisan group. When the residents of the ghetto were deported to concentration camps, Glick ended up in a camp in Estonia. In 1944, together with other partisans, he attempted to escape and was murdered by the Nazis. Glick wrote this poem while he was in the Vilna ghetto, and two Soviet composers set it to music. It became the anthem of the Jewish resistance movement throughout eastern Europe.

Never say that there is only death for you
Though leaden skies may be concealing days of blue —
Because the hour we have hungered for is near;
Beneath our tread the earth shall tremble: We are here!

From land of palm-tree to the far-off land of snow
We shall be coming with our torment and our woe,
And everywhere our blood has sunk into the earth
Shall our bravery, our vigor blossom forth!

We'll have the morning sun to set our day aglow,
And all our yesterdays shall vanish with the foe,
And if the time is long before the sun appears,
Then let this song go like a signal through the years.

Hirsh Glick, "Jewish Partisan Song," in *Anthology of Holocaust Literature*, ed. Jacob Glatstein, Israel Knox, and Samuel Margoshes, trans. Aaron Kramer (New York: Atheneum, 1982), 349.

This song was written with our blood and not with lead;
It's not song that birds sing overhead,
It was a people, among toppling barricades,
That sang this song of ours with pistols and grenades.

So never say that there is only death for you.
Leaden skies may be concealing days of blue —
Yet the hour we have hungered for is near;
Beneath our tread the earth shall tremble: We are here!

49

RUTH KLUGER

A Young Girl's "Lucky Accident" at Auschwitz in 1944

1992

The Nazis murdered as many as three million Jews in massive extermination facilities in Poland run by the SS. At the Wannsee Conference in 1942, Nazi leaders outlined the "final solution," authorizing the SS to begin committing mass murder on an unprecedented scale. The most famous killing facility was Auschwitz-Birkenau. Ruth Kluger (b. 1931), an Austrian Jew, grew up in Vienna in a middle-class home. She and her mother were deported to Theresienstadt, a Nazi concentration camp near Prague, in September 1942. In May 1944, they were transferred to Auschwitz, where SS officials used a selection process to determine which prisoners were physically able to work and which would be gassed. In this excerpt from her memoir, originally published in German in 1992, Kluger describes the "lucky accident" that led to her survival.

Selection, there was to be a selection. At a certain barracks at a certain time, women between the ages of fifteen and forty-five were to be

From Ruth Kluger, *Still Alive: A Holocaust Girlhood Remembered* (New York: Feminist Press, 2001), 103–8.

chosen for a transport to a labor camp. Some argued that up to now every move had been for the worse, that one should therefore avoid the selection, stay away, try to remain here. My mother believed— and the world has since agreed with her—that Birkenau was the pits, and to get out was better than to stay. But the word *Selektion* was not a good word in Auschwitz, because it usually meant the gas chambers. One couldn't be sure that there really was a labor camp at the end of the process, though it seemed a reasonable assumption, given the parameters of the age group they were taking. But then, Auschwitz was not run on reasonable principles. . . .

Two SS men conducted the selection, both with their backs to the rear wall. They stood on opposite sides of the so-called chimney, which divided the room. In front of each was a line of naked, or almost naked, women, waiting to be judged. The selector in whose line I stood had a round, wicked mask of a face and was so tall that I had to crane my neck to look up at him. I told him my age, and he turned me down with a shake of his head, simply, like that. Next to him, the woman clerk, a prisoner, too, was not to write down my number. He condemned me as if I had stolen my life and had no right to keep it, as if my life were a book that an adult was taking from me, just as my uncle had taken the Bible from me because I was too young to read it. . . .

My mother had been chosen. No wonder: she was the right age, a grown-up woman. Her number had been written down, and she would leave the camp shortly. We stood on the street between the two rows of barracks and argued. She tried to persuade me that I should try a second time, with the other SS man in the other line, and claim that I was fifteen.

The month of June 1944 was very hot in Poland, and therefore both the front and the rear doors of the barracks stood open. The back entrance was guarded, but the detail consisted of inmates, and my mother felt I could sneak by and take another turn. And this time, please don't be a fool and tell them your real age of twelve. I got angry and was half desperate. "I don't look older," I remonstrated. I felt she half wanted me to step in a pile of shit, like the time a few years earlier when she had urged me to go to the movies despite the legal prohibition. . . . The difference between twelve and fifteen is enormous for a twelve-year-old. I was to add a quarter of my entire life. . . . The lie which my mother proposed was so transparent: three years! Where was I to find them?

I was anguished and frightened, but this was not the profound fear that overwhelmed me when I looked at the chimneys, the crematoria, spitting flames at night and smoke by day. When that fear gripped me, it was like the psychological equivalent of epileptic fits. The fear I felt now was more like the bearable fear of malicious grown-ups, a fear with which I could cope. For what would become of me if I had to stay in Birkenau without my mother? Well, that was out of the question, she assured me. If I wouldn't try the selection a second time, she would stay, too. She'd like to see who could separate her from her child. Only it wasn't a good idea, and would I please listen to what she was telling me, she said, without paying attention to my conclusive counterarguments. "You are a coward," she said half desperately, half contemptuously, and added, "I wasn't ever a coward." So what could I do but go in a second time, but with the proviso that I would try thirteen, never fifteen. Fifteen was preposterous. And if I get into trouble, it's your fault.

The space between the barracks I was to invade in order to reach the back door was guarded by a cordon of men. My mother and I watched them carefully for a minute or so. "Now!" we realized, and I sneaked by as the two men in charge happened to call out to each other. I bent over a little to appear smaller, or to make use of the shadow of the wall, turned the corner, and entered through the door, unobserved.

The room was still full of women. A kind of orderly chaos reigned which I associate with Auschwitz. The much-touted Prussian perfection of camp administration is a German myth. Behind every good organization is the presumption that there is something worth keeping and organizing. Here the organization was superficial, because there was nothing valuable to organize or retain. We were worthless by definition. We had been brought here to be disposed of, and hence the waste of *Menschenmaterial*, human substance, as the inhuman German term has it, was immaterial, to use another inhuman term. Basically the Nazis didn't care what went on in the Jew camps, as long as they were no bother. The selecting SS officers and their helpers stood with their backs to me. I went unobtrusively to the front door, took off my clothes once more, and quietly went to the end of the line. I breathed a sigh of relief to have managed so far so well, and was happy to have been smarter than the rules. I had proved to my mother that I wasn't chicken. But I was the smallest, and obviously the youngest, female around, undeveloped, undernourished, and nowhere near puberty.

I have read a lot about the selections since that time, and all reports insist that the first decision was always the final one, that no prisoner who had been sent to one side, and thus condemned to death, ever made it to the other side. All right, I am the proverbial exception.

What happened next is loosely suspended from memory, as the world before Copernicus dangled on a thin chain from Heaven. It was an act of the kind that is always unique, no matter how often it occurs: an incomprehensible act of grace, or put more modestly, a good deed. Yet the first term, an act of grace, is perhaps closer to the truth, although the agent was human and the term is religious. For it came out of the blue sky and was as undeserved as if its originator had been up in the clouds. I was saved by a young woman who was in as helpless a situation as the rest of us, and who nonetheless wanted nothing other than to help me. The more I think about the following scene, the more astonished I am about its essence, about someone making a free decision to save another person, in a place which promoted the instinct of self-preservation to the point of crime and beyond. It was both unrivaled and exemplary. Neither psychology nor biology explains it. Only free will does. . . .

The line moved towards an SS man who, unlike the first one, was in a good mood. Judging from photos, he may have been the infamous Dr. Mengele,[1] but as I said, it doesn't matter. His clerk was perhaps nineteen or twenty. When she saw me, she left her post, and almost within the hearing of her boss, she asked me quickly and quietly and with an unforgettable smile of her irregular teeth: "How old are you?" "Thirteen," I said, as planned. Fixing me intently, she whispered, "Tell him you are fifteen."

Two minutes later it was my turn, and I cast a sidelong look at the other line, afraid that the other SS man might look up and recognize me as someone whom he had already rejected. He didn't. (Very likely he couldn't tell us apart any more than I had reason to distinguish among the specimens of his kind.) When asked for my age I gave the decisive answer, which I had scorned when my mother suggested it but accepted from the stranger. "I am fifteen."

"She seems small," the master over life and death remarked. He sounded almost friendly, as if he was evaluating cows and calves.

"But she is strong," the woman said, "look at the muscles in her legs. She can work."

She didn't know me, so why did she do it? He agreed—why not? She made a note of my number, and I had won an extension on life.

---

[1] Josef Mengele (1911–1979) was the chief medical doctor at Auschwitz. He participated in the selection of those to be killed and also conducted medical experiments on prisoners.

Every survivor has his or her "lucky accident"—the turning point
to which we owe our lives. Mine is peculiar because of the intervention of the stranger. Virtually all those still alive today who have the
Auschwitz number on their left arm are older than I am, at least by
those three years that I added to my age. There are exceptions, like
the underage twins on whom Dr. Mengele performed his pseudo-
medical experiments. Then there are some who were my age, but who
were selected at the ramp to be sent immediately on to the labor camps,
and who were thought to be older because they wore several layers of
clothing, by way of transporting a wardrobe. They were not tattooed
because they weren't in the camp. To get out of the camp, you really
had to have been alive longer than twelve years.

50

HANNA LÉVY-IIASS

The Bergen-Belsen Concentration Camp
1944–1945

*Hanna Lévy-Hass (1913–2001), a teacher, lived in Montenegro, part of
Yugoslavia, before World War II. She was Jewish. When the Nazis took
control of Yugoslavia, she joined the resistance. In 1943, she considered
flight into the mountains to join her comrades; but three Jews appealed to
her not to join the partisans, because they feared that the Nazis would
punish the village by killing all the Jews who remained. She stayed and
was deported to Bergen-Belsen, a concentration camp in Germany. (This
camp was also the final destination of Anne Frank, who died there in
March 1945.) In these diary entries, recorded secretly while she was at
Bergen-Belsen, Lévy-Hass provides insights into the difference between a
"death factory" such as Auschwitz and death at Bergen-Belsen. After the
war, Lévy-Hass returned to Yugoslavia and then immigrated to Israel in
1948.*

From Hanna Lévy-Hass, *Diary of Bergen-Belsen*, trans. Sophie Hand (Chicago: Haymarket Books, 2009), 93–101, 104, 119–21.

DECEMBER 1944

Starvation is everywhere; each of us is nothing more than a shadow. The food we receive gets scarcer each day. For three days we haven't seen a piece of bread. Some people have saved theirs and now they open up their miserable provisions and everything is moldy. Bread is gold. You can get anything with bread; you will risk everything for bread. And there are more and more thieves, especially at night. Some-one suggested we take turns staying up and keeping watch so we could catch them. The hunt lasted two nights in the densest darkness. It was very dramatic, very noisy. No one slept and the results were nil.

Anyone who has a little bit of bread keeps it under his pillow or rather makes a pillow out of it. That way they feel more secure when they sleep. The mothers, especially, resort to this method to ensure a few mouthfuls for their children. As for the workers who are out work-ing all day, they're forced to lug their entire stock with them every-where in their bag. And their entire stock means six days' rations, at most, which is about half a loaf. The temptation is strong. Every-one ends up at some point eating the entire six days' worth in one day. . . .

In order to mobilize the maximum number of internees possible for all kinds of work, the Germans have multiplied their terror tenfold. Each day, before dawn, at four o'clock in the morning, everyone must be up. We feel hunted. A feverish coming and going, marked by anguish and terror. . . . It's the middle of winter; it's bitterly cold. At five o'clock, the human columns must already be in perfect order in the *Appellplatz*. This is the first *Appell* of the day (*Arbeitsappell*—roll call for work). It's still completely dark out, we stand for at least two hours waiting for the officer in charge who has to count us and send us off to work. Frozen, extremely weakened, famished, we feel our strength abandon us. But no leaving the square, no moving, even.

Due to the icy cold and starvation, many faint and collapse to the ground. Twice, I myself became violently dizzy and nearly succumbed. At such times, the ground has a magical appeal. Oh, how nice it would be to rest! But I managed to gather myself one more time. Falling ill here is not a good thing. No one and nothing in the world can help us. We die, and that's it.

The German officer finally deigns to count us at seven or seven thirty. He begins with a hearty volley of insults and cursing directed at everyone, he starts to let fly, kicking people for no reason, randomly. Afterwards, he chooses his victims, those who dare to explain why they can't work. These are the ones he "sets right." Systematically, he lunges at them, gives them a back-breaking beating, drags them on the ground, and tramples them—after which he forces them to stand up and take their place in the ranks.

DECEMBER 1944

The camp commander was just dismissed. Kramer was appointed in his place. Kramer, however, is the former commander of Auschwitz. Ominous reminder. All commentary is useless. . . . The camp regime gets more atrocious by the day. Beatings are commonplace; punishments that in the past were given to individuals and meant depriving one person of bread or food are now collective measures meted out to the camp as a whole. What difference does it make if there are small children and sick people among us?. . .

An atrocious fright has gripped all of our hearts. We feel that no one looks after us any longer. We are completely at the mercy of the new commander, a villain and avowed anti-Semite. Absolute Master of the camp, he is subordinate to no one. No authority exists for us, except him. God Himself is powerless here.

Kramer does what he likes. Endless transports keep pouring in. Processions of strange creatures move constantly between the blocks and the barbed wire. Pitiful, their terrifying appearance so unlike that of human beings. Ghosts. They look at us with fright and we look at them the same way. Without a doubt we make the same impression on them as they do on us. There isn't enough room for all these people. We change places every day, each time more tightly squeezed together. Finally, they give the order that we are to sleep two to a bed, so the three-tiered bunks now contain six people. The space between the bunks is even narrower than before. This is how we emptied half of our barracks to make room for the new arrivals. . . .

DECEMBER 1944

. . . What is important to us at the moment is Kramer and his band. He has imposed a new command on us, composed of Aryans, common criminals (the *Häftlinge*) of German, Polish, or French nationality. They are well-fed types, big and strong as bulls. They continually strut among us with clubs, beating whomever they wish. They wear convict's clothes, those striped pants and long shirts with large numbers marked on the back. But the most tragic thing is that by their very nature, they are criminals in the worst sense of the word. Their body and soul sold to the devil—to Kramer—they have nothing of humanity left in them. Cynical, cruel, sadistic. You should see the perverse joy they take in beating people. I've noticed it clearly. They are wild animals disguised as men. This is what the Germans have done, what they have reduced them to. And it seems that it is on us that they intend to take their revenge.

These hardened criminals are our masters from this moment on, free to dispose of our lives, our souls, our children. We are enslaved under these vile serfs. What an infernal scheme! The Nazi brute is never short of ideas when it comes to finding a way to humiliate man better, to crush him better. The new command, these new *Kapos*[1] attack the male internees especially. They persecute them mercilessly. There is a place called the *Stuppenkommando*. It's the death commando. In the evening, after work, not one of the men who have worked there returns unscathed. There they are beaten to the point of being broken, bloody, and swollen. Yesterday, December 30, two men died under their bludgeons. The same day, two others were brought back to the camp on stretchers carried by their comrades. The "kapos" also strike the women or, worse yet, succeed in prostituting them. . . .

JANUARY 1945

I succeeded in talking to some of the women from the transport that came from Auschwitz. Most of them are Jewish women from Poland, Greece, or Hungary. They tell us what they've experienced at Auschwitz. In 1943 and 1944 alone, during the time they were there, hundreds of thousands of people were exterminated. They are among the few hundred who miraculously managed to get out of there.

"There are no words to describe what we went through," they tell us. And they tell us of mass murders, by gas, of 99 percent of the detainees who were eliminated in this way, of their executioners' depraved behavior. They tell us all this while scrutinizing us to see if we believe them; because, they say, they are beginning themselves to doubt the truth of what they say. They fear that no one will ever believe them, that their words will be taken as those of abberant, demented people. Only a few hundred women remain alive out of all those who were deported to Auschwitz. The men and the children were immediately eliminated, as were the elderly and the weak. A Jewish woman from Greece tells me that out of seventy thousand Greek Jews interned

---

[1] Prisoners in the camps who, within the limits clearly established by the SS, were given administrative authority over other prisoners. Jews, at the bottom of the camp hierarchy— below criminals, Communists, Jehovah's Witnesses, Gypsies, and homosexuals— were rarely *kapos*.

at Auschwitz with her, only three hundred women are still alive. She herself saw her parents and her entire family disappear in smoke.

It's strange. These women who have escaped from hell and who worked in the kitchens, in the depots, in the orchestra, even, seem relatively healthy. They're all robust, well preserved. It's bizarre, when you compare them to our own bodies. They tell us: Back there, in Auschwitz, people got enough to eat. On top of that, the internees themselves had organized a sort of mutual assistance program and made arrangements to procure what they needed. In general, they didn't suffer from hunger. On the other hand, the risk of death hovered over everyone, each person knew he was under constant threat of a sudden, irrevocable death, as each one imagined himself already consumed by the flames. . . .

The death factory functioned at full capacity every day. Columns of men, of women, several hundreds and sometimes even one or two thousand per day, waited their turn at the entrance to the gas showers. The crematory smoked right before their eyes, and they just watched, knowing exactly what it meant. The smoke spoke to them of the fire where their loved ones had burned and where they themselves would soon end their existence. No, they weren't hungry there, our companions from Auschwitz tell us, dismayed by our tales of the methodical hunger we are subjected to. All this just shows that the goal is the same, only the means vary. Back there, a brutal and cynical process, mass assassinations by gassing; here, a slow extermination, calculated in a cowardly way through hunger, violence, terror, consciously sustained epidemics. . . .

JANUARY 1945

Death has moved in to stay. It's our most loyal tenant. Always and ever present. Men die en masse due to vile treatment, hunger, humiliation, dysentery, and vermin. They fall, they collapse. Their number diminishes rapidly. Many of my acquaintances ended their lives in this manner. Every morning we find one or two corpses in the beds. One, two, three, four. . . . We end up confusing the living and the dead. Because in essence the difference between them is minimal; we are skeletons who still possess some capacity to move, they are immobile skeletons.

There is yet a third category: those who still breathe a little but remain lying down, unable to move. We wait for them to pass, to make room for others. It's not surprising that we confuse them with the dead and that we lose count. . . .

APRIL 1945

I am terribly ashamed to have lived through all this. Men are rotting and decomposing in the mud. There are reports that in one of the neighboring blocks acts of cannibalism have arisen. According to a personal statement by a German doctor who finally came to our block to take stock of the "progress" of mass deaths—according to his statement, then, over the past two months, February and March, more than seventeen thousand internees per month died—that is to say, thirty-five thousand out of forty-five thousand internees.

If only they had been simple, humane deaths. . . . Ah, no, I don't want to die like this. I don't want to! It would be better to die right away, as quickly as possible . . . like a human being. What? Allow your body and soul to putrefy and to wallow in their own filth, to slowly but irrevocably disappear from total starvation, to sink into nothingness, devoured by pus and stench and going through all the stages of ecomposition before rotting to death? Because that's exactly what it is: we don't die here, we rot to death. Why wait? That would be an affront to human dignity. What a disgrace, what an immense disgrace. . . .

I look at this gloomy barracks full of ghosts, humiliation, hatred, these motionless sick people reduced to total powerlessness, these living and already putrefied corpses . . . a dark abyss where an entire humanity founders. . . . Oh, no, as long as my brain can function normally, I will not allow myself to end like this. It is man's duty to die like a man, to avoid a death worse than all deaths, a death that isn't a death.

APRIL 1945

It's awful, what they have done to mankind. The darkest scenes from the Middle Ages or the Inquisition are reproduced and multiplied here to the extreme. Their monstrous "revival" will forever leave the mark of shame and infamy on the "civilized" and "cultured" Germany of the twentieth century.

This darkest and most degrading slavery imaginable has made it so that life in this camp has nothing in common with life as humans conceive it.

It is indeed a cruel plan aiming to cause the systematic and certain end of thousands of human lives. Of that, *there is not the slightest doubt, not the slightest doubt*. It requires nothing but to see clearly and to follow attentively everything that goes on in order to deduce, with no hesitation: this camp is not made to hold civilian deportees or prisoners of war for a specific period of time, to temporarily deprive them of freedom for whatever political, diplomatic, or strategic reasons with the intention of holding them and releasing them alive before or after the cessation of hostilities. . . . No: this camp is consciously and knowingly organized and arranged in such a way as to methodically exterminate thousands of human beings according to a plan. If this continues for only one more month, it is highly doubtful that one single person among us will come through.

5

The Limits to Resistance

51

NATIONAL SOCIALIST REICH YOUTH LEADERSHIP

Report on "Swing" Dancing as a Form of Resistance

1942

The Gestapo (Geheime Staatspolizei), the Nazi secret police that reported directly to SS leader Heinrich Himmler, and Hitler Youth leaders sought to root out any signs of nonconformity among young people. In the 1930s and 1940s, gangs made up of young working-class males caused particular concern, and for the Nazis, the best response to "youth cliques" was to throw members into jail or labor camps. Though less explicit in their opposition, upper-middle-class young people engaged in another form of resistance—on the dance floor. The so-called swing movement challenged the regime by rejecting its cultural prescriptions and dancing to American-style jazz. When public dances proved to be too popular and were banned, the "swing youth" formed "swing clubs." The following excerpts are from a 1942 report of the Reich Youth Leadership describing swing parties in Hamburg.

For the dance only English and American music was played. Only Swing and "hot" [jitterbug] dancing was engaged in. At the entrance to the hall was posted a sign upon which the inscription had been altered from SWING VERBOTEN [PROHIBITED]! to SWING ERBETEN [REQUESTED]!

From Benjamin C. Sax and Dieter Kuntz, eds., *Inside Hitler's Germany: A Documentary History of Life in the Third Reich* (Lexington, Mass.: D. C. Heath, 1992), 470–72.

The participants accompanied the dances and songs without exception by singing along with the English words. Moreover, throughout the entire evening they attempted to speak only English, except for a few tables where they even spoke French. The sight of those dancing was appalling. Not a single couple danced in a normal fashion; they all did the "swing" in the most vile manner. Sometimes two boys would dance with one girl, while sometimes several couples would form a circle and others would cut in and then hop around in a manner whereby they would slap each other's hands and even roll the backs of their heads together. Then in bent-over position they would let their upper bodies hang limply downward, their long hair wildly covering the face, knees half bent while legs are swung to and fro. When the band struck up a rumba, the dancers fell into a wild ecstasy. All ran around quite wildly and babbled the English refrain. The band played increasingly wilder music. None of those in the band remained seated, all jitterbugged about the stage wildly. Numerous boys danced with each other, all of them with two cigarettes in their mouths—one in each corner of their mouths. . . .

A subsequent dance party was prohibited by the police; thereupon the gangs dispensed with large crowd affairs and met only in small groups, such as at parties at home, and so forth. They would frequent small taverns in groups of 20 to 30 youths and dance to English music. . . . In October of 1940, the Security Police took steps against the members of the Swing Youth, as a result of which 63 youths were arrested. Four of their number were between the ages of 14 and 16, and 22 were between 16 and 18 years old. The investigation found the Swing Youth to be an illegal association of youths opposed to the Party and state, and which on a wholesale level practiced English life-styles while rejecting the German life-style. . . . In order to be considered a full member, every boy and girl had to acquire the mannerisms, clothing styles, and insignia of the Swing Youth. In order for males to legitimize their membership they wore long hair reaching down to the collar, . . . checkered English business suits, shoes with thick, light-colored crepe soles, conspicuous scarfs, diplomat-style hats, umbrellas on the arm (regardless of the weather), and serving as a piece of identifying insignia, a colorful gem or stone protruding from a dress-shirt buttonhole.

The girls too preferred to wear their hair in long wavy locks. Eyebrows were penciled, lips glossed, and fingernails were painted. . . .

Very much characteristic of the Swing-Youth is their form of expression. They address each other as "Swing-Boys," "Swing-Girls," or "Old-hot-Boy." Letters are concluded with "Swing Heil."

... The attitude of Swing Youth members toward today's Germany and its politics, the Party and its organizations, the Hitler Youth, the Labor Service, and military service, inclusive of the war, is one of rejection or at the best disinterest. They perceive the National Socialist orientation to be one of "mass coercion." The great accomplishments of our time do not stir them; the opposite is true, "they enthusiastically embrace all that is not German, but is instead English." The greeting "Heil Hitler" is rejected. On the occasion of the formation of a new gang, in the clubroom of a tavern, the picture of the Führer hanging on the wall was inverted, face to the wall. This was accompanied by the hooting of all participants. . . . Homosexuality also plays a role within these slovenly gangs. Among these youths, girls included, it was openly discussed that within the group there were several who were of a "different orientation." . . . In accordance with the general attitude of the Swing Youth, approximately ten half-Jews and Jewesses were allowed membership of the swing gangs. Male gang members even maintained friendly and in part intimate relationships with five full-blooded Jewesses (between the ages of fifteen and eighteen), even though they were aware of their racial identities.

52

Jokes about the Nazi Regime
1940–1943

Jokes about the regime represented one form of resistance to National Socialism. Although humor could not topple the Nazi state, making disparaging remarks about Hitler and the regime could lead to denunciation by a neighbor, interrogation by the Gestapo, and designation as an "asocial" element, best dealt with in a prison cell or concentration camp. The first two jokes come from William Shirer's diary (see Document 14) early in the war. The others come from reports by a number of regional

From William L. Shirer, *Berlin Diary: The Journal of a Foreign Correspondent, 1934–1941* (Boston: Little, Brown, 1941), 562–63; Benjamin C. Sax and Dieter Kuntz, eds., *Inside Hitler's Germany: A Documentary History of Life in the Third Reich* (Lexington, Mass.: D. C. Heath, 1992), 465–66.

Nazi leaders, collected in April 1943. Regional leaders warned that the enemy could use jokes "to shake the mood and attitude of the populace and its trust in the country's leadership."

The chief of the Air-Raid Protection in Berlin recently advised the people to go to bed early and try to snatch two or three hours of sleep before the bombings start. Some take the advice, most do not. The Berliners say that those who take the advice arrive in the cellar after an alarm and greet their neighbours with a "Good morning." This means they have been to sleep. Others arrive and say: "Good evening!" This means they haven't yet been to sleep. A few arrive and say: "*Heil Hitler!*" This means they have always been asleep.

An airplane carrying Hitler, Goering, and Goebbels crashes. All three are killed. Who is saved?
   Answer: The German people.

The difference between the sun and Hitler: The sun "rises" in the East, while Hitler "sinks" in the East.

The difference between India and Germany: In India one person starves himself for all, while in Germany all starve for one person.

Young Max tells at school that his cat at home gave birth to kittens. He composed a short rhyme about it: "Our cat had a litter, five in all, four meowed 'Heil Hitler,' while one said nothing at all." Several weeks later the principal came to visit the classroom and, calling on Max, said: "Not long ago you composed such a nice rhyme about your cat, please recite it again." Upon which little Max began: "Our cat had a litter, five in all, four meowed 'Heil Moscow,' while one said nothing at all." This shocked the teacher, who then demanded to know why the text had suddenly changed. Max answered that it was because four weeks ago the kittens were blind, but now four of them have had their eyes opened.

The Führer, Goering, and Mussolini are in a plane above Munich. They are discussing how they can best make themselves popular with the people of Munich. Goering decides that he is going to throw down lard ration coupons. The Führer decides he will throw down meat ration coupons. Mussolini goes up to the cockpit, pats the pilot on the shoulder, and says: "Give me some advice. I don't have any lard or meat ration coupons to throw down; what can I do to become popular with the people of Munich?" The pilot advised him to throw the other two passengers down.

53

THE WHITE ROSE

Resistance to the Nazi State

1942

There were few cases of organized resistance to the Nazi regime within Germany. In part, this reflected the fact that many of those who had opposed Hitler had been driven into exile or imprisoned after January 1933. Others kept silent for fear of being sent to a concentration camp or worse. But millions of Germans did not resist because they enthusiastically supported the Nazi state. There were important exceptions, most famously the White Rose, a secret organization of university students in Munich led by Sophie Scholl (1921–1943) and her brother Hans (1918–1943). In 1942 and 1943, this small group distributed leaflets protesting the regime's murder of Poles and Jews, and they called for resistance. The second and third leaflets, excerpted here, were written and distributed in the summer or fall of 1942. After the German defeat at Stalingrad in 1943, Sophie and Hans intensified their calls for open opposition to the Nazi state. In February 1943, they were arrested by the Gestapo and executed.

The Second Leaflet

It is impossible to engage in intellectual discourse with National Socialism because it is not an intellectually defensible program. It is false to speak of a National Socialist philosophy, for if there were such an entity, one would have to try by means of analysis and discussion

From Inge Scholl, *Students against Tyranny: The Resistance of the White Rose, Munich, 1942–1943*, trans. Arthur R. Schultz (Middletown, Conn.: Wesleyan University Press, 1970), 77–79, 82–84.

either to prove its validity or to combat it. In actuality, however, we face a totally different situation. At its very inception this movement depended on the deception and betrayal of one's fellow man; even at that time it was inwardly corrupt and could support itself only by constant lies. After all, Hitler states in an early edition of "his" book (a book written in the worst German I have ever read, in spite of the fact that it has been elevated to the position of the Bible in this nation of poets and thinkers): "It is unbelievable, to what extent one must betray a people in order to rule it." If at the start this cancerous growth in the nation was not particularly noticeable, it was only because there were still enough forces at work that operated for the good, so that it was kept under control. As it grew larger, however, and finally in an ultimate spurt of growth attained ruling power, the tumor broke open, as it were, and infected the whole body. The greater part of its former opponents went into hiding. The German intellectuals fled to their cellars, there, like plants struggling in the dark, away from light and sun, gradually to choke to death. Now the end is at hand. Now it is our task to find one another again, to spread information from person to person, to keep a steady purpose, and to allow ourselves no rest until the last man is persuaded of the urgent need of his struggle against this system. When thus a wave of unrest goes through the land, when "it is in the air," when many join the cause, then in a great final effort this system can be shaken off. After all, an end in terror is preferable to terror without end.

We are not in a position to draw up a final judgment about the meaning of our history. But if this catastrophe can be used to further the public welfare, it will be only by virtue of the fact that we are cleansed by suffering; that we yearn for the light in the midst of deepest night, summon our strength, and finally help in shaking off the yoke which weighs on our world.

We do not want to discuss here the question of the Jews, nor do we want in this leaflet to compose a defense or apology. No, only by way of example do we want to cite the fact that since the conquest of Poland *three hundred thousand* Jews have been murdered in this country in the most bestial way. Here we see the most frightful crime against human dignity, a crime that is unparalleled in the whole of history. For Jews, too, are human beings—no matter what position we take with respect to the Jewish question—and a crime of this dimension has been perpetrated against human beings. Someone may say that the Jews deserved their fate. This assertion would be a monstrous impertinence; but let us assume that someone said this—what position has he then taken toward the fact that the entire Polish aristocratic youth is being annihilated? (May God grant that this program has not fully achieved its aim as yet!) All male offspring of the houses of the nobility between the ages of fifteen and twenty were transported to concentration camps in Germany and sentenced to forced labor, and all girls of this age group were sent to Norway, into the bordellos of the SS! Why tell you these things, since you are fully aware of them — or if not of these, then of other equally grave crimes committed by this frightful sub-humanity? Because here we touch on a problem which involves us deeply and forces us all to take thought. Why do the German people behave so apathetically in the face of all these abominable crimes, crimes so unworthy of the human race? Hardly anyone thinks about that. It is accepted as fact and put out of mind. The German people slumber on in their dull, stupid sleep and encourage these fascist criminals; they give them the opportunity to carry on their depredations; and of course they do so. Is this a sign that the Germans are brutalized in their simplest human feelings, that no chord within them cries out at the sight of such deeds, that they have sunk into a fatal consciencelessness from which they will never, never awake? It seems to be so, and will certainly be so, if the German does not at last start up out of his stupor, if he does not protest wherever and whenever he can against this clique of criminals, if he shows no sympathy for these hundreds of thousands of victims. He must evidence not only sympathy; no, much more: a sense of *complicity* in guilt. For through his apathetic behavior he gives these evil men the opportunity to act as they do; he tolerates this "government" which has taken upon itself such an infinitely great burden of guilt; indeed, he himself is to blame for the fact that it came about at all! Each man wants to be exonerated of a guilt of this kind, each one continues on his way with the most placid, the calmest conscience. But he cannot be exonerated; he is *guilty, guilty, guilty*! It is not too late, however, to do away with this most reprehensible of all miscarriages of government, so as to avoid being burdened with even greater guilt. Now, when in recent years our eyes have been opened, when we know exactly who our adversary is, it is high time to root out this brown horde. Up until the outbreak of the war the larger part of the German people was blinded; the Nazis did not show themselves in their true aspect. But now, now that we have recognized them for what they are, it must be the sole and first duty, the holiest duty of every German to destroy these beasts. . . .

The Third Leaflet

... Many, perhaps most, of the readers of these leaflets do not see clearly how they can practice an effective opposition. They do not see any avenues open to them. We want to try to show them that everyone is in a position to contribute to the overthrow of this system. It is not possible through solitary withdrawal, in the manner of embittered hermits, to prepare the ground for the overturn of this "government" or bring about the revolution at the earliest possible moment. No, it can be done only by the cooperation of many convinced, energetic people—people who are agreed as to the means they must use to attain their goal. We have no great number of choices as to these means. The only one available is *passive resistance*. The meaning and the goal of passive resistance is to topple National Socialism, and in this struggle we must not recoil from any course, any action, whatever its nature. At *all* points we must oppose National Socialism, wherever it is open to attack. We must soon bring this monster of a state to an end. A victory of fascist Germany in this war would have immeasurable, frightful consequences. The military victory over Bolshevism dare not become the primary concern of the Germans. The defeat of the Nazis must *unconditionally* be the first order of business. The greater necessity of this latter requirement will be discussed in one of our forthcoming leaflets.

And now every convinced opponent of National Socialism must ask himself how he can fight against the present "state" in the most effective way, how he can strike it the most telling blows. Through passive resistance, without a doubt. We cannot provide each man with the blueprint for his acts, we can only suggest them in general terms, and he alone will find the way of achieving this end:

Sabotage in armament plants and war industries, sabotage at all gatherings, rallies, public ceremonies, and organizations of the National Socialist Party. Obstruction of the smooth functioning of the war machine (a machine for war that goes on solely to shore up and perpetuate the National Socialist Party and its dictatorship). *Sabotage* in all the areas of science and scholarship which further the continuation of the war—whether in universities, technical schools, laboratories, research institutes, or technical bureaus. *Sabotage* in all cultural institutions which could potentially enhance the "prestige" of the fascists among the people. *Sabotage* in all branches of the arts which have even the slightest dependence on National Socialism or render it service. *Sabotage* in all publications, all newspapers, that are in the pay of the "government" and that defend its ideology and aid in disseminating the brown lie. Do not give a penny to public drives (even when they are conducted under the pretense of charity). For this is only a disguise. In reality the proceeds aid neither the Red Cross nor the needy. The government does not need this money; it is not financially interested in these money drives. After all, the presses run continuously to manufacture any desired amount of paper currency. But the populace must be kept constantly under tension, the pressure of the bit must not be allowed to slacken! Do not contribute to the collections of metal, textiles, and the like. Try to convince all your acquaintances, including those in the lower social classes, of the senselessness of continuing, of the hopelessness of this war; of our spiritual and economic enslavement at the hands of the National Socialists; of the destruction of all moral and religious values; and urge them to *passive resistance*! . . .

Please duplicate and distribute!

54

FABIAN VON SCHLABRENDORFF

Account of the Military Conspiracy to Assassinate Hitler

1944

On July 20, 1944, Claus von Stauffenberg, an army colonel, carried a bomb in a briefcase into a meeting with Hitler with the goal of killing him. This act was the culmination of a conspiracy that involved a number of high-ranking military officers who believed that only by murdering Hitler would it be possible to bring the war to an end. When the bomb went off, Hitler was injured but not killed. This excerpt from the memoir of Fabian von Schlabrendorff (1907–1980), one of Stauffenberg's

From Fabian von Schlabrendorff, "Thunderclap in the 'Wolfsschanze' and the Activities in Bendlerstrasse," in *Germans against Hitler, July 20, 1944*, ed. Bundeszentrale für politische Bildung, trans. Allan Yahraes and Lieselotte Yahraes (Bonn: Press and Information Office of the Federal Government of Germany, 1969), 118, 120, 124.

co-conspirators, provides a detailed account of the planning that went into the assassination attempt. The excerpt ends with Stauffenberg's return from Hitler's headquarters to Berlin, where he was apprehended and executed by a firing squad.

The person who was to plant the bomb had to be gotten into Hitler's headquarters. That limited the selection at the outset to a relatively small group of persons, since the great majority of the conspirators had no admission privileges there, or could only be brought there by some pretext, and with difficulty. In order to clarify the preliminary question of the possibilities in Hitler's headquarters, I went there twice by plane, and talked over necessary details with Lieut. Col. Dietrich von Bose, who was familiar with the place.

Through him I got hold of an exact outline of Hitler's daily schedule. Hitler had a servant wake him at 10 o'clock in the morning. At the same hour, breakfast was sent to the bedroom by elevator. With breakfast, excerpts from foreign newspapers, selected by Ribbentrop,[1] were placed before Hitler. As he read no foreign language, the excerpts were translated into German. All items of writing that were presented to him were typed on a special typewriter that had unusually big letters. Hitler was near-sighted. Everything had to be written in such large characters that he could read it without spectacles. Nobody was to find out from the way he held the material that he had eye trouble. To look at a map, he used a magnifying glass or spectacles. It was strictly forbidden to photograph him with his glasses on. Hitler felt that a dictator wearing spectacles would lose authority.

At 11 A.M. he received his chief adjutant, who reported mainly on personnel matters. At noon the briefing began. During the briefing, various reports on the situation were made by the chief of the general staffs of the armed forces and the army. Other officers were called in as needed. On this occasion Hitler made military decisions personally. At 2 P.M. luncheon began. It dragged out until 4 P.M. because of the monologues that Hitler directed to the company. Then Hitler lay down for his afternoon nap, from which he arose between 6 and 7 P.M. After that, he granted audiences of a "representation" character. Dinner began at 8 P.M. and lasted until 10 P.M. Afterward Hitler surrounded himself with a circle of persons selected by himself. He talked with them until 4 A.M., usually leading the discussion himself. It was in

---

[1]Joachim von Ribbentrop was the foreign minister in the Nazi regime.

these night hours that he developed his "fortunate for the people" ideas in the company of his faithful.

Then, at 4 A.M., he went to bed. His two secretaries participated in his night-time discussions; otherwise he had no women who were close to him at his headquarters. These women, however, had access to the Obersalzberg. Only in very urgent cases was something changed in his daily schedule. While he was sleeping he was not to be awakened under any circumstances.

The only persons who had a chance to perform the assassination were those who succeeded in procuring an invitation to the nightly circle, or who had access to the briefing session. SS men who were constantly in the room with Hitler or near-by made it almost impossible to use a pistol to kill Hitler. Anyone who has used a weapon knows how difficult it is to shoot a man dead from the wrist. If on the other hand the killing is represented as an unpremeditated act, the difficulty is much less than if a frankly calculated attempt is made on the victim's life. Moreover, the stalker is seized by hunting fever when he sees the desired game within reach of his gun. How much greater this inner excitement is likely to be if one takes up arms after overcoming a thousandfold difficulties! And the tension is redoubled by the fact that one is risking one's life, with incalculable danger of failure, to carry out a deed the success or failure of which affects the destiny of millions. . . .

Stauffenberg himself had become chief of staff with General Fromm,[2] the commander of the reserve army, as of July 1. He had received this appointment by virtue of his outstanding organizational capacities. When General Fromm informed him that he had been selected for this key position, Stauffenberg refused, pointing out that he, Stauffenberg, no longer believed that the war could be won. He added that the guilt for the defeat, however, ought to rest on nobody else than Hitler. Fromm listened to this without contradicting, and then said that his, Fromm's, opinion was not very much different from that of Stauffenberg. Stauffenberg had the courage to put up the same objections with the chief of the general staff of the army, General Zeitzler. He, too, listened quietly to the protest, and then commented that he valued a subordinate who had the courage of his convictions and spoke his thoughts frankly. . . .

---

[2]General Friedrich Fromm (1888–1945) was the commander-in-chief of the Reserve Army in 1944. Stauffenberg was his chief of staff. Fromm knew about the plot, but when he learned that it had failed, he turned on the conspirators, although ultimately he, too, was tried by a Nazi court and executed.

Hitler's headquarters in East Prussia was surrounded by three restricted areas. These could be traversed only with difficulty, for a special pass was necessary at each barrier. The same difficulty was involved in leaving the headquarters. When Stauffenberg had reached the inner restricted area on July 20, 1944, shortly before noon, he noticed to his surprise that the briefing was not taking place in the concrete bunker, as usual, but in the so-called tea-house, the floor and ceiling of which were without solid stone covering. The conference room was located on the long corridor. In the room itself was a big table. Along its long side, there was room for five persons.

Hitler was present. With the exception of Himmler and Göring, who were absent, the usual circle of persons was there. Stauffenberg's seat was immediately to the right of Hitler on the long side of the table. After the report about the troop-replacement situation was finished, Stauffenberg made the excuse of a pretended telephone call in order to leave the room. He threw the ignition of the time bomb in his briefcase, put it beside the leg of the table which separated his chair from Hitler's, and went out of the room.

The time bomb exploded as Hitler stood at his place, bending over a map on the table. Because there was no stone frame around the building, the pressure from the explosion blasted its way out through the wall. Most of those present were hurled through the wall that gave way, and thus escaped with their lives. Four were killed. . . .

Hitler himself was hurled out of the room. Besides bruises and burns, he suffered only an injury to his right hand. In the wake of the explosion, the scene was terrible to contemplate. It appeared as if the persons who had been present in the room were lying dead, or dying, in their blood. Stauffenberg had stayed nearby. He waited until the explosion interrupted the silence of headquarters with its earsplitting crash. He saw that the participants of the conference—Hitler among them—were hurled from the room, and were lying there, bloody, their clothes in tatters. In the firm belief that the bomb had done its intended work, Stauffenberg headed back. But the alarm had already been sounded. The barriers were closed. With luck and cunning, however, Stauffenberg succeeded nevertheless in getting out of headquarters. He drove to the airport, flew to Berlin, and took over the leadership there.

55

SOVIET SLAVE WORKERS IN GERMANY

Anti-Nazi Leaflet

November 27, 1944

In the last year of the war, the greatest potential source of resistance to the Nazis came not from Germans, but from Soviet slave workers who had been deported to Germany to replace German workers who had been conscripted and sent to the front. In November 1944, the Gestapo in the city of Gummersbach rounded up a number of "female Eastern workers" for distributing the following document.

Women citizens of the Soviet Union who are under the yoke of the fascist hangmen and dogs in Germany!

Dearest daughters, sisters, women! I send you warmest greetings, and don't ever forget your beloved Ukraine,[1] where you were born and where you have lived, but these dogs have robbed you of your freedom because they have conquered you and not let you live. You were quickly loaded into goods-wagons and brought here, to work for cabbage for 3 or 2 weeks, which there was hardly any of. You have had to sleep in camps, first thing in the morning you heard the words "Out of bed!" and the police were already standing by the window where the bread rations were handed out. But now we won't have to wait much longer. If any of us who have been particularly worked up by the fascist dogs goes up to a German, he will say the whole wide world is free, there is no oppression. But they can't see their own hideous faces. They don't work with their own hands, they rob and steal, they invade weak countries, they plunder them and are satisfied. Well, I don't think [they] are going to [last very long]. They are being driven out like dogs. You already know their soldiers are struggling day and night, they have spilled their hot blood and are stained with it.

---

[1] Part of the Soviet Union that the Nazis invaded in 1941 (see Document 45).

From Detlev J. K. Peukert, *Inside Nazi Germany: Conformity, Opposition, and Racism in Everyday Life*, trans. Richard Deveson (New Haven, Conn.: Yale University Press, 1987), 133–34.

They took 2 years to conquer our beloved Ukraine, but the Red Army cleared them out in 3 months. They have no right to show their faces in a foreign country they have forced their way into. Our Bolsheviks will show them that spring follows winter as night follows day. I put this appeal to you: "Never betray your bleeding hearts, even if they maltreat you and drink your heart's blood—be stronger than steel! The enemy will be defeated and victory will be ours!" Their young people live the good life, they are young and happy, but we shall never know what happened to our youth, we shall only remember the life in prisons that we lived in our youth in Germany. Don't believe these enemies and parasites when they say our Bolsheviks will do you harm. . . . Read this sheet and think about your own young life. Have you had freedom under Hitler? That's right, we have had the freedom not to leave the prisons and concentration camps. We know very well what your lives are like in the camps. I am writing you this letter and I ask you to preserve it as you would your own heart, until we arrive.

This letter has been written by Russian people living under the fascist yoke in German hands.

6

The Last Days of the Nazi Regime

56

MELITA MASCHMANN

The Mobilization of Youth in the Winter of 1945

1963

Like millions of other Germans, Melita Maschmann (see Documents 9 and 36) fled westward in advance of the Red Army at the end of the war. By late 1944, the Soviets were pressing rapidly westward into Germany. In September 1944, Hitler ordered the creation of the Volkssturm, a militia whose membership included males from sixteen to sixty who had not yet been conscripted into the regular army. Its task was to offer a last-ditch defense of the home front. By March 1945, all boys age sixteen or older were subject to conscription into the regular army. Maschmann describes the mobilization of these young men, "still half children," in the last months of the war.

I did not make my westward escape out of some of the little towns in Lusatia until the first Russian tanks were already entering them from the east. I left one town pulling a cart containing a dozen small children. The staff of a home which had left had not been able to take them. A boy of perhaps fourteen or fifteen helped me. He had the energy and composure of a grown man. We kept blocking the path of the fleeing cars and wagons, forcing them to stop and handing children at random into the vehicles. There were two brothers amongst

From Melita Maschmann, *Account Rendered: A Dossier on My Former Self*, trans. Geoffrey Strachan (London: Abelard-Schuman, 1964), 156–57.

the children, one about seven and the other a little boy of two. The elder brother fought for the little one like a mother for her child. I came across the two of them again later in a refugee camp. I watched the elder brother stealing a sausage from a sack, biting it into pieces and pushing it bit by bit into his brother's mouth. Believe me, I saw more people helping one another during the last months of the war than ever before or since. Everywhere I met people who had left all they had behind them because the war had taken away their homes, their belongings and often their families as well. Now they were free to step in wherever they were needed. There were people among them who had been rich or poor; there were old people and young people; some were National Socialists and others made no bones about the fact that they were violently opposed to the régime.

I shall never forget my encounters with the youngest of them, still half children, who did what they believed to be their duty until they were literally ready to drop. They had been fed on legends of heroism for as long as they could remember. For them the call to the "ultimate sacrifice" was no empty phrase. It went straight to their hearts and they felt that now their hour had come, the moment when they really counted and were no longer dismissed because they were still too young. They shovelled away day and night on the East wall or the West wall—the system of earthworks and tank traps which was built along all the frontiers during the last months. They looked after refugees, they helped the wounded. During air raids they fought the fires and strove to rescue sick and wounded people. Finally they went in against the Russians with "panzer-fists,"[1] which were given out by the *Volkssturm*.

In one suburb of Berlin I saw a row of dead anti-aircraft auxiliaries lying side by side. It was just after an air raid. The anti-aircraft base where these schoolboys were serving had received several direct hits: I went into a barrack room where the survivors were gathered. They sat on the floor along one wall, and the white faces they turned towards me were distorted with fear. Many of them were weeping.

In another room lay the wounded. One of them, a boy with a soft round childish face, held himself rigid when the officer I was with asked him if he was in pain. "Yes, but it doesn't matter. Germany must triumph."

[1] Handheld antitank weapons.

57

ANNA SCHWARTZ

Account of the Entry of Soviet Troops into Danzig on March 27, 1945

1952

As they advanced into Germany in 1945, Red Army soldiers left a wake of mass rape and devastation. In front of this juggernaut, millions of Germans from eastern Europe and the eastern part of the Reich fled westward, abandoning their homes and belongings. In the early 1950s, the West German state conducted a massive documentation project to record the stories of those driven from their homes in eastern Germany and eastern Europe. The testimony from "tailoress" Anna Schwartz of Schönberg in West Prussia is typical of thousands of similar accounts. After the events described here, Schwartz was deported to the Soviet Union and not returned to Germany until 1948.

On the 27 March 1945 the Russians marched into Danzig. For days before the town had been a sea of flames, for days the bombs of aeroplanes and the shells of artillery had been bursting over us, and for days we had been living in air-raid shelters in fear of the future.

Russian loud-speakers, which had been erected on the walls of the town, kept calling upon the citizens of Danzig to capitulate. They were promised freedom and safety, and the announcements were accompanied by the most beautiful waltzes of Strauss. However, we did not believe all this, and prepared for the worst. Everyone used any chance possible to get out of this hell. However, the departing ships offered no guarantee for escape, as most of them were sunk. The German soldiers, fighting in Danzig, were confronted with the same fate as we were, that is to say, either to die or to be taken prisoner. Many men and women committed suicide, in order not to fall into the hands of the Russians.

From Anna Schwartz, eyewitness account, in *The Expulsion of the German Population from the Territories East of the Oder-Neisse-Line*, ed. Theodor Schieder, trans. Vivian Stranders (Bonn: Federal Ministry for Expellees, Refugees and War Victims, n.d.), 178–79.

On the 27 March, in the early morning, the shooting stopped. In the following calm we heard the Russian panzer[1] rolling in, and the first cheers of the Russian soldiers. Shortly afterwards Russian soldiers were heard coming down the steps of the cellar. The first Russian soldiers stood in front of us, and the first word we heard from them was: "Urr"! "Urr!"[2] There was a stink of alcohol, sweat and dirty uniforms. After they had robbed us of our watches, with machine-pistols in their hands, they hastily disappeared into the next cellar, and did the same there. After five minutes the next two came, and so it continued, until we had no more jewelry, and the contents of our trunks had been turned upside down.

In the meanwhile we heard the shrieks of women, who were being raped by Mongols.[3] Suddenly a Russian officer appeared, and called upon us in broken German, to leave the cellar at once. As quickly as we could, we took hold of our trunks and rucksacks, which had been searched over and over again, and rushed into the yard, which was full of guns and soldiers. All around the houses were burning, shells were exploding, and German low-flyers were attacking; wounded people and horses were screaming, and through this confusion we tried to make our way into the open. Paying no heed to the death around us, we went past burning houses, Russian panzer, guns and soldiers, who absolutely wanted to drag us into the houses.

When we had gone a distance, there was more room, but to our horror we saw Russian sentries in the street, who plundered our baggage. After taking everything they liked the look of, we were allowed to go further on. We, however, did not get far. Further on, there was a large detachment of Russian troops, who then took us prisoner. Two sentries, with fixed bayonets, brought us seven Germans to a farm in the neighbourhood; here there were already a great number of German men and women. We were brought to the loft of the house, had to seek room to sit down, and received a good meat soup. In the course of the afternoon, continually more prisoners came. We were guarded by sentries. In a state of terror, we waited for what was to happen.

[1]Panzer is the German word for tank.
[2]Many people reported that Red Army soldiers demanded watches—in German, *Uhr*. Schwartz records this as "Urr," suggesting that this was among the only words in the soldiers' limited German vocabulary.
[3]The Soviet army included some troops from Mongolia, but most came from other parts of the country. Schwartz's testimony suggests the ways in which Nazi racist ideology shaped the views of Germans.

58

GENE CURRIVAN

Report on a Visit to a Nazi Concentration Camp Liberated by the U.S. Army

April 18, 1945

Buchenwald, about five miles away from Weimar, the town where Germans had adopted a democratic constitution in 1919, was the site of one of the biggest concentration camps within Germany's borders. Established in 1937, it first contained primarily political opponents of the Nazi regime. They were joined by Jehovah's Witnesses, Gypsies (Sinti and Roma), criminals, homosexuals, and "asocials." After Kristallnacht in November 1938 (see Document 33), more and more Jews arrived, and once the war began, prisoners of war also were sent to the camp. In early 1945, prisoners from Auschwitz and another concentration camp, Gross-Rosen, were led on a forced march to Buchenwald in advance of the Red Army. U.S. Army forces liberated Buchenwald in April 1945. The American commander ordered residents of Weimar to visit the camp. These excerpts from Currivan's account, published in the New York Times, *record the residents' reactions.*

BUCHENWALD, GERMANY, April 16 (Delayed)—German civilians— 1,200 of them—were brought from the neighboring city of Weimar today to see for themselves the horror, brutality and human indecency perpetrated against their "neighbors" at the infamous Buchenwald concentration camp. They saw sights that brought tears to their eyes, and scores of them, including German nurses, just fainted away.

They saw more than 20,000 nondescript prisoners, many of them barely living, who were all that remained of the normal complement of 80,000. The Germans were able to evacuate the others before we overran the place on April 10.

From Gene Currivan, "Nazi Death Factory Shocks Germans on a Forced Tour," *New York Times*, April 18, 1945.

There were 32,705 that the "visiting" Germans didn't see, although they saw some of their bodies. It was this number that had been murdered since the camp was established in July, 1937. There was a time when the population reached more than 110,000, but the average was always below that. It included doctors, professors, scientists, statesmen, army officers, diplomats and an assortment of peasants and merchants from all over Europe and Asia. . . .

It had its gallows, torture rooms, dissection rooms, modern crematoria, laboratories where fiendish experiments were made on living human beings and its sections where people were systematically starved to death.

This correspondent made a tour of the camp today and saw everything herein described. The statistics and an account of the events that happened before our troops liberated the camp were obtained from a special committee of prisoners, some of whom had been in the camp since its inception and others who had been German prisoners for twelve years. Their information was documented and in most cases confirmed by the records.

This story has already been told in part, but not until today has the full import of the atrocities been completely felt.

One of the first things that the German civilian visitors saw as they passed through the gates and into the interior of the camp was a display of "parchment." This consisted of large pieces of human flesh on which were elaborate tatooed markings. These strips had been collected by a German doctor who was writing a treatise on tatooes, and also by the 28-year-old wife of the Standartenfuehrer or commanding officer. This woman, according to prisoners, was an energetic sportswoman who, back in Brandenburg, used to ride to hounds. She had a mania for unusual tattooes, and whenever a prisoner arrived who had a rare marking on his body, she would indicate that that trophy would make a valuable addition to her collection.

In addition to the "parchments" were two large table lamps, with parchment shades also made of human flesh.

The German people saw all this today, and they wept. Those who didn't weep were ashamed. They said they didn't know about it, and maybe they didn't, because the camp was restricted to Army personnel,[1] but there it was right at their back doors for eight years.

The visitors stood in lines, one group at a time passing by the table on which the exhibits were displayed. A German-speaking American

[1]Currivan's observation is inaccurate; Buchenwald was run by the SS.

sergeant explained from an adjacent jeep what they were witnessing, while all around them were thousands of liberated "slaves" just looking on. Even the barracks roof was crowded with them. They watched silently. Some of them looked as if they were about to die, but this assemblage of "slaves" constituted the more healthy elements of the camp.

In barracks farther down the line were 3,000 sick who could not move and 4,800 aged who were unable to leave their squalid quarters. In addition, there were untold hundreds just roaming around, not knowing where they were or what was going on.

There were human skeletons who had lost all likeness to anything human. Most of them had become idiots, but they still had the power of locomotion. Those in the sick bay were beyond all help. They were packed into three-tier bunks, which ran to the roof of the barnlike barracks. They were dying there and no one could do anything about it. . . .

Some Germans were skeptical at first as if this show had been staged for their benefit, but they were soon convinced. Even as they had milled along from one place to another, their own countrymen, who had been prisoners there, told them the story. Men went white and women turned away. It was too much for them.

These persons, who had been fed on Nazi propaganda since 1933, were beginning to see the light. They were seeing with their own eyes what no quantity of American propaganda could convince them of. Here was what their own Government had perpetrated. . . .

This sight was too much for many German housewives, especially a little farther on, where only the children were kept. One 9-year-old boy, who had had only the first few injections, seemed quite chipper. He was Andor Gutman, a Hungarian Jew of Budapest. He had been in the camp three years. When asked where his parents were, he replied, without any emotion: "My father was killed and my mother was burned to death."

As one watched the Germans filing out of this building there was hardly a dry eye, although some tried to maintain their composure. There was real horror ahead, but some of them just couldn't go on.

From there they were taken to the living quarters. The stench, filth and misery here defied description. Those human wrecks standing in the corridor were beyond the stage where any amount of hospitalization could restore them to normal, while others peering helplessly from their bunks would be fortunate when they died.

There was a still lower grade in another barracks, where the prisoners were alive but could not rouse themselves. They were living skeletons. This was Barracks 58, and it was from here that they were taken to the crematory. This was the end of the road, and for them it was probably a godsend. The Germans saw this, too—and there was more to come.

The next exhibit was the most ghastly of all, although it was merely the disposal of the dead. . . .

The camp was liberated April 10 by the Eightieth Division. Two days later President Roosevelt died, and the liberated prisoners unfurled a large black flag over the building at the entrance way. It still flies as a memorial to his death and to the dead within the camp. Those still living realize what he tried to do, and they doff their caps every time they see an American uniform.

As the sun went down tonight, and its last glow gave a softer touch to this distorted scene, which, paradoxically, is in a magnificent setting on a hilltop overlooking a valley, the German visitors were taken back to their homes. If they still think that Hitler and what he stands for is supreme, then we have lost the war. But observations made by this correspondent indicate that they are chastened people who have suffered today, but who will benefit by reflection in the long run.

59

ADOLF HITLER

My Political Testament

April 29, 1945

In April 1945, the Allies were closing in on Berlin. On April 29, a little over a week after his fifty-sixth birthday in his well-fortified bunker in the German capital, Hitler dictated his political testament. The same day, as Allied bombs and Soviet shells continued to level the capital, he married his longtime partner, Eva Braun, and the next day they committed suicide together. On May 8, 1945, Admiral Karl Dönitz, Hitler's successor, accepted the only terms the Allies had to offer—unconditional surrender.

From Adolf Hitler, "My Political Testament," doc. 3569-PS, in Office of the United States Chief of Counsel for Prosecution of Axis Criminality, *Nazi Conspiracy and Aggression* (Washington, D.C.: U.S. Government Printing Office, 1946), 6:260–61, 263.

More than thirty years have now passed since I in 1914 made my modest contribution as a volunteer in the first world-war that was forced upon the Reich.

In these three decades I have been actuated solely by love and loyalty to my people in all my thoughts, acts, and life. They gave me the strength to make the most difficult decisions which have ever confronted to mortal man. I have spent my time, my working strength, and my health in these three decades.

It is untrue that I or anyone else in Germany wanted the war in 1939. It was desired and instigated exclusively by those international statesmen who were either of Jewish descent or worked for Jewish interests. I have made too many offers for the control and limitation of armaments, which posterity will not for all time be able to disregard for the responsibility for the outbreak of this war to be laid on me. I have further never wished that after the first fatal world war a second against England, or even against America, should break out. Centuries will pass away, but out of the ruins of our towns and monuments the hatred against those finally responsible whom we have to thank for everything, International Jewry and its helpers, will grow.

Three days before the outbreak of the German-Polish war I again proposed to the British ambassador in Berlin a solution to the German-Polish problem.... This offer also cannot be denied. It was only rejected because the leading circles in English politics wanted the war, partly on account of the business hoped for and partly under influence of propaganda organized by international Jewry.

I also made it quite plain that, if the nations of Europe are again to be regarded as mere shares to be bought and sold by these international conspirators in money and finance, then that race, Jewry, which is the real criminal of this murderous struggle, will be saddled with the responsibility. I further left no one in doubt that this time not only would millions of children of Europe's Aryan peoples die of hunger, not only would millions of grown men suffer death, and not only hundreds of thousands of women and children be burnt and bombed to death in the towns, without the real criminal having to atone for this guilt, even if by more humane means.

After six years of war, which in spite of all set-backs, will go down one day in history as the most glorious and valiant demonstration of a nation's life purpose, I cannot forsake the city which is the capital of this Reich. As the forces are too small to make any further stand against the enemy attack at this place and our resistance is gradually being weakened by men who are as deluded as they are lacking in initiative, I should like, by remaining in this town, to share my fate with those, the millions of others, who have also taken upon themselves to do so. Moreover I do not wish to fall into the hands of an enemy who requires a new spectacle organized by the Jews for the amusement of their hysterical masses.

I have decided therefore to remain in Berlin and there of my own free will to choose death at the moment when I believe the position of the Fuehrer and Chancellor itself can no longer be held.

I die with a happy heart, aware of the immeasurable deeds and achievements of our soldiers at the front, our women at home, the achievements of our farmers and workers and the work, unique in history, of our youth who bear my name.

That from the bottom of my heart I express my thanks to you all, is just as self-evident as my wish that you should, because of that, on no account give up the struggle, but rather continue it against the enemies of the Fatherland, no matter where, true to the creed of a great Clausewitz.[1] From the sacrifice of our soldiers and from my own unity with them unto death, will in any case spring up in the history of Germany, the seed of a radiant renaissance of the National-Socialist movement and thus of the realization of a true community of nations.

Many of the most courageous men and women have decided to unite their lives with mine until the very last. I have begged and finally ordered them not to do this, but to take part in the further battle of the Nation. I beg the heads of the Armies, the Navy and the Air Force to strengthen by all possible means the spirit of resistance of our soldiers in the National-Socialist sense, with special reference to the fact that also I myself, as founder and creator of this movement, have preferred death to cowardly abdication or even capitulation.

May it, at some future time, become part of the code of honour of the German officer—as is already the case in our Navy—that the surrender of a district or of a town is impossible, and that above all the leaders here must march ahead as shining examples, faithfully fulfilling their duty unto death. . . .

Above all I charge the leaders of the nation and those under them to scrupulous observance of the laws of race and to merciless opposition to the universal poisoner of all peoples, international Jewry.

Given in Berlin, this 29th day of April 1945.   4:00 A.M.

Adolf Hitler.

---

[1]Carl von Clausewitz, a general and military theorist of the Prussian army in the early nineteenth century.

A Chronology of the Rise and Fall
of the Nazi State (1914–1945)

1914   *August* Germany declares war on Great Britain and enters World War I.

1918   *November* Declaration of German republic; armistice ending World War I.

1919   *June* Germany accepts terms of Versailles treaty.

      July Weimar constitution adopted.

1922   *October* Mussolini's "march on Rome."

1923   *October* Germany gripped by severe inflation.

      November Hitler's Beer Hall Putsch and failed march on Berlin.

1924   *April* Hitler sentenced to five years in prison for his involvement in Beer Hall Putsch.

      December Hitler released on probation.

1925   *July Mein Kampf* published.

1928   *May* NSDAP wins 2.6 percent of vote in national elections.

1930   *September* Nazis win 18.3 percent of vote in national elections.

1932   *January* One in three German workers unemployed.

1933   *January* Hindenburg names Hitler chancellor.

      February At Hitler's behest, Hindenburg dissolves parliament and calls for new elections; Reichstag building torched by former Dutch Communist; Hitler suspends freedom of expression, press, and assembly.

      March Nazis receive 43.9 percent of vote in national elections; Joseph Goebbels named minister for popular enlightenment and propaganda; concentration camp opened at Dachau; Reichstag passes Enabling Act.

      April Jews excluded from all forms of civil service employment.

May Students and others organize book burnings throughout Germany.

July All parties except NSDAP banned; Law for the Prevention of Genetically Diseased Offspring passed; Vatican signs concordat with Germany.

November "Strength through Joy" (KdF) movement announced.

1934 *June* Night of Long Knives.

1935 *March* Hitler publicly announces rearmament and conscription for army, openly violating Treaty of Versailles.

September At annual party congress, Hitler announces Nuremberg Laws.

1936 *March* In violation of Treaty of Versailles, German troops occupy demilitarized side of Rhine River.

1937 *July* The "Degenerate Art" exhibition and the House of German Art open in Munich.

1938 *March* German army marches into Austria.

October German army marches unopposed into Sudetenland.

November Herschel Grynszpan assassinates German embassy official Ernst vom Rath in Paris, setting off Kristallnacht.

1939 *January* Hitler announces that should war break out, it would lead to "annihilation of the Jewish race in Europe."

March German army occupies all of Czechoslovakia; membership in Hitler Youth made mandatory for all German youths ages ten and older.

August Signing of German-Soviet nonaggression pact.

September Germany invades Poland; Britain and France declare war on Germany.

1940 *May* German army invades Holland, Belgium, and Luxembourg.

June German army conquers France.

October Jewish ghetto created in Warsaw, Poland.

November Warsaw ghetto sealed off.

1941 *June* German army invades Soviet Union in Operation Barbarossa.

September All Jews in Germany over age six ordered to wear yellow "Jewish star" when in public.

December First mass killing facility opened at Chelmno; Japanese attack on Pearl Harbor brings United States into Second World War; Germany declares war on United States.

1942   *January* Nazis lay out plans for Final Solution at Wannsee Conference in Berlin.

   July Mass deportations from Warsaw ghetto begin.

1943   *February* Germans defeated by Red Army at Stalingrad; Hans Scholl and Sophie Scholl arrested and executed in Munich.

   May Nazis crush all resistance in Warsaw ghetto.

   July–August British and American planes drop incendiary bombs on Hamburg.

1944   *June* Allied invasion of western Europe begins.

   July Colonel Claus von Stauffenberg unsuccessfully attempts to assassinate Hitler.

   September Order creating the *Volkssturm*, popular militias for men ages sixteen to sixty not yet conscripted.

1945   *March* Boys age sixteen or older subject to military conscription.

   April Buchenwald liberated by U.S. Army forces; Hitler issues final political testament and commits suicide.

   May German army surrenders.

   July–August Big Three meet in Potsdam.

   November Nazi war criminals go on trial in front of international tribunal in Nuremberg.

Questions for Consideration

1. Discuss the relationship between the Nazis' anti-Communist and anti-Semitic views (Documents 4 and 38). What evidence can you find to demonstrate how Hitler and the Nazis tied their critique of the Weimar Republic to their hatred of the Jews?

2. How did the Nazis' idea of womanhood differ from the "new woman" described by Elsa Herrmann? Why would the Nazis reject the image of the new woman? (See Documents 3, 6, and 22–24.)

3. What arguments does Magnus Hirschfeld offer in defense of the decriminalization of male homosexual activity (Document 2)? What arguments does Heinrich Himmler make against homosexuality (Document 28)?

4. Historians debate whether the Nazi regime was pronatalist—encouraging more births—or antinatalist—introducing measures that prevented some Germans from having children. Compare the evidence on both sides of this debate. (See Documents 22, 23, and 26–30.)

5. Some of the eyewitness accounts included in this book are diaries and letters, written at the time of the events they describe. Others are memoirs and court testimony, written long after the events they describe. What distinguishes these different types of sources? Are some sources more credible than others? Why or why not? (See Documents 8, 9, 14, 20, 25, 31, 32, 36, 37, 39, 41, 42, 44, 45, 47, 49, 50, 56, and 57.)

6. What did Hitler find so abhorrent about swing dancing (Document 51) and the "degenerate" art and music put on display by the Nazis in 1937 and 1939 (Documents 17 and 18)? What do his observations tell us about a Nazi aesthetic?

7. How did the Nazis appeal to voters on the eve of the 1930 parliamentary elections (Document 7)? Using Documents 8, 9, 12, and 21, explain why many Germans supported the Nazis.

8. Historian Marian Kaplan describes the "social death" of German Jews that preceded the Nazi attempt to exterminate them physically. What

evidence can you find in the documents of this social death? What forms did it take? (See Documents 20, 31, 32, and 44.)

9. Explain the different strategies used to resist the Nazi state (Documents 11, 16, 20, and 47–55). What evidence can you find of nonviolent forms of resistance to the Nazi state? Of violent forms of protest?

10. We usually think of propaganda as something that is insidious, intended to warp our minds and unfairly influence our opinions. Would Joseph Goebbels have agreed (Document 13)? Why or why not?

11. Not all Nazi concentration camps were alike. How were the camps described in Documents 20, 49, 50, and 58 similar, and how were they different? How did the Nazis' use of the camps compare to other tactics used in the Final Solution (Documents 45–47)?

12. After 1945, many Germans who met the racial, political, sexual, and religious criteria of the regime would argue that they, too, were victims of the Nazis. Based on the experiences described in documents 41, 56, and 57, how would you assess these claims? Can people who shared responsibility for the triumphs of the Nazi regime also claim status as victims of it? Explain.

13. The idea of the "national community," or *Volksgemeinschaft*, was vital to Nazi ideology. It depended on defining clearly both those who belonged and those who did not. Based on Documents 11, 17–33, 35, 36, and 39, who were the insiders and why? Who were the outsiders, and why were they excluded?

14. A defining characteristic of the Second World War is that it erased the boundary between the military front and the home front. What evidence can you find in Documents 40, 41, 56, and 57 of the ways in which the military front and home front ceased to be clearly divided?

15. Karl Fuchs and Melita Maschmann came of age in the Nazi state. What evidence can you find in their eyewitness accounts that they embraced Nazi ideology? (See Documents 9, 36, 37, 39, and 56.)

16. How did Nazi racial policy affect military strategy in Poland and the Soviet Union? (See Documents 35, 36, 38, and 39.)

Selected Bibliography

GENERAL HISTORIES OF NAZI GERMANY

Burleigh, Michael. *The Third Reich: A New History*. New York: Hill & Wang, 2000.

Burleigh, Michael, and Wolfgang Wippermann. *The Racial State: Germany, 1933–1945*. Cambridge: Cambridge University Press, 1991.

Caplan, Jane, ed. *Nazi Germany, 1933–1945*. Oxford: Oxford University Press, 2008.

Childers, Thomas, and Jane Caplan, eds. *Reevaluating the Third Reich*. New York: Holmes & Meier, 1993.

Crew, David F., ed. *Nazism and German Society, 1933–1945*. New York: Routledge, 1994.

Evans, Richard J. *The Coming of the Third Reich*. New York: Penguin Press, 2004.

———. *The Third Reich in Power, 1933–1939*. New York: Penguin Press, 2005.

———. *The Third Reich at War, 1939–1945*. London: Allen Lane, 2008.

Kershaw, Ian. *Hitler, 1889–1936: Hubris*. New York: W. W. Norton, 2000.

———. *Hitler, 1936–1945: Nemesis*. New York: W. W. Norton, 2001.

Stackelberg, Roderick. *Hitler's Germany: Origins, Interpretations, Legacies*. London: Routledge, 1999.

THE LEGACY OF THE FIRST WORLD WAR AND THE WEIMAR REPUBLIC

Bessel, Richard. *Germany after the First World War*. Oxford: Clarendon Press, 1993.

Mommsen, Hans. *The Rise and Fall of Weimar Democracy*. Translated by Elborg Forster and Larry Eugene Jones. Chapel Hill: University of North Carolina Press, 1996.

Peukert, Detlev J. K. *The Weimar Republic: The Crisis of Classical Modernity*. Translated by Richard Deveson. New York: Hill & Wang, 1993.

THE RISE OF NATIONAL SOCIALISM

Allan, William Sheridan. *The Nazi Seizure of Power: The Experience of a Single German Town, 1922–1945*. New York: F. Watts, 1984.

Childers, Thomas, ed. *The Formation of the Nazi Constituency, 1919–1933*. London: Croom Helm, 1986.

———. *The Nazi Voter: The Social Foundations of Fascism in Germany, 1919–1933*. Chapel Hill: University of North Carolina Press, 1983.

Fritzsche, Peter. *Germans into Nazis*. Cambridge, Mass.: Harvard University Press, 1998.

EVERYDAY LIFE, CULTURE, AND RELIGION IN THE THIRD REICH

Baranowski, Shelley. *The Confessing Church: Conservative Elites and the Nazi State*. Lewiston, N.Y.: E. Mellen Press, 1986.

———. *Strength through Joy: Consumerism and Mass Tourism in the Third Reich*. Cambridge: Cambridge University Press, 2004.

Barron, Stephanie, ed. *Degenerate Art: The Fate of the Avant-Garde in Nazi Germany*. Los Angeles: Los Angeles County Museum of Art, 1991.

Bergen, Doris L. *Twisted Cross: The German Christian Movement in the Third Reich*. Chapel Hill: University of North Carolina Press, 1996.

Conway, J. S. *The Nazi Persecution of the Churches, 1933–45*. London: Weidenfeld & Nicholson, 1968.

Hake, Sabine. *Popular Cinema of the Third Reich*. Austin: University of Texas Press, 2001.

Kater, Michael H. *Different Drummers: Jazz in the Culture of Nazi Germany*. New York: Oxford University Press, 1992.

———. *Hitler Youth*. Cambridge, Mass.: Harvard University Press, 2004.

———. *The Twisted Muse: Musicians and Their Music in the Third Reich*. New York: Oxford University Press, 1997.

Mason, Timothy W. *Nazism, Fascism and the Working Class*. Edited by Jane Caplan. Cambridge: Cambridge University Press, 1995.

Peukert, Detlev J. K. *Inside Nazi Germany: Conformity, Opposition, and Racism in Everyday Life*. Translated by Richard Deveson. New Haven, Conn.: Yale University Press, 1987.

Phayer, Michael. *Protestant and Catholic Women in Nazi Germany*. Detroit: Wayne State University Press, 1990.

Potter, Pamela Maxine. *Most German of the Arts: Musicology and Society from the Weimar Republic to the End of Hitler's Reich*. New Haven, Conn.: Yale University Press, 1998.

Rentschler, Eric. *The Ministry of Illusion: Nazi Cinema and Its Afterlife*. Cambridge, Mass.: Harvard University Press, 1996.

Steigmann-Gall, Richard. *The Holy Reich: Nazi Conceptions of Christianity, 1919–1945*. New York: Cambridge University Press, 2003.

Welch, David. *Propaganda and the German Cinema, 1933–1945*. Oxford: Clarendon Press, 1983.

———. *The Third Reich: Politics and Propaganda*. 2nd ed. London: Routledge, 2002.

GENDER AND SEXUALITY

Bridenthal, Renate, Atina Grossmann, and Marion Kaplan, eds. *When Biology Became Destiny: Women in Weimar and Nazi Germany.* New York: Monthly Review Press, 1984.

Herzog, Dagmar, ed. *Sexuality and German Fascism.* New York: Berghahn Books, 2005.

———. *Sex after Fascism: Memory and Morality in Twentieth-Century Germany.* Princeton, N.J.: Princeton University Press, 2005.

Koonz, Claudia. *Mothers in the Fatherland: Women, the Family, and Nazi Politics.* New York: St. Martin's Press, 1987.

Pine, Lisa. *Nazi Family Policy, 1933–1945.* Oxford: Berg, 1997.

Stephenson, Jill. *Women in Nazi Germany.* New York: Longman, 2001.

GERMAN JEWS AND NAZI ANTI-SEMITISM

Friedländer, Saul. *Nazi Germany and the Jews.* Vol. 1, *The Years of Persecution, 1933–1939.* New York: HarperCollins, 1997.

Kaplan, Marion A. *Between Dignity and Despair: Jewish Life in Nazi Germany.* New York: Oxford University Press, 1998.

———, ed. *Jewish Daily Life in Germany, 1618–1945.* Oxford: Oxford University Press, 2005.

Koonz, Claudia. *The Nazi Conscience.* Cambridge, Mass.: Belknap Press, 2003.

Roseman, Mark. *A Past in Hiding: Memory and Survival in Nazi Germany.* New York: Metropolitan Books, 2001.

TERROR, REPRESSION, AND THE PERSECUTION OF NON-JEWS IN THE THIRD REICH

Berenbaum, Michael, ed. *A Mosaic of Victims: Non-Jews Persecuted and Murdered by the Nazis.* New York: New York University Press, 1990.

Gellately, Robert. *Backing Hitler: Consent and Coercion in Nazi Germany.* Oxford: Oxford University Press, 2001.

Gellately, Robert, and Nathan Stoltzfus, eds. *Social Outsiders in Nazi Germany.* Princeton, N.J.: Princeton University Press, 2001.

Wachsmann, Nikolaus. *Hitler's Prisons: Legal Terror in Nazi Germany.* New Haven, Conn.: Yale University Press, 2004.

THE SECOND WORLD WAR, GERMAN EXPANSION, AND THE WAR ON THE HOME FRONT

Bartov, Omer. *Hitler's Army: Soldiers, Nazis, and War in the Third Reich.* New York: Oxford University Press, 1991.

Bessel, Richard. *Nazism and War.* London: Weidenfeld & Nicolson, 2004.

Harvey, Elizabeth. *Women and the Nazi East: Agents and Witnesses of Germanization.* New Haven, Conn.: Yale University Press, 2003.

Overy, Richard. *Why the Allies Won*. London: Jonathan Cape, 1995.

Stargardt, Nicholas. *Witnesses of War: Children's Lives under the Nazis*. New York: Alfred A. Knopf, 2006.

Steinert, Marlis G. *Hitler's War and the Germans: Public Mood and Attitude during the Second World War*. Translated by Thomas E. J. de Witt. Athens: Ohio University Press, 1977.

Stephenson, Jill. *Hitler's Home Front: Württemberg under the Nazis*. London: Hambledon Continuum, 2006.

Weinberg, Gerhard L. *A World at Arms: A Global History of World War II*. Cambridge: Cambridge University Press, 1994.

THE NAZI WAR AGAINST THE JEWS AND THE FINAL SOLUTION

Bartov, Omer. *Germany's War and the Holocaust: Disputed Histories*. Ithaca, N.Y.: Cornell University Press, 2003.

Bergen, Doris L. *War and Genocide: A Concise History of the Holocaust*. Lanham, Md.: Rowman & Littlefield, 2003.

Browning, Christoper R. *Ordinary Men: Reserve Police Battalion 101 and the Final Solution in Poland*. New York: HarperCollins, 1992.

————. *The Origins of the Final Solution: The Evolution of Nazi Jewish Policy, September 1939–March 1942*. With contributions by Jürgen Matthäus. Lincoln: University of Nebraska Press, 2004.

Friedlander, Henry. *The Origins of Nazi Genocide: From Euthanasia to the Final Solution*. Chapel Hill: University of North Carolina Press, 1995.

Friedländer, Saul. *The Years of Extermination: Nazi Germany and the Jews, 1939–1945*. New York: HarperCollins, 2007.

Herf, Jeffrey. *The Jewish Enemy: Nazi Propaganda during World War II and the Holocaust*. Cambridge, Mass.: Belknap Press, 2006.

Roseman, Mark. *The Wannsee Conference and the Final Solution: A Reconsideration*. New York: Metropolitan Books, 2002.

RESISTANCE TO NATIONAL SOCIALISM

Hamerow, Theodor S. *On the Road to the Wolf's Lair: German Resistance to Hitler*. Cambridge, Mass.: Belknap Press, 1997.

Mommsen, Hans. *Alternatives to Hitler: German Resistance under the Third Reich*. Translated by Angus McGeoch. London: I. B. Tauris, 2003.

THE LEGACIES OF NATIONAL SOCIALISM AND
THE SECOND WORLD WAR IN GERMANY

Biess, Frank. *Homecomings: Returning POWs and the Legacies of Defeat in Postwar Germany*. Princeton, N.J.: Princeton University Press, 2006.

Fehrenbach, Heide. *Race after Hitler: Black Occupation Children in Postwar Germany and America*. Princeton, N.J.: Princeton University Press, 2005.

Frei, Norbert. *Adenauer's Germany and the Nazi Past: The Politics of Amnesty and Integration*. Translated by Joel Golb. New York: Columbia University Press, 2002.

Moeller, Robert G. *War Stories: The Search for a Usable Past in the Federal Republic of Germany*. Berkeley: University of California Press, 2001.

Niven, Bill, ed. *Germans as Victims: Remembering the Past in Contemporary Germany*. Basingstoke, England: Palgrave Macmillan, 2006.

Olick, Jeffrey K. *In the House of the Hangman: The Agonies of German Defeat, 1943–1949*. Chicago: University of Chicago Press, 2005.

PRIMARY SOURCE COLLECTIONS

Crew, David F., ed. *Hitler and the Nazis: A History in Documents*. New York: Oxford University Press, 2005.

Grau, Günter, ed. *Hidden Holocaust? Gay and Lesbian Persecution in Germany, 1933–1945*. Translated by Patrick Camiller. London: Cassell, 1995.

Kaes, Anton, Martin Jay, and Edward Dimendberg, eds. *The Weimar Republic Sourcebook*. Berkeley: University of California Press, 1994.

Meyer, Henry Cord, ed. *The Long Generation: Germany from Empire to Ruin, 1913–1945*. New York: Walker, 1973.

Noakes, Jeremy, and Geoffrey Pridham, eds. *Nazism, 1919–1945: A History in Documents and Eyewitness Accounts*. Vol. 1, *The Nazi Party, State and Society, 1919–1930*. New York: Schocken Books, 1983.

———. *Nazism, 1919–1945: A History in Documents and Eyewitness Accounts*. Vol. 2, *Foreign Policy, War and Racial Extermination*. New York: Schocken Books, 1988.

Sax, Benjamin C., and Dieter Kuntz, eds. *Inside Hitler's Germany: A Documentary History of Life in the Third Reich*. Lexington, Mass.: D. C. Heath, 1992.

Snyder, Louis L., ed. *Hitler's Third Reich: A Documentary History*. 1981. Reprint, Chicago: Nelson-Hall, 1988.

Stackelberg, Roderick, and Sally A. Winkle, eds. *The Nazi Germany Sourcebook: An Anthology of Texts*. London: Routledge, 2002.

Acknowledgments (continued from p. iv)

Document 1: Adolf Hitler, "On His Hopes for Germany in 1914 from *Mein Kampf*," 1925, from Adolf Hitler, *Mein Kampf,* translated by Ralph Manheim, published by Pimlico. Copyright © 1943, renewed 1971 by Houghton Mifflin Company. Reprinted by permission of The Random House Group Ltd.

Document 2: Magnus Hirschfeld, "Sexual Catastrophes" (translated by Don Reneau). *The Weimar Republic Sourcebook,* edited by Anton Kaes, Martin Jay, and Edward Dimendberg, © 1994 Regents of the University of California. Published by the University of California Press.

Document 3: Elsa Herrmann, "This Is the New Woman" (translated by Don Reneau). *The Weimar Republic Sourcebook,* edited by Anton Kaes, Martin Jay, and Edward Dimendberg, © 1994 Regents of the University of California. Published by the University of California Press.

Document 4: Adolf Hitler, "Anti-Semitic Speech." From Louis L. Snyder, ed., *Hitler's Third Reich,* 1e. © 1981 Wadsworth, a part of Cengage Learning, Inc. Reproduced by permission. www.cengage.com/permissions.

Document 5: Adolf Hitler, "On the Use of Mass Meetings from *Mein Kampf*," 1925, from Adolf Hitler, *Mein Kampf,* translated by Ralph Manheim, published by Pimlico. Copyright © 1943, renewed 1971 by Houghton Mifflin Company. Reprinted by permission of The Random House Group Ltd.

Document 6: Elsbeth Zander, "Tasks Facing the German Woman." From Detlef Mühlberger, *Hitler's Voice: The Völkischer Beobachter, 1920–1933,* Vol. II, *Nazi Ideology and Propaganda* (Oxford: Peter Lang, 2004), 326–27.

Document 7: Adolf Hitler, "Adolf Hitler's Manifesto." From Detlef Mühlberger, *Hitler's Voice: The Völkischer Beobachter, 1920–1933,* Vol. I, *Organisation and Development of the Nazi Party* (Oxford: Peter Lang, 2004), 395–405.

Document 8: Reprinted with the permission of Scribner, a Division of Simon & Schuster, Inc., from *Inside the Third Reich* by Albert Speer, translated from German by Richard and Clara Winston. Copyright © 1969 by Verlag Ullstein GmbH. English Translation copyright © 1970 by Macmillan Publishing Company. All Rights Reserved. Copyright © 1970 by Weidenfeld and Nicolson, an imprint of The Orion Publishing Group, London.

Document 9: Melita Maschmann, "A German Teenager's Response to the Nazi Takeover in January 1944," from *Account Rendered: A Dossier on My Former Self.* Abelard-Schuman/Anderson Press Ltd.

Document 10: "Germany Ventures." From the *New York Times,* January 31, 1933. © 1933 The New York Times. All rights reserved. Used by permission and protected by the Copyright Laws of the United States. The printing, copying, redistribution, or retransmission of the Material without express written permission is prohibited.

Document 12: "Reports on the Sources of Working-Class Support for the Nazis and the Limits to Opposition," 1935–1939, excerpted from Detlev J. K. Peukert, *Inside Nazi Germany: Conformity, Opposition, and Racism in Everyday Life* (Yale University Press, 1987); and Jeremy Noakes and Geoffrey Pridham, eds., *Nazism, 1919–1945: A Documentary Reader,* vol. 2, *State, Economy, and Society, 1933–1939* (University of Exeter Press, 2000), 159, 397. Reprinted by permission of the publishers.

Document 13: Joseph Goebbels, "The Tasks of the Ministry for Propaganda," in David Welch, *The Third Reich: Politics and Propaganda,* 2nd ed. (Routledge, 2002).

Document 14: William Shirer, "Description of the Nazi Party Rally in Germany," from *Berlin Diary: The Journal of a Foreign Correspondent, 1934–1941.* Reprinted by permission of Don Congdon Associates, Inc. Copyright © 1941, renewed 1968 by William L. Shirer.

Document 15: Sally Winkle, trans. "Concordat between the Holy See and the German Reich," July 20, 1933, in *The Nazi Germany Sourcebook: An Anthology of Texts,* ed. Roderick Stackelberg and Sally A. Winkle. London: Routledge, 2002, 150–60. Reproduced by permission of the translator.

Document 16: "Protestant Church Leaders' Declaration of Independence from the Nazi State," October 21, 1934, excerpted from Jeremy Noakes and Geoffrey Pridham, eds., *Nazism,*

1919–1945: A Documentary Reader, vol. 2, *State, Economy, and Society, 1933–1939* (University of Exeter Press, 2000), p. 390. Reprinted by permission of the publisher.

Document 17: Adolf Hitler, "Opening Address at the House of German Art in Munich," July 19, 1937, excerpted from Jeremy Noakes and Geoffrey Pridham, eds., *Nazism, 1919–1945: A Documentary Reader*, vol. 2, *State, Economy, and Society, 1933–1939* (University of Exeter Press, 2000), 205–6. Reprinted by permission of the publisher.

Document 19: "Report on a Visit to a Reich Prison Camp." From the *New York Times*, July 26, 1933. © 1933 The New York Times. All rights reserved. Used by permission and protected by the Copyright Laws of the United States. The printing, copying, redistribution, or retransmission of the Material without express written permission is prohibited.

Document 20: Gabriele Herz, "Description of an Early Concentration Camp for Women," from *The Women's Camp in Moringen*. Reproduced by permission of the Publisher. All rights reserved.

Document 21: SOPADE, "Reports of the Social Democratic Party in Exile on Working-Class Attitudes toward the Nazis," in Detlev J. K. Peukert, *Inside Nazi Germany: Conformity, Opposition, and Racism in Everyday Life* (Yale University Press, 1987).

Document 22: Sally Winkle, trans. "Hitler's Speech to the National Socialist Women's Organization," September 1934 in *The Nazi Germany Sourcebook: An Anthology of Texts*, ed. Roderick Stackelberg and Sally A. Winkle. London: Routledge, 2002, 182–84. Reproduced by permission of the translator.

Document 24: Jutta Rüdiger, "On the League of German Girls," in Michael Burleigh and Wolfgang Wippermann, *The Racial State: Germany 1933–1945* (Cambridge: Cambridge University Press, 1991), 235–36. Copyright © 1991 Cambridge University Press. Reprinted with the permission of Cambridge University Press.

Document 25: Peter Gay, "A Jewish Teenager Remembers the 1936 Berlin Olympics," 1998. Excerpt from pp. 78–80 of *My German Question: Growing Up in Nazi Berlin* by Peter Gay (Yale University Press, 1998). Copyright © 1998 by Peter Gay. Reprinted by permission of Yale University Press.

Document 26: "Law for the Prevention of Genetically Diseased Offspring," July 14, 1933, excerpted from Jeremy Noakes and Geoffrey Pridham, eds., *Nazism, 1919–1945: A Documentary Reader*, vol. 2, *State, Economy, and Society, 1933–1939* (University of Exeter Press, 2000), 263–64. Reprinted by permission of the publisher.

Document 27: SS Security Service, "Report Assessing Popular Response to the Film *I Accuse*" in Michael Burleigh and Wolfgang Wippermann, *The Racial State: Germany 1933–1945* (Cambridge: Cambridge University Press, 1991), 158–61. Copyright © 1991 Cambridge University Press. Reprinted with the permission of Cambridge University Press.

Document 28: Heinrich Himmler, "On the Question of Homosexuality," in Michael Burleigh and Wolfgang Wippermann, *The Racial State: Germany 1933–1945* (Cambridge: Cambridge University Press, 1991), 192–93. Copyright © 1991 Cambridge University Press. Reprinted with the permission of Cambridge University Press.

Document 29: Heinrich Himmler, "Fight against the Gypsy Nuisance," in Michael Burleigh and Wolfgang Wippermann, *The Racial State: Germany 1933–1945* (Cambridge: Cambridge University Press, 1991), 120–21. Copyright © 1991 Cambridge University Press. Reprinted with the permission of Cambridge University Press.

Document 30: Otto D. Tolischus and Frederick T. Birchall, "Reports on the Introduction of Anti-Semitic Laws." From the *New York Times*, September 16, 1935 © 1935 The New York Times. All rights reserved. Used by permission and protected by the Copyright Laws of the United States. The printing, copying, redistribution, or retransmission of the Material without express written permission is prohibited.

Document 31: Marta Appel, from *Jewish Life in Germany: Memoirs from Three Centuries*, ed. Monika Richarz, trans. Stella P. Rosenfeld and Sidney Rosenfeld (Bloomington: Indiana University Press, 1991). Copyright © 1991 Indiana University Press. Reprinted with permission of Indiana University Press.

Document 36: Melita Maschmann, "A German Colonizer of Poland in 1939 or 1940," from *Account Rendered: A Dossier on My Former Self*. Abelard-Schuman/Anderson Press Ltd.

Document 37: Karl Fuchs, "A German Soldier's Letters from France." Reprinted with permission of Horst Fuchs Richardson.

Document 39: Karl Fuchs, "A German Soldier's Letters from the Eastern Front." Reprinted with permission of Horst Fuchs Richardson.

Document 41: Käthe Ricken, "Diary Entries about Life under the Bombs," 1943. Excerpt from *War Wives* by Colin and Eileen Townsend, published by Grafton Books. Copyright © Colin and Eileen Townsend 1989. Reproduced by permission of Sheil Land Associates Ltd.

Document 42: Victor Klemperer, "Reflections on the Meanings of the Yellow Star for Jews in Germany in 1941." Excerpted from Victor Klemperer, *The Language of the Third Reich*, trans. Martin Brady (London: Continuum, 2006). By kind permission of Continuum International Publishing Group.

Document 43: Jewish Cultural Association of Württemberg, "Circular on Deportation, November 17, 1941," excerpted from Jeremy Noakes and Geoffrey Pridham, eds., *Nazism, 1919–1945: A Documentary Reader*, vol. 3, *Foreign Policy, War, and Racial Extermination* (University of Exeter Press, 2000), 523–24. Reprinted by permission of the publisher.

Document 44: Ria Bröring, "A German Woman's Account of Jewish Deportations," April 23, 1942. Excerpt from *War Wives* by Colin and Eileen Townsend, published by Grafton Books. Copyright © Colin and Eileen Townsend 1989. Reproduced by permission of Sheil Land Associates Ltd.

Document 47: Excerpts from *Scroll of Agony : The Warsaw Diary of Chaim A. Kaplan,* trans. and ed. Abraham I. Katsh. Copyright © 1965, 1973 by Abraham I. Katsh. Reprinted with the permission of Scribner, a Division of Simon & Schuster, Inc., and the Estate of Abraham I. Katsh. All rights reserved.

Document 48: "Song of the Partisans" or "Jewish Partisan Song" (*Zog Nit Keynmol*) by Hirsh Glick (1943), translation by Aaron Kramer. Reprinted from the April 1947 issue of *Jewish Life*, now publishing as *Jewish Currents* (www.jewishcurrents.org). Reprinted with the permission of *Jewish Currents*.

Document 49: Ruth Kluger, excerpts from *Still Alive: A Holocaust Girl Remembered*, 103–8. Copyright © 2001 by Ruth Kluger. Copyright © 1992 by Wallstein Verlag, Gottingen, Germany. Reprinted with the permission of The Feminist Press at the City University of New York, www.feministpress.org. All rights reserved.

Document 50: Copyright 2009 Amira Hass. Translation copyright Sophie Hand and Amira Hass. Reprinted with permission of Haymarket Books and the author from Hanna Lévy-Hass, *Diary of Bergen-Belsen*, trans. by Sophie Hand and Amira Hass, with a foreword and afterword by Amira Hass (Chicago: Haymarket Books, 2009).

Document 51: Benjamin C. Sax and Dieter Kuntz, eds., from *Inside Hitler's Germany*, 1e. © 1992 Wadsworth, a part of Cengage Learning, Inc. Reproduced by permission.

Document 52: Benjamin C. Sax and Dieter Kuntz, eds., from *Inside Hitler's Germany*, 1e. © 1992 Wadsworth, a part of Cengage Learning, Inc. Reproduced by permission.

Document 53: Inge Scholl, pp. 77–79 and 82–84 from *Students against Tyranny: The Resistance of the White Rose, Munich, 1942–1943* © 1970 by Inge Scholl and reprinted by permission of Wesleyan University Press.

Document 55: "Anti-Nazi Leaflet." From Detlev J. K. Peukert, *Inside Nazi Germany: Conformity, Opposition, and Racism in Everyday Life* (Yale University Press, 1987).

Document 56: Melita Maschmann, "The Mobilization of Youth in the Winter of 1945," from *Account Rendered: A Dossier on My Former Self*. Abelard-Schuman/Anderson Press Ltd.

Document 58: Gene Currivan, "Nazi Death Factory Shocks Germans on a Forced Tour." From the *New York Times*, April 18, 1945. © 1945 The New York Times. All rights reserved. Used by permission and protected by the Copyright Laws of the United States. The printing, copying, redistribution, or retransmission of the Material without express written permission is prohibited.

Index

THE LEARNING CENTRE
HAMMERSMITH AND WEST
LONDON COLLEGE
GLIDDON ROAD
LONDON W14 9BL